The Origins of Scottish Nationhood

Neil Davidson

The Origins of
Scottish Nationhood

Pluto  **Press**
LONDON • STERLING, VIRGINIA

First published 2000 by Pluto Press
345 Archway Road, London N6 5AA
and 22883 Quicksilver Drive,
Sterling, VA 20166–2012, USA

British Library Cataloguing in Publication Data
A catalogue record for this book is available from
the British Library

ISBN 0 7453 1609 3 hbk

Library of Congress Cataloging in Publication Data
Davidson, Neil, 1957–
    The origins of Scottish nationhood / Neil Davidson.
        p. cm.
    Includes bibliographical references (p.) and index.
    ISBN 0–7453–1609–3
        1. Scotland—History—18th century. 2. Nationalism—Scotland—
    History—18th century. 3. National characteristics, Scottish—History—
    18th century. 4. Scotland—History—The Union, 1707. I. Title.

DA809 .D38 2000
941.107—dc21
                                                                99–089799

Designed and produced for Pluto Press by
Chase Production Services, Chadlington, OX7 3LN
Typeset from disk by Stanford DTP Services, Northampton
Printed in the European Union by TJ International Ltd, Padstow

Contents

Preface, Acknowledgements, Dedication

This book was originally part of a study of the Scottish bourgeois revolution which I began early in 1993 and completed late in 1998.[1] It became apparent during my research that the Scottish experience was distinct in two ways from that of the other European countries which underwent their revolutions before 1848. In the United Netherlands, England and France the transition to a capitalist economy and the formation of national consciousness were *preconditions* for their respective revolutions taking place, in Scotland they were *outcomes* of the revolution. My attempt to deal with these issues began to extend the chronological and thematic boundaries of the work in successive drafts. The first (1995) did not deal with them at all. In the second (1997) they shared a final chapter on post-revolutionary developments. By the third (also 1997) they demanded a chapter each, but the chapter on the nation could no longer be accommodated in that book and had itself to be expanded to book length. The reasons why this aspect of the Scottish Revolution required such expansion are set out in the Introduction.

Any writer who uses the word 'origins' in the title of a book should keep in mind what the French historian, Marc Bloch, called 'the idol of origins'. Bloch complained that his fellow-historians failed to clarify whether they used the term 'origins' to mean 'beginnings' or 'causes'.[2] I am concerned with both. The Scottish nation did not always exist (it began during a specific historic period), nor was it inevitable that it should exist (it was caused by a specific combination of economic, social and political events). My precise title, *The Origins Of Scottish Nationhood*, is a *homage* to an important essay of the same name by George Kerevan which appeared in *The Bulletin Of Scottish Politics* during 1981. Given the limited circulation of that journal, it is unlikely that more than a few hundred people ever read the piece, but when I first came across it in the second-hand box of Clyde Books in Glasgow early in the 1990s, it impressed me as one of the few serious attempts to outline a Marxist analysis of Scottish historical development.[3] It remained in outline since Kerevan ultimately abandoned his original orthodox Trotskyism (which was not without its own problems) for the free-market Scottish nationalism he currently advocates through his weekly column in *The Scotsman*. Nevertheless, it would be sectarian folly not to acknowledge that his earlier incarnation at least asked the right questions of Scottish history, some of which I have tried to answer here.

Those answers were presented publicly as contributions to three very different events: the London Socialist Historians Society annual conference, *Political Change*, at the Institute of Historical Research in May 1998; the Supplementary Studies Programme of the Open University Foundation Course *Society And Social Science* Summer School, at Stirling University in August 1998; and the week-long event, *Marxism At The Millennium*, organised by the Socialist Workers Party at the University of London in July 1999. I am grateful to the organisers and to the historians, students and comrades who attended these meetings and participated in the discussions. Parts of my argument were rehearsed in two articles for the journal *International Socialism*. The editor, John Rees, was kind enough to allow me to reproduce passages which originally appeared there.[4]

My thanks are particularly due to the two people who, more than any others, were on the receiving end of my pleas for fraternal criticism. Alex Law read and commented on the various drafts and his intellectual solidarity with the entire project was invaluable to me throughout. Cathy Watkins read the final draft with a view to improving my English (although I fear this may have proved beyond even her powers) and asked the kind of sensible questions of the contents that a normal person who is neither an academic nor a political activist might ask.

I knew three of my four grandparents: Helen and William Farquhar and Mary Davidson. They belonged to a generation which formed perhaps the last direct link with a rural Scotland – the farming communities of Aberdeenshire – that came to an end during their youth in and around the First World War, a process later recorded in literature by Lewis Grassic Gibbon and in historiography by Ian Carter.[5] All three lived in the great metropolis of Aberdeen from the 1920s onwards, but to me, growing up in the town during the 1960s, their cultural identities always seemed to be that of the countryside from which they came, rather than those of the Scottish or British nations whose origins are discussed here. This book is dedicated to their memory.

Neil Davidson
Edinburgh
22 December 1999

Introduction

If it were possible to draw a graph showing the strengthening of Scottish national consciousness over the last 20 years, it could be charted in relation to the Conservative party general election victories of 1979, 1983, 1987 and 1992, and would show the curve ascending more steeply with the announcement of each result. The latter two were particularly significant in this respect, for the moment when our imaginary graph would take the sharpest upward swing would be after the 1987 election, when the cycle by which Labour governments replaced Conservative ones in succession appeared to have been permanently broken. In other words, this heightened sense of Scottishness was not an assertion of primordial being but a response to a particular political conjuncture, often described as involving a 'democratic deficit' whereby the majority of Scots regularly voted for parties other than the Conservatives, but nevertheless ended up with Conservative governments. There is nothing unusual or shameful about this: nationhood is never asserted for its own sake, but always in order to achieve some economic, social or political goal. Opposition to Thatcherism was, however, probably no greater across Scotland as a whole than it was in, say, northeast England or Inner London. (It is worth noting, in this connection, that although the Conservative party received the largest number of votes in England between 1979 and 1997, the majority of English people also voted for other parties throughout that period.) Because Scotland is a nation, however, and not a region or an urban district, opposition took a form which was impossible in most other parts of Britain. The key issue was less the abstract question of democracy and more the concrete consequences of continued Conservative rule, in the shape of increased unemployment, attacks on the welfare state and the introduction of the Poll Tax. Since the Labour party seemed unable to win general elections (and how often was the impossibility of a Labour victory asserted as an incontrovertible fact during these years!) for many Scots the only solution seemed to be a national one, in the form of a devolved Scottish Parliament or an independent Scottish state.

For some writers, such as Tom Nairn, the Thatcher and Major years had the effect of awakening a nationalism that was missing, presumed dead, but in fact merely sleeping.[1] Yet what was interesting about the 'awakening' was the form which it took. Over the last 20 years there has been a greater flourishing of Scottish culture than at any time since the 1920s and 1930s, and on a far broader basis than the largely literary focus of those decades. Yet this has not been accompanied by any significant or sustained increase in support for the Scottish National Party, which has never returned to, let alone surpassed, the high point of 30.4 per cent of the vote in the general election of October 1974, several years before the renaissance of national identity began. This is not to suggest that Scottishness is only registered at a cultural level, but at the political level it focussed on the demand for a Scottish Parliament, not a Scottish state. In other words, there appears to be a division between Scottish national consciousness, which has grown, and Scottish nationalism, which has not.

The apparent paradox between a strong and growing sense of Scottish national consciousness which nevertheless remains attached to the British nation state was not (for me, at any rate) adequately explained in the existing literature. Thomas Devine, in his monumental history of modern Scotland, published while this book was in the final stages of preparation, criticises fellow-historians for writing exclusively for an audience of other academics and neglecting to make their work accessible to the broader public.[2] It is difficult to disagree with this assessment. As Ian Bell writes: 'there has been an all but unnoticed golden age in the field of Scottish history while the nation itself has muddled along with its baggage of myths, half-truths and other people's interpretations.'[3] Yet in one sense historians and academics in other fields have contributed to the 'baggage of myths and half-truths', not by commission but by omission. Most discussions of Scottish nationhood are conducted, not by historians, but by sociologists, political scientists and – above all – by journalists. To that extent Bell is correct. The latter profession tend however to take the historical material on which they base their work from the former, and it is here that the sins of omission have their effect.

Since the late 1960s, historians of Scotland have produced a substantial body of work which has both increased our knowledge in many areas and exposed several long-held positions as untenable.[4] I do not intend to diminish their achievement, to which I am personally indebted, by pointing out that the vast majority of these historians do not situate themselves openly within any explicit theoretical framework. If several intellectually destructive systems of thought, from structuralism to postmodernism, have failed to take root in Scottish history departments, it is not because they have found the soil already permeated by Weberianism or Marxism, but because it has been resistant to any systematic theoretical approach to the discipline. While this resistance has spared us from the type of work where endless theoretical preliminaries take precedence over substantive analysis, it has also led to several difficulties.

No work is (or could be) completely without theoretical foundations, but these are rarely acknowledged and still more rarely brought into conflict with alternative positions.[5] At the most fundamental level, the refusal of theory means that the very concepts which historians of Scotland regularly use remain largely unexamined. Key amongst these are the 'nation' and its derivatives – 'nationhood', 'nationalism', 'national identity', 'national consciousness' and so on. These are historical concepts in another sense – they themselves have a history during which their meanings have changed over time – but one characteristic of Scottish historical writing is precisely the assumption that the concept 'nation' will fundamentally have the same meaning in 2001 as it did in 1320, 1560 or 1707.

Behind this assumption about the linguistic sign lies another about the referent, the nation itself. Devine's own work, both contribution to and culmination of the Scottish historical renaissance, carries the message explicitly in the title, *The Scottish Nation, 1700–2000*. Was there a Scottish nation in 1700? To answer this question would involve defining a nation, a national identity and all the other terms which have tripped so easily from my own keyboard in the course of this Introduction, yet it is precisely this is which is hardly ever done.[6] Theoretically, deficient history informs a sociology and political science which are – as a result – profoundly ahistorical, and both then support the commonsense notion of the nation reproduced day-in, day-out in the Scottish media. A correspondent to *Scotland On Sunday* in 1999 praised the newspaper for publishing a six-part history of Scotland, *The Story Of A Nation*, but complained about the decision to begin in 1707: 'If the Scottish nation didn't exist before the Act of Union then what was it that was "united" with England [?]'[7] The answer is, of course, the Scottish state – and historically, states have no more always embodied nations than nations have always sought to be embodied in states.

In what follows I will argue that a Scottish nation did not exist in 1320, nor in 1560, nor yet in 1707. The Lowlands were in the process of developing a sense of nationhood by the latter date, but this was a process from which the Highlands were largely excluded and which was in any event cut short by the Treaty of Union. It follows then that the Scottish national consciousness we know today could not have been preserved by institutions carried over from the pre-Union period, but arose after the Union and as a result of the Union, for only after 1707 were the material obstacles to nationhood – most notably the

Highland/Lowland divide – overcome. The historical events that are supposed to prove the existence of Scottish nationhood before 1707 were in fact presented in this way only after that date, when they were retrospectively assimilated into the national myth. The Scottish nationalism which arose in Scotland during the twentieth century, particularly in the 1960s, was not therefore a revival of a pre-Union nationalism after 300 years – since no such nationalism existed – but an entirely new formation. This has as many implications for British history as it does for Scottish. The 'four nations' history called for by John Pocock in 1975 involves historians of Britain abandoning their Anglocentric focus and taking all the nations of the British Isles into account.[8] This is now an academic growth area, at least as far as the history of British identities is concerned, but the majority of contributors tend to assume the existence of the four nations before the formation of Britain itself. If what I argue about Scotland is correct, however, then the British nation state was as much responsible for shaping the nations of which it consists as it was shaped by them. The Scottish nation was only formed in the late eighteenth century, so too was the British nation, and these two processes were not simply chronologically coincident, but structurally intertwined. What we are concerned with is not simply the origins of Scottish national consciousness, but the origins of national consciousness *in* Scotland, since it had two aspects, both Scottish and British. Let me make the point absolutely clear: it is not simply that Scottishness is part of Britishness – a point most people would concede – it is also that Britishness is part of Scottishness and the latter would not exist, at least in the same form, without the former.

There is another disabling assumption in Scottish intellectual life, although responsibility for this cannot be laid solely at the door of the historical profession. Because the Scottish nation has not been embodied in its own state since 1707, it has supposedly produced a 'civic' form of nationalism which is often contrasted favourably with the 'ethnic' nationalism of, for example, the Serbs. During the Kosovan conflict of 1999 George Kerevan used his column in *The Scotsman* to distinguish the nationalism of his party from that of the Milosevic regime:

> There is nationalism in the sense it applies to Hitler or Milosevic. Call it ethnic or tribal nationalism. In fact, don't call it nationalism at all, because it's not about building modern nations. This is a reactionary, tribal, exclusive ideology espoused in times of economic and political change by those social orders who are being usurped or threatened by the process of modernisation. ... But there is another, totally different meaning of the word nationalism – nation building. Building the common institutions of an inclusive civil society that alone mobilises the talents, energies, and co-operation of the population to create a modern industrial society.[9]

Note that the nationalisms of which Kerevan disapproves (not least because they threaten to discredit his own nationalism by association) are dismissed as mere 'tribalism'. This is self-serving in the extreme. Ethnicities can be invented to categorise groups by their enemies, or as self-identification by those groups themselves. Precisely because ethnicity is a socially constructed category, ethnic categorisations can be produced anywhere with the same disastrous results that we have seen for the last ten years in the Balkans. Consequently there is no reason why 'civic' nationalism cannot be transformed into 'ethnic' nationalism in its turn under certain determinate conditions, just as it did in Germany – a modern, developed and highly cultured capitalist society – during the 1930s.[10] This is a conclusion that adherents of 'civic' nationalism are, of course, most anxious to avoid. The contemporary situation in Europe contains all the elements for 'ethnic' nationalisms to arise – and in this Scotland is no different from other European nations, although it tends to evade the scrutiny to which the nations (including England) are subjected.

More to the point, whatever the future may hold in this respect (and nothing I have written here should be taken as endorsing *Daily Record*-style hysteria about the likely trajectory of Scottish nationalism), study of the Scottish historical past demonstrates that even this most civil of societies emerged from a sea of ethnic blood. The Scottish nation was partly created through two linked processes. First, the destruction of the Highland society and the incorporation of its imagery into the Scottish (and British) national self-image. Second, the consolidation of that image through participation in the conquest and colonisation of North America and India. Both included ferocious episodes of what we would now call 'ethnic cleansing'.

Our first task is therefore to define our terms. What theory underlies these arguments? I intend to argue in defence of a Marxist position, but to say that this tradition is not highly regarded by the majority of writers on nationalism would be an understatement. Indeed, it was an erstwhile Marxist from among their number, Tom Nairn, who famously declared that 'the theory of nationalism represents Marxism's greatest historical failure'.[11] This is a verdict which non-Marxist writers have been generally happy to accept.[12] Richard Finlay asserts, with specific reference to Scotland, that Marxism has the 'simplest', 'easiest', but 'least convincing' explanation of Scottish national identity. Apparently Marxism has nothing useful to say about 'the relationship of Scottish identity to the emergence of the newly created British state and the evolution of its particular national identity'. Why?

It is argued that national identity is a bourgeois construct which does not figure until the time of the French revolution. So for most of the eighteenth century, the Scots do not have a national identity until one is invented for them in the period of the turn of the nineteenth century. Apart from displaying an appalling ignorance of Scottish history and the popular character and mass participation of the Anglo Scottish wars of the fourteenth century, the Reformation, the Covenanting wars and the evidence of medieval and popular culture, the analysis is crude and rudimentary and does not command, nor deserve, serious attention from most historians.[13]

In the essay which follows this diatribe Finlay goes on to make some useful, if exaggerated, points about the continuing influence of the Covenanting tradition in Scottish social life during the eighteenth century. It is not clear whether he is arguing that Scotland is unique in having a national identity so long before the eighteenth century (and that it is simply Scottish Marxists who are at fault) or whether the Scottish experience is typical (and that Marxist theory itself is deficient). Most likely the latter. Either way, although I intend to argue a version of the position caricatured by Finlay, I am not aware that Marxists have done so before me, at least in any detail. In fact, the very few to have discussed the subject have tended – in my view quite wrongly – to date the origins of the Scottish nation nearer to the thirteenth than the eighteenth century. The references cited by Finlay himself make this quite clear, since not only do they reject the position he ascribes to them, but in fact take one close to his own.[14] Finlay is boxing with shadows, so perhaps it is time to provide him, and those who think like him, with an opponent made of flesh and blood.

Although I am confident that I can defend the positions I have taken in Chapters 1 and 2, in one sense it is less important that they meet with general approval (unlikely in any event) than that other writers on Scotland are encouraged to begin defining their terms in turn, if only in order to criticise the claims made here. Some writers of historical sociology have been known to advise their readers to skip introductory theoretical chapters, returning to them only if they require to know what the author means by a particular concept.[15] That is not a course of action I recommend for this book. Since I intend to criticise many received opinions about the Scottish nation, readers should be aware from the start that such criticism is based on a consistent theoretical position, not mere iconoclasm, or the desire to generate controversy. The first issue before us is one to which I have already alluded: the difference between national consciousness and nationalism.

1

What Is National Consciousness?

The purpose of this chapter is to produce a conceptual framework within which the Scottish experience can be discussed. Where I use the terms 'nation', 'national consciousness' and 'nationalism' in what follows, I am not, however, using concepts to which the Scottish experience is *external*, but concepts into which the Scottish experience has been *incorporated*, as subsequent chapters will demonstrate. The reader should bear three points in mind during what follows. First, although the theoretical basis of this chapter is the classical Marxist tradition, that has not prevented my drawing from the literature of 'nation theory' where it is compatible with historical materialism, however unwelcome that affinity may be for the writers concerned. Second, that literature is now extensive and continues to grow, but rather than provide yet more commentary on the major contributors or, worse still, commentary on their commentators, I have referred to their work only where it usefully illustrates positions that I want to accept or reject: this chapter is a framework; it is not intended to be a comprehensive survey. Third, for the purposes of clarity many of these positions are posed in starkly antithetical terms which will require subsequent qualification. The first concerns the definition of nationhood.

Defining a Nation

Definitions of nationhood tend to fall into one of two categories, which rely on either objective or subjective criteria. There is no agreed Marxist position and little help to be gained from Marx or Engels themselves since, as Michael Lowy noted, 'a precise definition of the concept of "a nation"' is absent from their writings on the national question.[1]

Consequently, their successors have tended to take one of the existing sides in the debate.

On the objective side the most famous definition was given by Stalin in an article of 1913 called 'Marxism and the National Question', which unfortunately has exerted an influence over the Left far in excess of its theoretical merits, which are slight. Stalin writes: 'A nation is a historically evolved, stable community of language, territory, economic life and psychological make-up manifested in a community of culture.' Furthermore, we learn that 'it is sufficient for a single one of these characteristics to be absent and the nation ceases to be a nation.'[2] These positions have been accepted by many who would otherwise have nothing to do with Stalinist politics. In an article discussing the Scottish national question Bob Mulholland quotes part of the above passage then writes of Stalin that 'his succinct definition makes sense and undoubtedly applies to the national characteristics of the Scottish people.'[3] In fact, 'his succinct definition' is merely an extensive checklist of criteria, against which can be matched the attributes of those peoples seeking the status of 'nation'. Eric Hobsbawm has noted the 'shifting and ambiguous' quality of all objective criteria, which 'makes them unusually convenient for propagandist and programmatic, as distinct from descriptive purposes', and these characteristics are clearly present here.[4] Perhaps the most obvious deficiency of these specific criteria, however, is that many nations which are currently recognised as such would be denied the title, and contrary to what Mulholland says, one of these would be Scotland. Many nations which have successfully attained statehood would also have to admit that they had attained their position through false pretences. Take Switzerland as an example.

Switzerland fails the Stalinist criteria on at least two counts: those of language (there are five official languages – German, French, Italian and two dialects of Romanish) and religion (there are two major religions – Roman Catholicism and Calvinist Protestantism). Yet the territory of Switzerland did not change from 1515 to 1803 and, during those three centuries the vast majority spoke dialects of German, only at the latter date incorporating Italian speakers. Only in 1815 did it acquire territories with significant French speaking populations in Valais, Geneva and Neuchatel, courtesy of the Holy Alliance. The state itself was only established in 1815 and as late as 1848 it was still enforcing religious divisions within the cantons: Protestantism being unlawful in Catholic areas and Catholicism being illegal in Protestant ones. After the revolutions of that year (which actually began in Switzerland), these restrictions were lifted and the territory of the state divided on a linguistic basis instead. In was only in 1891 that the state decided that the 600th anniversary of the founding of the original Confederation of Schwyz, Obwaldemn and Nidwalden in 1291 constituted the origin of the Swiss nation.[5] It should be clear even from this brief account that the Swiss nation exists *in the absence of* the elements which are supposed to constitute nationhood, not because of them. It might be protested that Switzerland is an exceptional case, but as we shall see in Chapter 3, Scotland faced similar (and in some respects even more extreme) difficulties, yet also succeeded in becoming a nation.[6]

The specific reasons why the Swiss, the Scots or any other people originally came to feel themselves a nation have to be separately discovered in each case, but this subjective feeling of identification is the only attribute which all have in common. In the words of the Zionist Ahad Ha'am:

> If I feel the spirit of Jewish nationality in my heart so that it stamps all my inward life with its seal, then the spirit of Jewish nationality exists in me; and its existence is not at an end even if all my Jewish contemporaries should cease to feel it in their hearts.

As Elie Kedurie, who quotes this passage, adds: 'Here are no superfluous appeals to philology or biology, no laborious attempts to prove that because a group speaks the same language, or has the same religion, or lives in the same territory, it is therefore a nation.'[7] As Hugh Seton-Watson writes: 'a nation exists when a significant number of people in a community consider themselves to form a nation, or behave as if they form one.'[8]

Do we need to make such a stark choice between objective and subjective definitions? Might not the notion of 'ethnicity' provide a way of transcending their opposition? Anthony Smith has argued that an ethnic community – that is, a community whose members have not had their 'ethnicity' imposed on them from outside, but distinguish *themselves* in this way – has six main attributes: 'a collective proper name, a myth of common ancestry, shared historical memories, one or more differentiating elements of common culture, an association with a specific "homeland", and a sense of solidarity for significant sectors of the population'.[9] Smith sees ethnicity as being the basis of national consciousness (or 'national identity', as he and most other writers call it) in most cases. 'Ethnicity' can be defined in three ways.

First, where members of a group have a common line of descent and consequently a shared *kinship*. Social groups who share a common line of descent are usually referred to in anthropology as endogamous groups, or groups whose members interbreed exclusively with each other, thus maintaining the same genetic inheritance. Such groups would have been universal at the origins of human evolution but are, however, virtually impossible to find today and have been since before the rise of capitalism. Second, where they have a common position within the international division of labour and consequently a shared *occupation*. Existing occupational patterns in pre-capitalist societies were used by European colonists to classify the population as supposedly endogamous groups. In other circumstances the migrations set in train by colonialism had led groups to define themselves as either endogamous, or in possession of some quality or characteristic which distinguished them from the native populations around them. Third, where they have one or more cultural attributes in common and consequently a shared *identity*. This could be national identity, or it could be religious, linguistic, regional or indeed virtually any other sort of identity. Ethnicity in this sense is simply a way of labelling people through the use of an ideological super-category that includes virtually any characteristic they might conceivably possess and is consequently quite useless for analytic purposes.[10]

In the context of this discussion, the first and second definitions are irrelevant. There are no longer any endogamous groups and have not been for centuries, or possibly even millennia (although there are, of course, groups which *believe* that they share the same genetic inheritance). There are certainly occupational groups, but these are by no means all 'national', and even those which are can never be the *basis* of nations, precisely because their definition as such is only possible in relation to a pre-existing external national homeland: Chinese traders in Indonesia can only be defined as Chinese because 'Chinese' is already a recognised national category. The third definition is the only relevant one and, as Smith's own checklist makes clear, it is entirely subjective. Assuming therefore that there is no third way between objective and subjective definitions, therefore, two difficulties are commonly raised in relation to the latter.

The first tends to be raised on the Left. Does granting national status to any group (Zionists like Ha'am, South African white supremacists, Ulster Loyalists and other groups whose goals socialists oppose) automatically imply support? This objection is based on a misunderstanding. Recognising that the aforementioned groups consider themselves to be nations does not in any way imply *support* for them. Whether or not one supports a national group surely depends on an assessment of the role it plays in world politics, not the mere fact of its existence. The distinction between oppressor and oppressed nations, first drawn by Marx and later refined by Lenin, is obviously a helpful guide in making such an assessment, although it is clear that many nations in dispute – of which Scotland is one – fall into neither of these categories.[11] The point is perhaps made clearer if considered in relation to existing imperial powers: I am, generally speaking, opposed to the activities of the French state; I do not for that reason seek to deny the existence of the French nation.

The second is less concerned with the theoretical than the political implications of subjectivism. According to Hobsbawm, subjective definitions are 'open to the objection that defining a nation by its members' consciousness of belonging to it is tautological and provides only an a posteriori guide to what a nation is.'[12] Such definitions would, however, be tautological *only if group members did not already know what a nation was.* Since they do, a group which decides it is a nation is saying, in effect, 'we are the same kind of group as these other groups which have declared themselves nations'. The only group of which this could not have been true would have been the first to declare itself a nation, since it would have had nothing to measure itself against. Once a group decides that it is a nation then it usually also discovers that it has always been one, or at least that it has been one since 1291, or perhaps 1320.

In the discussion that follows the word 'nation' will therefore be used to describe a human community that has acquired national consciousness. Benedict Anderson famously wrote of the nation which exists in this consciousness that: 'It is *imagined* because the members of even the smallest nation will never know most of their fellow-members, meet them, or even hear of them, yet in the minds of each lives the image of their communion.' According to Anderson all communities beyond the original tribal groupings (and perhaps even they) have faced this problem of numbers and consequently have had to 'imagine' themselves as a collective, although in different ways depending on the nature of the community. Consequently, he argues, 'imagining' in this sense is neutral and does not involve 'falsity' or 'fabrication'.[13] Leave aside whatever value judgements we may wish to make for the moment; it is nevertheless clear that national consciousness is *different* from other forms of collective consciousness. In what way? It is first necessary to identify what they all have in common.

The Russian Marxist Valentin Voloshinov wrote that: 'The only possible objective definition of consciousness is a sociological one.' By this Voloshinov means that consciousness is not an individual but a collective attribute. It is produced by people internalising the meaning of the ideological signs that their social group has produced and used over time in the process of interaction. As a result: 'Individual consciousness is not the architect of the ideological superstructure, but only a tenant lodging in the social edifice of ideological signs.'[14] We distinguish between specific forms of consciousness not by the way that they come into being or the way that the community is 'imagined', which are the same in each case, but by the relationships they bear to external social reality, which are different. These distinctions can be seen most readily if we compare national consciousness to another form of consciousness: class.

National Consciousness and Class Consciousness

All the analytic concepts that we use to describe certain types of social relationship – class, nation, state – are abstractions. What is crucial is their underlying relationship to the reality from which they are abstracted. For Marxists, 'class' is an objective condition independent of what a person perceives their condition to be. In the classic statement of this position, Geoffrey de Ste. Croix writes:

> A class (a particular class) is a group of persons in a community identified by their position in the whole system of social production, defined above all according to their relationship (primarily in terms of the degree of ownership or control) to the conditions of production (that is to say, the means and labour of production) and to the other classes.'[15]

For a class in a subordinate position within 'the whole system of social production' to become an effective contender for power it must first become *conscious*, both of its own position and of the antagonistic relationship that this involves with the dominant class. As Marx explains in relation to the working class:

> Economic conditions had first transformed the mass of the people of the country into workers. The domination of capital had created for this mass a common situation, common interests. This mass is thus already a class against capital, but not yet for itself. In the struggle...the mass becomes united and constitutes itself as a class for itself.[16]

It may be, as Georg Lukacs once suggested, that in situations where the process has not taken place, it is nevertheless possible to imagine what type of consciousness the working class might have if its members were collectively aware of their position.[17] Their position as workers does not, however, *depend* on their awareness of it, for it is certain that many, perhaps most, workers under capitalism have never achieved full awareness of their position; indeed, this is one of the necessary conditions of their remaining workers under capitalism.

There is, however, another position, also claiming to be Marxist, which argues against an objective definition of class. Edward Thompson has given it the clearest expression: 'And class happens when some men, as a result of common experiences (inherited or shared), feel and articulate the identity of their interests as between themselves, and against other men whose interests are different from (and usually opposed to) theirs.'[18] Some writers have used this definition of class to argue for the essential similarity between the processes by which classes and nations are formed.[19] In fact, Thompson's original definition does not relate to the formation of classes at all, but to the formation of class *consciousness*, the process of becoming a 'class for itself'.[20] Nevertheless, with the necessary adjustments it does indeed become an excellent definition of how *nations* 'happen': 'And nationhood happens when some people, as a result of common experience (inherited or shared), feel and articulate the identity of interests as between themselves, and against other nations whose interests are different from (and usually opposed to) theirs.' The point here, and the reason why I have stressed the objective nature of social class, is that where nations are concerned, the situation is reversed. Contrary to what is written by Stalin and all other objectivist theorists of the nation, there is no underlying reality of nationhood that can be brought to the level of consciousness. Consequently, to revert to the Marxist distinction between a class 'in itself' and a class 'for itself', we can say that a national group becomes 'a nation for itself' when members of the group learn to think of themselves and each other as members of the same nation, but can never be 'a nation in itself'.[21] As George Kerevan once pointed out, national consciousness 'is materially determined by the external appearance of bourgeois society', class consciousness is materially determined 'by its essence'.[22] Class consciousness arises through a process of *recognising* real common interests, a recognition which is only possible as a *result of* social classes having a material reality prior to consciousness. National consciousness arises through a process of *constructing* imaginary common interests, a construction which can *result in* the establishment of a territorial nation state, but only at that point will the nation have a material reality outside of consciousness. The resulting difference in aspiration may be summed up schematically by saying that a member of a social class *may* achieve class consciousness (bring their consciousness in line with reality) and a group with national consciousness *may* achieve statehood (bring reality in line with their consciousness).

National Consciousness and Nationalism

I have suggested that national consciousness does not always involve the objective of attaining statehood. In his attempt to specify what distinguishes the nation from other 'imagined communities', Benedict Anderson stresses the existence of both territorial limits 'beyond which lie other nations', and sovereignty embodied in a state, which suggest the opposite.[23] In this Anderson stands in a long tradition within social science. Max Weber wrote that 'a nation is a community [of culture] which normally tends to produce a state of its own'.[24] Albert Cobban concluded, still more decisively, that: 'A nation is a community which is, or wishes to be, a state'.[25] For John Breuilly the active participation in realising that wish is decisive:

> The constant reiteration of the statement 'I am French' is empty unless linked to some notion of what being French means. In turn, that meaning can become politically effective only if shared by a number of people with effective organisation. It is the shared meanings and their

political organisation that constitute a form of nationalism rather than the purely subjective choices of individual Frenchmen.[26]

Other writers have gone still further. According to Anthony Smith: 'A nation can...be defined as *a named human population sharing an historic territory, common myths and historical territories, a mass, public culture, a common economy and common legal rights and duties for all members.*'[27] The difficulty with this definition is that if nationhood is even partly dependent on economic and legal factors then – contrary to what Smith says elsewhere in his writings – nationhood must involve not only the desire for statehood, not only participation in or support for the struggle to achieve it, but its actual attainment, for it is difficult to see how else 'a common economy and legal rights and duties' could have any reality.

All the writers cited directly above fail to distinguish between what I have defined as national *consciousness* and national*ism*, and treat the former merely as an aspect of the latter. Montserrat Guibernau, for example, writes that:

The fragmentary nature of current approaches to nationalism originates from their inability to merge its two fundamental attributes: the political character of nationalism as an ideology defending the notion that state and nation should be congruent; and its capacity to be a provider of identity for individuals conscious of forming a group based upon a common culture, past, project for the future and attachment to a concrete territory.[28]

And, in the context of Scotland, Tom Nairn has written of the difference between what he calls 'Upper Case Nationalism' and 'lower case nationalism'; the first representing the specific political demand for a nation state, although not necessarily membership of the Scottish National Party, and the second a more general identification with the Scottish people, compatible with a variety of political positions, but both can be accommodated under the heading of nationalism.[29]

In fact, the sense of mutual recognition implied by the term 'national consciousness' is different from nationalism. It is perfectly possible for a people to develop national consciousness without subsequently becoming nationalists – and the majority of modern Scots are the living proof of this contention, at least as far as Scottish, as opposed to British, national consciousness is concerned – but it is *not* possible to build a nationalist movement without (at least a minority of) people previously developing national consciousness. The two have also been known to develop simultaneously, but for the purposes of clarity I will treat national consciousness as a more or less passive expression of collective identification among a social group, and nationalism as a more or less active participation in the political mobilisation of a social group for the construction *or* defence of a state.

Anthony Smith has argued against purely political definitions of nationalism on the grounds that 'not all nationalisms have in practice opted for independent statehood', citing the Scottish and Catalan examples. Smith asserts that a consequence of defining nations politically is that they can only then be said to exist when embodied in a state, leading to a situation where 'Scotland cannot become a "nation" until the majority of Scottish voters agree with the Scottish National Party's platform and vote for an independent Scottish "nation-state"'.[30] Here we see the consequences of failing to distinguish between national consciousness and nationalism. The Scottish people already have national consciousness and would therefore constitute a nation even if there were no organisations committed to Scottish statehood – as indeed was the case prior to the 1920s. Similarly, Michael Biddiss asks rhetorically whether 'a deep pride in Welshness only be accorded the status of nationalism proper when it is harnessed to the programme of Plaid Cymru?'[31] The answer is, not necessarily, but it must be harnessed to *some* programme for the establishment of a Welsh state, otherwise 'deep pride' remains an expression of national consciousness, rather than nationalism.

What National Consciousness Is Not

Nationalism is not the only concept to be confused with national consciousness. In the following section I want to distinguish between national consciousness and four related concepts – national identity, 'banal nationalism', patriotism and cultural nationalism – to which it bears a superficial resemblance and with which it often used interchangeably. This will have the added advantage of showing what I mean by these concepts when I use them in the chapter that follows.

National Identity

The most widely used of these concepts is that of 'national identity', which is unsurprising, given the totemic authority with which the concept of identity in general is currently endowed. The supposed transition from modernity to postmodernity, whose precise date is disputed but most commonly placed in the first half of the 1970s, is held to have produced a number of unprecedented social effects: 'Postmodernism argues that late or post-modern societies are impelled by constant and rapid social change which makes a fixed and immutable sense of self redundant.' According to this argument, there has not only been an increase in the *speed* with which identities can be exchanged, but also a change in the *type* of identities associated with modernity – principally those of class – to others which are the basis of the 'new social movements such as feminism, black struggles, nationalist and ecological movements'.[32] As John Shotter says: '"identity" has become the watchword of the times', but as Michael Billig adds: 'The watchword, however, should be watched, for frequently it explains less than it appears to.'[33] There are a number of reasons why the current significance ascribed to identity requires that we mount a watchtower, but two are particularly relevant to this discussion.

The first is that the significance of identity is not new. One of the chief characteristics of modernity was precisely 'constant and rapid social change' in which, as one moderately well-known text of 1848 has it, 'all that is solid melts into air'. It is therefore curious that these characteristics are now being claimed for postmodernity. It may be therefore that people who lived during earlier stages of industrial capitalism had a wider and more fluid range of identities (religious, regional, artisanal, stadial) than is sometimes patronisingly assumed by modern social theorists: it was certainly during this period that national identity became available for the first time, at least for the majority of the populations of Europe and the Americas.[34]

The second is that, even if we accept that identities have some increased significance in contemporary social life, some are of greater significance than others and cannot be exchanged for others. As Michael Billig has stressed:

> Not all identities should be considered as equivalent and interchangeable. Perhaps the postmodern consumer can purchase a bewildering range of identity-styles. Certainly, the commercial structures are in place for the economically comfortable to change styles in the Western world. ...national identity cannot be exchanged like last years clothes. ... One can eat Chinese tomorrow and Turkish the day after; one can even dress in Chinese or Turkish styles. But *being* Chinese or Turkish are not commercially available options.[35]

National identity is therefore of great significance, but is it the same as national consciousness? For some writers it is. Take, for example, the following – and in most respects unexceptionable – passage by Guibernau:

> In my view nationalism is a sentiment that has to do with attachments to a homeland, a common language, ideals, values and traditions, and also the identification of a group with symbols (a flag, a particular song, piece of music or design) which defines it as 'different' from others. The attachment to all these signs creates an identity; and the

appeal to that identity has had in the past, and still has today, the power to mobilise people.[36]

My objection is not, at this point in the argument, with the concept of nationalism outlined here, but with the concept of national identity. As Billig writes: 'One should not presume that an identity is a hidden psychological state, as if there is a wordless, psychological or neurological state of "having an identity"'.[37] The signs to which Guibernau refers do not *create* an identity, they *are* themselves an identity, or rather, they are part of one. Identities are the *ensemble* of all the external signs through which people show both to themselves and to other people that they have chosen to be identified in that particular way. These signs can be as visible as particular types of clothing or as audible as particular ways of speaking, but most often they are simply the ways in which people respond to being addressed in a particular way. If, for example, I began to wear the kilt as my regular form of dress, where I had previously worn trousers, began to include Scottish words in my conversation, where I had previously spoken only English, and began to hail the abilities of the Scottish national football team, where I had previously expressed admiration for the Italian side, the observer might reasonably conclude that – questions of my sanity apart – I was asserting my Scottish national identity by displaying the signs which are generally recognised as carrying this message.

Ross Poole has noted the variety of ways in which the term 'identity' has been used and the consequent ambiguity which has arisen over its meaning. As far as national identity is concerned, he discerns two dominant uses. The first corresponds to the way in which I understand national identity:

In one sense, identity refers to what is characteristic of and perhaps specific to a particular group or community: in this sense, national identity designates the particularities of tradition, politics, history, geography and culture insofar as these enter into a prevailing conception of a nation.

The second corresponds to the way in which I understand national consciousness:

On the other hand, the term is often used to refer to a mode of individual existence – a way in which individuals conceive themselves and others. In this sense it is individuals who have identities (or sometimes search for them), and national identity is a certain kind of shared self-awareness.[38]

As Billig notes:

> National identities are forms of social life, rather than internal psychological states; as such, they are ideological creations, caught up in the historical processes of nationhood. ... A 'national identity' is not a thing; it is a short-hand description for ways of talking about the self and community.[39]

National *consciousness*, however, is precisely the 'internal psychological state' which then seeks expression in the outward signs of identity. This does not mean that for every form of consciousness there is a corresponding 'identity' which one 'has' (recall Billig's strictures about identity not being a *thing*): Edward Thompson wrote of the 'robustness' of 'customary consciousness' in eighteenth century England, but the people of whom he writes did not have a 'customary identity'. Rather they took part in certain rituals, gave utterance to certain types of speech, or had certain expectations of how much should be charged for staple goods, all of which they recognised as 'customary'.[40] Similarly, there is class consciousness but there is no 'class identity', at least for the working class. The outward signs of class-belonging change as the class itself is restructured and as new and different occupations – with corresponding forms of dress and speech – arise to replace the old, which are then invariably lamented as 'traditional', even though they may only have existed since the latter half of the nineteenth century.

'Banal Nationalism'

If the concept of 'national identity' is virtually omnipresent in the contemporary discourse of the nation, then that of 'banal nationalism' is unique to its creator, the social psychologist, Michael Billig, from whose work I have already drawn. Billig uses the concept to stress both the ubiquity of nationalism and its unexceptional quality: 'The metonymic image of banal nationalism is not the flag which is being consciously waved with fervent passion; it is the flag hanging unnoticed on the public building.'[41] Billig appears to consider 'banal nationalism' an example of what Voloshinov calls a 'behavioural psychology': 'Behavioural psychology is that atmosphere of unsystematised and unfixed inner and outer speech which endows our every instance of behaviour and action and our every "conscious" state with meaning.'[42] I have found this to be a useful concept, particularly in deflating the assumption within long-established nation states (which often happen to be the most powerful states in the world system) that they are immune from nationalism: '"Our" nationalism is not presented as nationalism, which is dangerously irrational, surplus and alien': only other people have nationalism. Billig aims his comments specifically at the situation in the USA, but they have a broader applicability: 'The wars waged by US troops; the bombing in Vietnam and Iraq; the bombast of successive US presidents; and the endless display of the revered flag; all of these are removed from the problems of over-heated nationalism.'[43] Banal nationalism is not, however, the same as national consciousness. No matter how everyday or undemonstrative the former is, it is still an expression of loyalty to the nation as a *state*, as the image of the flag employed by Billig makes clear, whereas the latter is an expression of identification with the nation as a *social group* who may not have attained statehood and may not even aspire to do so.

Patriotism

'Patriotism' in the modern sense seems to have come into use in the late seventeenth century, but was first systematically formulated in England by Henry St. John, Lord Bolingbroke, during the 1720s. He drew on three sources. The first was the tradition of Greek and Roman thought, reclaimed from Antiquity by Machiavelli, where political 'virtue' was ensured by balancing between the different elements of the constitution, namely king, lords and commons. 'Corruption' was the consequence of any of these elements attaining ascendancy over the others and patriotism was the expression of resistance to this imbalance. The second was the notion that the ancient constitution of the English itself was handed down from the unsullied period of the Anglo-Saxons, before the Norman conquest. The third was the belief that, with the Reformation, England became an elect nation, not necessarily in a religious sense, but one in which England is seen as the home of liberty.[44]

Bernard Crick writes of this period in British history that: 'Patriotism could, indeed, positively adhere to the Dynasty, Parliament, the Protestant religion and the rule of law (or negatively to hating and fearing Papists and the French) in both England and Scotland, but patriotism does not always imply nationalism.'[45] This is plausible if we are simply using the term 'patriotism', as the late Ernest Gellner did, to refer to any of the different feelings of group loyalty possible before nationalism came into being.[46] In eighteenth century England, however, the term did not denote any old loyalty, but exactly the same loyalty as is now denoted by the term 'nationalism': it is how people spoke of nationalism before that term came into common use during the early nineteenth century. This is certainly how it was received in France where, in 1750, the treatise by Bolingbroke in which his ideas were expounded was translated and published anonymously as *Lettres sur l'esprit de patriotisme et sur l'idée d'un roi patriot*. As Robert Palmer notes:

> Patriotism was invoked in 1789 because the course of eighteenth-century thought had prepared and developed it. ...it was nationalism,

if we take the word in its larger sense to mean the idea that a man depends for his well being, his possession of rights, his hope for self-improvement, his duties and obligations, his faith in a cause for which he is willing to die, not on God, the king, humanity, class, or something vaguely called society, but on his nation or *patrie*. And this idea showed a remarkable growth in the forty years before the Revolution.[47]

This usage became general in Europe and North America following the French Revolution of 1789. In their address to the Scottish Society of the Friends of the People in 1792, for example, the United Irishmen quite naturally discussed the constitutional changes of the previous decade in these terms: 'The patriots won reform, but the revolution itself was nominal and delusive.'[48] It is therefore quite wrong to argue, as for example Peter Taylor does, that it was only the Anglo-British who claimed to be patriots rather than nationalists.[49] During the classic period of bourgeois revolution, from 1776 to 1848, it was the term used by both those who wished to reform the existing capitalist states (in the United Netherlands and Britain) and those seeking to create new capitalist states on their model (in the American Colonies and France).[50]

What has confused the question of patriotism is that the meaning of the term underwent a change during 'the long nineteenth century'. Crick is, of course, the biographer of George Orwell, and he has praised the distinction which his subject drew between 'patriotism' and 'nationalism' as one of 'extraordinary importance'.[51] Yet if we turn to the essay from 1945 in which he makes this distinction we find the following definitions:

By 'patriotism' I mean devotion to a particular place and way of life, which one believes to be the best in the world but has no wish to force upon other people. Patriotism is of its nature defensive, both militarily and culturally. Nationalism, on the other hand, is inseparable from the desire for power.[52]

As Orwell explains elsewhere in this essay he is using 'nationalism' in a highly personal way, nevertheless it is clear that he is using the term patriotism quite differently from a British patriot urging war on France in the 1740s or, for that matter, a French patriot urging war on Britain in the 1790s, neither of which could remotely be called 'defensive'.

In fact, the distinction drawn by Orwell between patriotism and nationalism had already been formalised by the Dutch historian Johan Huizinga in a lecture given under German occupation in 1940. According to Huizinga, the former corresponds to 'the will to maintain and defend what is one's own and cherished' and the latter to 'the powerful drive to dominate, the urge to have one's own nation, one's own state assert itself above, over and at the cost of others.' Superficially, this distinction appears close to that which I have drawn between national consciousness and nationalism, an impression strengthened by the existence of several Dutch terms for 'national awareness', 'sense of nationality' and 'national consciousness' which Huizinga sees as affinal with patriotism, but not with 'nationalism': 'The dividing line between patriotism and nationalism, however one may understand the latter, is in theory absolutely clear: the one is a subjective feeling, the other an objectively perceptible attitude.' In practice, however, he concedes that the distinction is less clear.[53]

Both writers were displaying an attitude, which crystallised in the face of Fascism, common where members of the Allies in particular defined their own nationalism as inward-looking and pacific, or at any rate defensive, compared to the aggressive imperialism of the Axis powers. Indeed, so different was this feeling, that it should not be classified as nationalism at all, but as patriotism. This may be understandable, but it is scarcely very plausible, given the way in which nationalist rhetoric was used to rally the defence of the Dutch and British Empires, and would shortly be invoked again during the Cold War to justify massive levels of arms spending 'in defence of British values' – something of which Orwell, in his more acute moments at least, was painfully aware.[54] The distinction between good 'patriotism' and bad 'nationalism' is now in general use, but is totally meaningless – except to indicate which nationalism the users themselves support, since they will refer to it as 'patriotism'.[55]

During the eighteenth century the term 'patriotism' was therefore a *precursor* to 'nationalism' because the latter term was not yet available. During the twentieth century it was used as an *alternative* to 'nationalism', because of the disgrace into which the phenomenon had fallen, partly as a result of the hysteria which accompanied the First World War, but even more so because of the way in which the Axis powers used nationalism to justify their conquests and the horrors which ensued. In both cases it is a thoroughly political concept.

Cultural Nationalism

The distinction between cultural nationalism (emphasising the 'ethnic characteristics' of a people) and political nationalism (expressing the 'collective will' of a people) first emerged, respectively, in works by J.G. Herder and Jean Jacques Rousseau during the third quarter of the eighteenth century.[56] The distinction between *Kulturnation* and *Staatsnation* was systematised by Freidrich Meinecke in 1907:

We may distinguish between an earlier period, in which nations on the whole had a more plantlike and impersonal existence and growth, and a later period, in which the conscious will of the nation wakens in that it feels itself to be a great personality (even if only through the

instrumentality of its leaders) and claims the hallmark and right of the developed personality, namely, self-determination.[57]

These remarks suggest a distinction very close to mine, between cultural identification and political mobilisation, which is reinforced by John Plamenatz:

> ...nationalism is primarily a cultural phenomenon, though it can, and often does, take a political form. It is related to, but different from, both patriotism and national consciousness. ... And national consciousness is only a lively sense of, and perhaps also a pride in, what distinguishes one's own from other peoples. It is a sense of cultural identity. It was as strong among the Greeks, the Romans and the Italians of the Renaissance as it had been anywhere in the last two centuries. But these three peoples were free of nationalism because they felt no need to preserve a threatened culture... Nationalism, as distinct from mere national consciousness, arises when people grew aware, not only of cultural diversity, but of cultural change and share some idea of progress which moves them to compare their own achievements and capacities with those of others.[58]

There are two reasons for doubting the assimilation of national consciousness to cultural nationalism.

The first is the assumption that culture is by definition unpolitical. Smith has argued that to deny movements intent on renegotiating their position within a multinational state the title of nationalism is untenable because it 'overlook[s] the centrality of national culture and social regeneration in their movements, an ideal that is common to so many other "nationalisms".'[59] Accordingly culture may in certain circumstances be as central to a nationalist movement as political activity, for example, 'where political nationalism fails or is exhausted, we find cultural nationalists providing new models and tapping different kinds of collective energies, thereby mobilising larger numbers of hitherto unaffected members of the community.' Smith cites the Irish Gaelic revival after the fall of Parnell in 1891 as an example of this.[60] These movements are nationalisms, but not because culture in itself has the same significance as politics. On the contrary, it is because cultural mobilisation in these circumstances is simply *politics carried on by other means*, where normal means are no longer available, but this is still a political project. And it is possible to generalise the argument still further. Barnard has argued that the distinction between cultural and political nationalism is in every circumstance untenable, and was so even when Herder and Rousseau set out their respective positions. Both men 'were equally anxious to advance a doctrine of nationhood which involved the transformation of both culture and politics':

...the significance of 'cultural nationalism' is not in its being apolitical or non-political but in directing attention to a profound change in the source of political legitimisation. Culture now emerges as something not only potentially relevant to politics but something indispensably *necessary*. A nation is no longer simply a community bound by spiritual ties and cultural traditions. Indeed...it is precisely the infusion of culture with political content, which characterises modern nationalism. Nationalism, on this view, is unthinkable without the appeal to cultural values. But for this change to come about, for culture to be invoked in the making of political claims, culture must itself be viewed in its political contexts.[61]

The second reason is the period during which cultural nationalism is said to have existed. In the quotation from Meinecke he is discussing the failure of – amongst other *Kulturnations* – the ancient Greeks to form a *Staatsnation*. As we have seen, Plamenatz discusses not only the Greeks but the Romans and – with slightly more plausibility – the Italians of the Renaissance. Both writers imply, in other words, that nations have always existed, but have not always succeeded in forming states. As Moses Finley acidly observes: 'Modern critics of Greek particularism should first decry their failure to have an industrial revolution.' The ancient Greeks, in other words, did not have the structural capacity to form a nation state:

If one asks, Of what nation, territory or country was Ptolemy king?, the answer is that he was not king 'of' anywhere, neither in his titulary nor on his coins nor in any official documents, whether edicts, letters or treaties. He was just 'King Ptolemy', of wherever his writ ran at any moment. And the same was true of the other Hellenistic rulers, major or minor. That is what *dynasteia* signified.[62]

As this suggests, certain forms of consciousness only become possible when the historical conditions are ready for their appearance. When were the conditions ready for the appearance of national consciousness and how did it then become transformed into nationalism?

2

From National Consciousness to Nation States

'The surest sign that a society has entered into the secure possession of a new concept', writes Quentin Skinner, 'is that a new vocabulary will be developed in terms of which the concept can then be publicly articulated and discussed.' He takes the example of how the term 'state' emerged during the Reformation to describe 'a form of public power separate from both the ruler and the ruled, and constituting a supreme political authority within a certain defined territory'.[1] Yet the state had existed for thousands of years before the concept was required. With 'nation' the situation is reversed. The word 'nation' had existed for hundreds, if not thousands of years before it acquired its current meaning, but as Voloshinov explains: 'the word is the most sensitive index of social changes, and what is more, of changes still in the process of growth, still without definitive shape and as yet not accommodated into already regularised and fully defined ideological systems'.[2] We can see the social changes to which the word 'nation' provides an index by briefly surveying how the word was used in the medieval period.

The Vulgate Bible, for example, when first produced in the third century rendered the original Greek 'ethnos' as the Latin 'natio', although in the New Testament the terms 'gens' and 'populus' are also used interchangeably – understandably, since these all refer to the original Middle Eastern tribal formations whose dismal fate the authors of the Book of Jeremiah take such delight in recounting. 'Natio' was in turn translated as 'nacioun' in the first English versions of the Bible produced in the fourteenth century, and this passed into the Authorised Version of 1611 as 'nation'.[3] What did 'natio' mean in late medieval and early modern Europe?:

A kingdom was never thought of merely as the territory which happened to be ruled by a king. It comprised and corresponded to a 'people' (*gens, natio, populus*), which was assumed to be a natural, inherited community of tradition, custom, law, and descent. [4]

'Natio' was therefore one of a variety of terms, along with 'gens' and 'populus', used to designate a people. 'Peoples' were in turn defined by two characteristics, which Susan Reynolds calls 'common biological descent' on the one hand and 'common culture' on the other.

The origin myths which established 'common biological descent' had three main sources, all of which had been established by the sixth or seventh centuries. The first was developed in sixth century Byzantium to classify the barbarian peoples by their supposed descent from the Germanic god Mannus. The second, which was first set down in a seventh century Frankish chronicle, traced the Franks back to the arrival of exiled Trojans in the Rhineland following the fall of their city, a lineage which was quickly claimed by other peoples for themselves. The third, created in the seventh century by Isidore of Seville, claimed that the peoples of Europe were descended from Japheth, son of Noah. By the first millennium the three genealogies were increasingly being combined into one:

> By the eleventh century, the *Historia Brittonum*, with its various additions, derived the British from the Trojan Brutus, taking in Alanus/Alaneus (i.e. the deutero-Mannus) by the way, then showing the descent of the Trojans from Noah, and adding Noah's descent from Adam and from God for good measure. [5]

The most significant aspects of the 'common culture' were language and law. More precisely, if the feudal idea of nation was essentially defined racially, then the feudal idea of race was itself defined linguistically: 'Language makes race', wrote one medieval writer, Claudius Marius Victor. [6] It was on this basis of common language that the student fraternity in medieval universities was usually, if not exclusively, divided into 'nations' from the thirteenth century onwards. Indeed, the first recorded use of the term 'nationalism' was in relation to the founding of Leipzig University in 1409, as the result of an academic dispute between the Bohemian 'nation' and the three other 'nations' at Prague University. As Anthony Smith reports, however: 'The sense in which the term was used was restricted: a union to defend the common interest of one of the four "nationes" among the Leipzig professors.' [7] Nor was it only academic communities which were defined in this way, so too were the knightly orders: 'The Hospitallers in the Levant were grouped into tongues according to their place of origin in Western Europe.' [8] Identification of language with race is close to what we would now call 'ethnic', rather than 'national', identity. Robert Bartlett has noted the emergence of a 'politicised linguistic consciousness' during the later middle ages in which the word for 'language' also comes to mean 'the people', leading to a situation where 'ethnic and linguistic identity tended to blur into one another'.[9] As late as the publication of the French *Dictionnaire de l'Academie* in 1694 the nation was still defined as those who spoke the French language and were subject to French laws.[10] In the words of John Hale: '"Nation" then meant, as it had in the organisation of the General Councils of the church in the fifteenth century and still did in the social organisation of universities, a group of individuals with a common place of origin.' And as Hale makes clear, such 'nationalism' as did exist was the cultural expression of xenophobia towards other 'races'.[11]

These racial distinctions did not necessarily imply any degree of solidarity between their members. The international ruling class and its clerical ideologues communicated with each other in Latin and would have had more in common with each other than the peasant masses over whom they ruled, even supposing – and this is a major supposition – that they shared the same vernacular in the first place. One basis for the myth of the Norman Yoke in English history – of a Saxon 'race' oppressed by Normans – is the fact that the court did indeed speak in Norman French until the mid-fourteenth century. There were, of course, particular group loyalties in the premodern epoch, but these cannot be equated with nationalism. Susan Reynolds has criticised the view that European medieval kingdoms were 'predestined "nation-states"' which are 'seen as moving through the attainment of "national consciousness" to find [their] own rightful boundaries in the nation-state'. Leaving aside the fact that not all succeeded in doing so, this perspective assumes that the 'values and solidarities' of medieval Europeans were the same as our own: 'Language like this casts a blanket of muddled anachronisms over medieval institutions and ideas.' In their place, Reynolds uses the term 'regnal' to describe the kind of solidarity felt by the inhabitants of a kingdom towards the monarch or – more important in the context of Scotland after 1286 or even 1603 – the *institution* of monarchy.[12] As Brendan O'Leary has written: 'Most of those who discuss "nations" before "nationalism" are in fact establishing the existence of cultural precedents, and ethnic and other materials subsequently shaped and re-shaped by nation-builders.' Those who do so, and 'assimilate the materials upon which nationalists will draw, to nationalism itself' are both falling victim to and contributing to a 'conceptual confusion'.[13] In some cases regnal solidarity is one of the 'other materials' out of which nationalism was constructed: it should not be confused with the finished product.

What other forms of consciousness were available during the medieval period? Everyone was a believer in the Christian faith and, as a necessary concomitant of this, a member of a Christian congregation. Everyone also belonged to one of the Three Estates, but, with the exception of the merchants, it is unlikely that many of the Third Estate regarded themselves in this way. Identification with your Estate was the preserve of members of the First (clergy) and the Second (nobility), not the Third (commons). Both religion and rank were universal sources of identity, unconnected with belonging to particular locations or populations. At the local level all territories and peoples were subjects of one royal dynasty or another, who often ruled over widely disparate languages and cultures without attempting to unify them into one. For the vast majority of the population who lived on the land, the apex of the feudal pyramid represented by the monarch would have been unimaginably distant. Unavoidably, their identities would have been suffocatingly local.

Even if one accepts that 'the nation' in contemporary usage is an aspect of modernity whose appearance as a general movement can be traced no further back than the second half of the eighteenth century, one must still choose between alternative versions of the modernist case.

On the one hand, the sociological tradition derived in equal parts from Durkheim and Weber emphasises the need for societies to achieve cohesion during the process of *industrialisation*, overcoming its disintegrative impact on agrarian society by imposing a common culture coincident with the territory of the state. The key figure here is neither Durkheim nor Weber, but Ernest Gellner, for whom: 'The roots of nationalism in the distinctive structural requirements of industrial society are very deep indeed.' At least three aspects of industrial society produce this requirement: 'mobility', 'communication' and 'size due to refinement of specialisation'. These constitute a particular kind of culture:

> The maintenance of this kind of inescapably high (because literate) culture requires protection by a state, a centralised order-enforcing agency or rather group of agencies, capable of garnering and deploying the resources which are needed both to sustain a high culture, and to ensure its diffusion through an entire population, an achievement inconceivable and not attempted in the pre-industrial world.[14]

Nationalism here is essentially a substitute for the role of religion in what Weberians call traditional or agrarian societies. In effect they dismiss the idea that nations are permanent aspects of the human condition *before* industrialisation, only to reintroduce it as applicable *after* the process has begun.

On the other hand, Marxists emphasise not industrialisation as such but the dominance of *the capitalist mode of production*. This recognises that, because some areas were dominated by the capitalist mode long before industrialisation proper, national consciousness – and in some cases a fully formed nationalism – existed there before the second half of the eighteenth century. Given the frequency with which the existence of nationalism before 1789 is offered as a supposedly devastating critique of the Marxist position, it is perhaps necessary to elaborate on the latter point. As Michael Mann has noted, industrialisation simply arrives too late to play the role Gellner assigns to it. To argue that nations only appeared at some stage in the later eighteenth century would be as absurd as arguing that capitalism only appeared at the same period.[15] (It should be noted, however, that towards the end of his life, Gellner tended to argue that with 'industrialisation' he also included the earlier 'commercialisation' of society before large-scale production had been introduced – a position closer to the Marxist one.[16]) In fact, national consciousness took as many centuries to become the dominant form of consciousness as the capitalist mode of production did to become the dominant mode of production, and it did so as a *consequence* of the latter.

National consciousness developed in three stages. In the first, which I call that of *psychological formation* (c.1450–1688), it emerged unevenly across Europe (and its colonial extensions) among the most advanced economic groups as a response to socioeconomic changes set in train by the transition to capitalism. In the second, which I call that of *geographical extension* (1688–1789), the success of groups with an emergent national consciousness in the Netherlands and England in elevating this new psychological state into political movements led others (first in North America, Ireland and France, then generally) to aspire to national status, even if their level of social development had not previously allowed national consciousness to arise. In the third, which I call that of *social diffusion* (1789–1848), national consciousness begins to emerge in the social classes below the rulers of the new nation states, partly as the result of deliberate indoctrination, but far more so as the by now inevitable pattern of life experience within societies shaped by the nation state form.

Psychological Formation

Four main elements combined at the origin of national consciousness: all reflect to a greater or lesser extent the impact of capitalism on feudal society.

The *first* element was the formation of externally demarcated and internally connected areas of economic activity. Europe had emerged from the first crisis of feudalism by the second half of the fifteenth century as a system of states which, the Swiss Confederation apart, was still dominated by the feudal mode of production. It was a system, however, increasingly adapted to elements of capitalism. In *this* context, the importance of capitalist development is less in the domain of production than that of circulation, for it was in the creation of trade networks that merchant capital began to link up dispersed rural communities both with each other and with the urban centres to form an extensive home market.

Linked directly to this element was a *second*, the adoption of a common language by the communities that were being connected to each other at the economic level. During the mid-sixteenth century Charles de Roulles complained that while travelling across France he encountered eight different ways of saying 'yes' and 'no'.[17] The need to communicate for the purposes of market exchange began to break down the distinctiveness of local dialects, forging a language common, or at least comprehensible, to all. Language in this way began to set the boundaries of the economic networks referred to above, boundaries that did not necessarily coincide with those of medieval kingdoms. Clearly such economic and linguistic unification was far easier in a small centralised kingdom like England than in a territory like the German Empire. As Hale writes: 'In practice Germany was a congeries of independent units comprising some thirty principates...fifty ecclesiastical territories, about one hundred counties and sixty self-governing cities.'[18] Indeed, establishment of state frontiers often determined the boundary between a dialect of a particular language and another language. As J. Derrick McClure has pointed out, Flemish and Dutch are now considered no less than separate languages, and both are as near (or as far) from German as the English spoken in London is from the English spoken in Cornwall. If the German state had evolved to include Flemish-speaking Belgium and the Netherlands, however, then Flemish and Dutch would now be considered no more than dialects of German.[19] Any standard form is, as McClure nicely puts it, usually 'one out of a number of dialects which has, for fortuitous reasons, undergone a process of social climbing', usually because it happened to be the dialect spoken in the commercial and administrative centre of the state.[20] Billig has suggested that the concept of 'a language' is an invention of the epoch of the nation state, and: 'If this is the case, then language does not create nationalism, so much as nationalism creates language; or rather nationalism creates "our" common-sense, unquestioned view that there are, "naturally" and unproblematically, things called different "languages", which we speak.' The same is true for dialect: 'The notion of "dialect" becomes crucial to maintain the idea of separate languages: it seems to account for the fact that not all speakers of a language speak in the same way.'[21]

The formation of standard forms of language was immeasurably aided by the invention of printing and the possibilities it presented for the codification of language in mass-produced works. Of the 20,000,000 books published by 1500, 23 per cent were already in the vernacular, rather than Latin.[22] These would not have been produced unless an audience of the literate already existed which understood their contents, but their effect was to extend the size of that audience, since printers could not produce works in *every* local dialect, only in the one which had emerged as the standard form, or in those which were in competition to do so. The first north German translation of the Bible in 1479 had to be produced with double columns, one each for the Saxon and Frankish dialects of the language: an edition which extended to even the main south Germany dialects would have been impossible to produce in readable form.[23] The increasing standardisation of language then fed back into its original economic formation, as the merchants whose trading networks had originally defined the territorial reach of linguistic comprehensibility increasingly identified themselves with that territory, to the exclusion of rivals who spoke a different language. The rise of the vernacular was accompanied by the decline of Latin as a *lingua franca*, a process virtually complete by the mid-sixteenth century and expressed in the new profession of interpreter, now necessary to make vernacular diplomatic exchanges mutually comprehensible.[24]

As this reference to international relations suggests, the *third* element was the character of the new absolutist states. Absolutism was the form taken by the feudal state during the economic transition from feudalism to capitalism. Yet the absolutist states did not arise automatically as the expression of some immanent tendency within this process. The replacement of the estates monarchy of the earlier feudal period by this more centralised apparatus was rather the political response of the feudal ruling class to the social and economic pressures – different in degree and combination throughout Europe – set in train by the first crisis of the feudal system and the greater significance of capitalist production in the economies which emerged from it.

The fourteenth century crisis of the feudal system involved a generalised fall in rural productivity followed by demographic collapse, as the combined effects of famine and disease afflicted the inhabitants of town and country alike. In these circumstances the landowning nobility could only maintain – let alone increase – their level of income by systematically *extending* the area controlled by the state to which they owed allegiance (thus increasing the number of peasants under seigniorial control) and *intensifying* the level of exploitation for both long standing and newly conquered peasant communities. One brought conflict *between* those states who encroached on each other's territories, a process exemplified by the Hundred Years War between England and France (1337–1453). The other brought conflict *within* states, between the lords and the peasantry, who violently opposed increased exactions in a great series of risings which began in maritime Flanders in the 1320s and ended (in western Europe at least) in Catalonia in the 1470s. Both the effective pursuit of external military aggression and suppression of internal revolt required the agency of a centralised coercive state power greater than the territorially dispersed structures typical of the first period of feudalism proper (c.1000–1450). For our purposes two main characteristics of this emergent state form were of central importance.

One was the relative autonomy of the absolutist states from their class base – the nobility. The collective interests of the feudal ruling class did not necessarily correspond to the individual interests of its constituent feudal lords. Consequently the latter did not, in the main, directly control the state apparatus, either through inherited membership of their feudal estate or appointment to regal office. On the contrary, since they regularly went to war with each other and, less regularly, combined to make war on the monarch, it was essential that the apparatus was operated by a bureaucracy responsible to the crown and not to specific noble interests. Inseparable from this strengthening of central power was a weakening of the power of the lords in two areas. *Collectively*, the lords were invariably the dominant estate within any parliament, and could use this position to thwart the wishes of the monarch. The relative success of the absolutist monarchies therefore depended on (and could almost be measured by) the extent to which they managed to suppress their particular national assembly – the longevity of French absolutism compared to the English variant being very marked in this respect. *Individually*, the lords held jurisdictional authority within their own superiorities, which provided, on the one hand, a (theoretically) untrammelled supremacy over the peasants and, on the other, a territorial base for resistance to the monarch, particularly when combined with a system of military land tenure. Aspirant absolutists therefore sought to dominate the peasantry directly, without relying on local noble intermediaries. By 1688, where this displacement of power had been achieved successfully – as it had in France, Spain, Prussia and Sweden – the responsibility for extracting the surplus from the peasantry had been assumed by the central state and the mechanism of surplus extraction changed from rent to tax: the local autonomy of the nobles was thereby greatly reduced.

The other characteristic was the hegemony that the absolutist states exercised over the class that would eventually overthrow them – the bourgeoisie. For the bourgeoisie, the absolutist state was important as a means of controlling civil disorder within the towns and protecting the towns themselves from the demands of individual nobles; for the absolutist state, the bourgeoisie were important as a source of revenue, as personnel to fill the offices of state and, most importantly, as a social force which the monarchy could muster in the face of collective noble opposition. Yet this dependent relationship left the bourgeoisie as an *influence* upon the state, not a co-determinate (with the nobility) of its class nature. Absolutism placed the bourgeoisie in a protected but subordinate place within the social order, which had the paradoxical effect of allowing socioeconomic advance while imposing political retardation.

In the context of this discussion, it is important that in several respects these invested the territorial state with far greater political significance than did the estates monarchies that preceded them. The local jurisdictions that characterised the classic epoch of military feudalism began to give way to greater concentration of state power, notably through the introduction of standing armies and, partly in order to pay for them, regular centralised taxation. Death and taxes both involved bureaucracies that required a version of the local language, comprehensible across the state territory, with which to conduct their business, thus strengthening the second, 'linguistic', element referred to above. They also had two unintended effects. On the one hand, the introduction of regular taxation and the adoption of mercantilist policies reinforced the economic unity that had begun to emerge spontaneously from the activities of merchant capitalists. On the other, the military rivalry that characterised the new system necessitated mobilising the active support of the bourgeois minority as a source of financial backing and administrative expertise. Despite these innovations it is nevertheless important not to mistake the role of absolutism in the birth of nationhood, which was that of a midwife, not that of a mother. The issue is often elided by reference to the influence of 'the modern state' in the creation of nations, but this is to dissolve the difference between the absolutist state and its genuinely modern bourgeois successor.[25] The law is important in this respect. John Cairns writes of the rise of the legal works titled 'institutes' or 'institutions' in the seventeenth century:

> This element of national unification in law, the creation of a common law within one nation state, is found in the French institutional writers, who, while France was a country with a multiplicity of differing laws and jurisdictions, felt able to produce institutions of the law of all France.[26]

This process was not one of unifying the law, however, but of adding together all the different laws which pertained throughout the territory of the state. It would take the revolution of 1789 to establish a unified French law. More generally, the arrival of nationhood coincided not with the establishment of the absolutist states but with their overthrow.

The *fourth* and final element is an example of what Eric Hobsbawm calls 'protonationalism', or what I prefer to call 'protonational consciousness'. Under this heading Hobsbawm describes several types of 'collective belonging'. The most relevant to this discussion are 'supralocal forms of popular identification which go beyond those circumscribing the actual spaces in which people passed most of their lives', examples of which might be local manifestations of a global religious belief.[27] The ideology of absolutism involved stressing the deeds of religious figures such as saints who were associated with the territory of the realm, but it was the Reformation which made religion more than an ideologically pious enhancement to the image of the ruling dynasty. Wherever Protestantism became the dominant religion within a given territory after 1517, it contributed to the formation of national consciousness by allowing communities of belief to define themselves against the intraterritorial institutions of the Roman Catholic Church and the Holy Roman Empire. In part, this was through the availability of the bible in the vernacular, but this in turn was dependent on the existence of pre-existing linguistic frameworks in which market transactions and state administration could be carried out. In short, Protestantism acted as a stimulus to national consciousness only to the extent that the development of capitalism had provided it with the framework to do so. Naturally the process went furthest in England, but even there it was not until after the death of Elizabeth in 1603 that Protestantism came to be separated from regnal solidarity with the monarch.[28] Eventually, Catholicism would play the same role, but as Josep Llobera writes: 'religion was not sufficient to define national identity, particularly in religiously homogeneous areas, where there was more than one nation competing for hegemony.' Llobera uses the example of Catalonia in the nineteenth century to illustrate how 'the local church, and particularly the rank and file clerics – who were closer to the people – might have helped to vehiculate a nationalist ideology which went against state nationalism', but it is important to note that because the Catalan church was the same as that of the central Spanish state, it could not act as a focus for Catalan nationalism until the epoch of nationalism had arrived in the eighteenth century, when its continued use of the language made it the main vehicle for preserving Catalonian national consciousness.[29]

Geographical Extension

What precipitated the formation of national consciousness out of these four different elements? It was the bourgeois revolutions which effected the final transformation of the term 'nation' from one which signified '*a* people' as a racial group to one which stood for '*the* people' as a community – although one of the most divisive issues within all bourgeois revolutionary movements was precisely how 'the people' should be defined. As late as 1743, Jean-Francois Melon could define the French nation as 'about a thousand men as against twenty million others'.[30] In one respect, therefore, the great French Revolution was about extending – forcibly, in some cases – the definition of 'the French nation' to include the twenty million others. Yet whatever limits were set on membership, the struggle against absolutism required the mobilisation of at least a large minority of 'the people' to achieve the expulsion or destruction of the royal dynasty. This could only be done by providing some form of identity which could embrace the often very different forms of opposition to the crown, regardless of whether the ruler in question was foreign (as in the case of Spanish Hapsburg dynasty in the Netherlands) or native (as in the case of the Stuart dynasty in England).[31] Nationalism provided this identity.

Initially, it was an identity adopted principally by the bourgeoisie. Since the very term 'bourgeoisie' is frequently subjected to ridicule, it is perhaps worth explaining what is meant by the term. Ellen Meiksins Wood has attacked the notion, allegedly held by more orthodox Marxists than her, of 'the bourgeois as an agent of progress':

> We have got so used to the identification of bourgeois with capitalist that the presuppositions secreted in this conflation have become invisible to us. The burgher or bourgeois is, by definition, a town dweller. Beyond that, specifically in its French form, the word used to mean nothing more than someone of non-noble status who, while he worked for a living, did not generally dirty his hands and used his mind more than his body for work. That old usage tells us nothing about capitalism, and is likely to refer to a professional, an office-holder, or an intellectual no less than to a merchant.

Meiksins Wood calls attention to the flawed 'logic' whereby 'the ancient town-dweller gives way to the medieval burgher, who in turn develops seamlessly into the modern capitalist' and endorses 'a famous historian' who regards this view of history as involving 'the perennial rise of the middle classes'.[32] It is true that the origins of capitalism had no necessary connection with the growth of the towns. (This is a position associated with the thinkers of the Scottish Enlightenment and with the Marx and Engels of *The German Ideology*, where that work displays the Scottish influence.) It seems to me, however, that dislodging the bourgeoisie from the position they have occupied in Marxist accounts of the rise of capitalism gives far too much ground to anti-Marxist historians who wish to expunge from the historical record not only the 'rising bourgeoisie', but any notion that fundamental social change takes place through class struggle.[33] Some Marxists have responded to such attacks, not by effectively conceding the argument, like Meiksins Wood, but by avoiding the contested terminology, like Christopher Hill.[34] Neither of these options is satisfactory. The term 'bourgeoisie', like a number of terms (one of which, as we have seen, is 'nation') changed in meaning over time. By the time Marx used the term in the 1840s, it stood, in relation to town-dwellers, for something both shallower than previously (because it excluded the new class of industrial labourers) but also something wider (because it included rural capitalists). In short it meant capitalists, both rural and urban, in the literal sense of the those who owned or controlled capital, but also a larger social group over which capitalists as such were hegemonic. Hal Draper describes the bourgeoisie in this sense as 'a social penumbra around the hard core of capitalists proper, shading out into the diverse social elements who function as servitors or hangers-on of capital without themselves owning capital.'[35] These social elements tended to include lawyers and – in eighteenth century Scotland at least – ministers of religion.

Recognising the role of the bourgeoisie as the initial bearers of national identity can prevent historical misunderstandings. I wrote earlier of the need to distinguish between national consciousness and nationalism for analytic purposes. Nevertheless at the point of origin the two are inseparable. This is important since, as we saw when considering 'cultural nationalism', some writers have argued that national consciousness existed long before nationalism. Breuilly – who is a modernist – uses two essays by Dante to argue that national consciousness could be found as early as the thirteenth century. In one, 'On Vernacular Language', Dante claims to have discovered an Italian language, which he in turn identifies with the Italian nation and argues for its use by poets. In the other, 'On the Monarchy', Dante argues for the establishment of a universal monarchy to establish harmony across Christendom as a whole, not only in the Italian Peninsula. Breuilly argues that the divergence between these two positions is proof of both 'the existence of some kind of national consciousness and concern with national language and cultural identity in late thirteenth and early fourteenth century Europe' and 'the non-existence of nationalist consciousness'.[36] The 'illustrious vernacular' of which Dante spoke was in fact the Florentine dialect adopted by intellectuals like himself who belonged to the bourgeois of the most advanced Italian city-state. As Gramsci asked: 'Does not this mean that two conceptions of the world were in conflict: a bourgeois-popular one expressing itself in the vernacular and an aristocratic-feudal one expressing itself in Latin and harking back to Roman antiquity?' With the decline of the Communes and the reimposition of feudalism, the attempt to establish a vernacular means of expression was destroyed along with its social basis:

> After a brief interlude (the communal liberties) when there is a flourishing of intellectuals who come from the popular (bourgeois) classes, the intellectual function is reabsorbed into the traditional caste, where the individual elements come from the people but where the character of the caste prevails over their origins.[37]

In other words, the national consciousness expressed by Dante was linked to the very early development of capitalism in Italy, whose defeat meant that the possibility of national unification was taken off the historical agenda for another 500 years. In these circumstances the aspiration for a universal monarchy was an *alternative* to a nationalism which had been blocked, and whose literary manifestations would soon themselves be abandoned. National consciousness could not flourish, or even take root, where the conditions for capitalist development were no longer present, and for it to be consolidated across Europe, even if only among the bourgeoisie, there had to be at least one case where it successfully made the transition to nationalism and then became embodied in a nation state. Only when there were concrete examples of nationhood could different groups know what they were conscious *of*, regardless of whether they then went on to develop nationalisms of their own or not.

The capitalist nation state became a permanent feature of the international state system only towards the end of the hundred years between the end of the English Revolution in 1688 and the beginning of the French Revolution in 1789. Thereafter, new nations could be manufactured regardless of whether the original elements were present or not – although an economic infrastructure and common language would, of necessity, have to be introduced at some point for a sense of national consciousness to be consolidated. As Billig writes of the construction of the French nation during the revolutionary years after 1789: 'Because the project was being pursued in its own name (policies were to be justified in the name of "the nation"), it had to assume its own reality before being effected in practice.'[38] The ideological dominance of nationalism over the population depended, however, on *when* a particular revolution occurred in the overall cycle of bourgeois revolutions. In the two states where bourgeois revolutions were successfully completed before or during 1688 – the Dutch and the English – the existence of national consciousness was directly proportional to the extent that the post-revolutionary state developed a centralised apparatus, rather than a federal or confederal structure. In this respect English nationalism – 'God's firstborn', as Liah Greenfield calls it[39] – was as far in advance of its Dutch predecessors as it was of its American successor, which similarly remained an alliance of semi-autonomous states down to 1865.[40]

Three American academics have recently argued that the view of nineteenth century Europe as the epoch of nationalism must be abandoned. During the French Revolution: 'The nation is divided by class and regional strife, widely unsupported or even resisted by a disenchanted or uninterested population, and ruled by narrowly based governments dependent on terror, conscription and foreign wars.' The Italian Risorgimento and German Unification were similarly empty of national content:

> Nationalism was limited and contradictory in both cases, sometimes exploited, usually disregarded; not only the masses but also even the elites had little choice. The appeal of unification to these elites may in fact have been more economic than nationalist. The course of events was governed by traditional cabinet diplomacy in pursuit of great power interests, specifically the goals of Prussia and Piedmont as determined by Bismarck and Cavour. In their calculations, nationalism played no significant role.[41]

The problem with this analysis is that the authors treat nationalism as an independent political variable, a 'thing in itself', so to speak. If it transpires that other interests may have been involved then nationalism must therefore be of no account. But nationalism can only ever be a vehicle by which 'other' interests are advanced; to believe otherwise is to accept the myth of nationalism itself, which these authors evidently do. It is of course true that the majority of these elites were concerned to build states, rather than nations, but the latter was a necessary concomitant of the former, in conditions of industrialisation; this is the meaning of the famous quip by the Piedmontese politician Massimo d'Azeglio, which they quote, but evidently fail to understand: 'we have made Italy, now let us make Italians'.[42] As the great nationalist leader Giuseppe Mazzini wrote before Italy was 'made':

> The nation is the universality of Italians, united by agreement and living under a common law. ... Without unity of belief and a social consensus, without unity in political, civil and penal legislation, without unity in education and representation, there is no nation.[43]

After 1848 all ruling classes intent on creating states on the British or French models were forced to embrace nationalism, not because they personally were capitalists, or even, more broadly, members of the bourgeoisie, but because all of them – Prussian Junkers, Japanese Samurai, Italian monarchists and, eventually, Stalinist bureaucrats – were engaged in building industrial societies dominated by the capitalist mode of production. The example of Italy, cited above, is typical of how ruling classes were faced with the need to diffuse consciousness of being a nation down from elite level into the mass of the population, a large and growing proportion of whom were not the bourgeoisie and petty bourgeoisie who had originally formed the nation, but workers. The difficulties involved should not be underestimated: as late as the 1860s as many as a quarter of the inhabitants of the French state did not speak French: 'French was a foreign language for a substantial number of Frenchmen [sic], including almost half of the children who would reach adulthood in the last quarter of the century.'[44] In many respects, however, the difficulties involved in developing such a consciousness among workers were less extreme than among peasants.

Social Diffusion

Before discussing the nature of national consciousness among the working class, it will be necessary to return to the concept of class consciousness, or more precisely, that of *reformist* class consciousness, since this provides the context within which national consciousness and nationalism develop.

Ralph Miliband has argued that class consciousness at the individual level operates at a series of four 'distinct and ascending levels', rising from 'perception of class membership', to a perception of the immediate interests of that class, to possessing 'the *will* to advance the interests of the class', to a 'perception of what [the advancement of class interests] requires, not simply in immediate terms, but in more general, global terms'.[45] Miliband rightly says that the degree to which classes become conscious of their position varies according to what kind of class they are. Exploiting classes have always displayed a far greater awareness of their position than the majority of those whom they exploit – indeed, this is a precondition of their continuing to exploit them. Exploited classes, on the other hand, have shown far less awareness. He is wrong, however, to say, in relation to the working class, that any worker who is not committed to the revolutionary overthrow of capitalism is not class conscious.[46] On the contrary, the levels of consciousness between failing to even recognise oneself as a member of the working class and recognition of the revolutionary role of the working class are occupied by a particular form of class consciousness produced by the tension between accepting the system as an unchanging feature of human society and rejecting the way in which specific aspects of it negatively impact on the lives of working class people. For most workers, most of the time, it is the norm, not the exception.[47] The ascent to revolutionary class consciousness occurs when workers see both that these negative aspects are neither accidental nor incidental, but direct effects of how the system operates, and see that it is possible to replace that system in its totality.

Reformist consciousness was originally a historical product of the social conditions produced by the transition to capitalism, or, more precisely, by the process of capitalist industrialisation, first in Britain and subsequently wherever the process took place. It is sometimes said that the industrial working class in Britain was revolutionary at the moment of its formation and subsequently *became* reformist through a combination of political defeat in 1848 and economic expansion thereafter. But while the working class was certainly *insurrectionary* in its formative years, this is not the same as being revolutionary. The restricted nature of politics in the late eighteenth and early nineteenth centuries meant that even *reforms* had to be fought for with arms in hand – the debates about moral versus physical force in both the Chartist and earlier Radical movements were in some respects not about reform *versus* revolution, but about how best to achieve reform, through peaceful means or otherwise. In fact, reformist consciousness was established very early in the history of the British working class and will be reproduced as long as capitalism exists, but we are concerned here with its origins. Four developments lay behind it.

First, once the initial shock of industrialisation passed, workers came to accept that capitalism was not a passing aberration, but a new form of society which might have many years of vitality ahead of it. The apparent permanence of the system forced accommodation and adaptation, however grudgingly, from the new exploited class, whose horizons were anyway limited by the 'dull compulsion' to work, raise families and recover from the savage exertions demanded by the factory system.

Second, although these conditions provoked resistance, the fact that the new system generated its own defensive illusions made the possibility of a generalised revolutionary class consciousness emerging out of this resistance struggle less likely. Under slavery, feudalism, or any other class society before capitalism, the direct producers are forced to hand over all or part of the surplus they have produced to the exploiter by the threat or reality of force. Under early capitalism, exploitation was accompanied, not usually by the threat or actuality of direct physical violence, but rather by the economic discipline instilled by fear of the poverty which would result from being sacked. It could be argued that this, or at least the result in terms of hunger and general deprivation, was also a form of violence, but the impact on consciousness was different, at least partly because workers appeared to engage in fair exchange with the capitalist: he or she contracted to work for a certain number of hours and was paid accordingly. The actual process of exploitation, the fact that the worker produced more than that for which she or he was rewarded, was hidden from view.[48] As a result, although workers were usually hostile to their own particular boss, this did not necessarily generalise into opposition to the system as a whole, since meanness or ill-treatment of the workforce could be put down to his personal qualities (or the lack of them), rather than to the necessities of exploitation.

Third, since workers would nevertheless not come to a conditional acceptance of capitalism purely by the illusions thrown up by the economic operation of the system, a conscious effort was made by both the capitalist state and individual capitalists to persuade workers of the virtues of the system, a project rehearsed in church sermons and classroom lessons well before the advent of the mass media to whom such instruction is left today.

Fourth, although trade unions grew out of worker resistance, the goal of these new organisations, whatever rhetoric was employed about (invariably distant) overturning of the system, was improving the condition of the working class within the system itself.

In Britain, where both industry and the working class developed first, reformism as a form of working class consciousness was a fact by 1832, although it took another 50 years before it became embedded in political organisations. In other words it clearly predates the extension of representative democracy, the advent of imperialism, the creation of the welfare state, or any of the other mechanisms which are often cited as having secured the consent of the working class. The resulting form of consciousness was famously described by Gramsci as 'dual' or 'contradictory'; on the one hand accepting the permanence of the system, on the other rejecting the effect of its operation.[49] The most basic expression of this contradiction is an acceptance by workers of the wages system accompanied by a rejection of the particular level of wages which they are being offered, but it extends to all aspects of social life. The following incident, recorded by Wilhelm Reich after an encounter on an Austrian train during the 1930s, illustrates these contradictions in perhaps their most extreme form:

A young worker, clearly a married man, was saying that all the laws were made for the rich and were rigged against the poor. I pricked up my ears to hear what else this class-conscious worker might have to say. He went on: 'Take the marriage laws, for example. They say a man's entitled to beat his wife. Well I can tell you, only a rich man can beat his wife. If you're poor, you always get pulled up for it.' Whether what he was saying is correct or not isn't the point. It is highly indicative of what goes on inside an average worker's head. As a poor man, he contrasts himself with a rich man and senses his inequality: so far as that goes, he has the beginnings of a class conscious mentality. But at the same time he would dearly love to be able to *beat his wife within the law*! And his class sense makes him feel at a disadvantage in this particular respect. Bourgeois sexual morality fights class consciousness in his mind.[50]

What then is the relationship of national consciousness to this reformist consciousness? As Kerevan points out, workers are confronted by 'two materially conditioned allegiances'. On the one hand: '*Nationalism*, reflecting the social position of the individual caught in the allegiances of civil society and its exterior state.' On the other: '*Proletarian internationalism*, reflecting the class position of the worker and the kernel of the socialist mode of production developing within capitalism.'[51] But precisely because nationalism reflects the position of the worker in civil society, it never manifests itself in a pure form. Alex Callinicos points out that:

Dual consciousness within the Western working class is characterised by the acceptance of two identities – as worker and as citizen, as member of a class and as member of a nation state. These identities imply an involvement in different kinds of social conflicts, the class struggle between capital and labour and the power struggle between nation states.[52]

As the reference to dual consciousness here suggests, national consciousness does not compete with revolutionary class consciousness *directly* for the allegiance of workers, but as a key element in reformist class consciousness. Indeed, one might say that workers remain nationalist to the extent that they remain reformist. And from the point of view of the capitalist class in individual nations it is absolutely necessary that they do so, or the danger is always that workers will identify, not with the 'national' interest of the state in which they happen to be situated, but with that of the class to which they are condemned to belong, regardless of the accident of geographical location. Nationalism should not therefore be seen as something which only 'happens' during separatist movements on the one hand, or during fascist and imperialist manifestations on the other: the capitalist system generates nationalism as a necessary, everyday condition of its continued existence.

Benedict Anderson once argued that the origins of national consciousness lay in the collapse of 'three fundamental cultural conceptions' during the rise of capitalism: the identification of 'a particular script-language' (such as Latin in Christendom) with access to religious truth; the belief that society was organised in a natural hierarchy, at the summit of which were 'monarchs who were persons apart from other human beings'; and a view of the inseparability of cosmology and history which rendered 'the origins of the world and of men essentially identical'. The interconnected decline of these three meant that human beings required 'a new way of linking fraternity, power and time meaningfully together'.[53] As Chris Harman has noted, however, this argument makes the connection of nationhood with capitalist development contingent rather than necessary, with the former simply allowing expression for an 'existential yearning' and providing an outlet for 'the satisfaction of innate psychological needs.'[54] It is possible, however, to reformulate the position held by Anderson in a way that does not assume an eternal human condition, but looks to how it answers particular social needs which are produced by the atomised nature of capitalist society.

In one respect Gellner is right to say that mass nationalism was a product of industrialisation, but his insight was too focussed on the functionality of nationalism for industrial societies. At least as much attention should be paid to the way in which industrialisation, and the related process of urbanisation, together produced the changes in human consciousness which made nationalism *possible* (for the subordinate classes), as to the way in which the more complex societies they produced made nationalism *necessary* (for the dominant class). It is all too easy to ignore how unprecedented these experiences were (and still are) for the people undergoing them. Take a relatively late, but well documented example of industrialisation.

During the early 1930s the Russian psychologist A.R. Luria undertook a number of studies of behaviour in Uzbekistan and Kirghizia, both areas of what was then Soviet Central Asia. These were areas where the economy was largely pre-capitalist and the majority of the population were illiterate. The first five-year plan provided for more intensive industrialisation of regions like Central Asia than in the USSR more generally. Accordingly: 'Industrial production, and numbers of workers employed in industry, expanded more rapidly in Central Asia and Kazakhstan, and in the Urals and West Siberia, than in the rest of the USSR.' Furthermore, this was from a lower level: 'While 9.4 per cent of the Soviet population lived in these republics, they contained only 1.5 per cent of those employed in large-scale industry; and most industrial workers were Russians.' By 1934 this had completely changed, with the number employed in large-scale industry nearly trebling from 53,000 to 158,000: 'The increase in the working class in these areas took place against the background of the forcible transfer of a large part of Central Asian agriculture to the production of cotton, and the forcible settlement of the nomadic Kazakhs, many of whom died from starvation in the subsequent famine, or emigrated from Kazakhstan.'[55]

Both regions were therefore experiencing what Luria later called 'a radical restructuring of their socioeconomic system and culture' as a result of Stalinist collectivisation and the industrialisation process. The economy was based on cotton, with some transhument cattle-rearers who spent part of the year in the mountains. The population was dominated by Islam, in respect of whose tenets women were confined to their own quarters, from which they could only emerge if draped in the veil. 'The radical changes in class structure were accompanied by new cultural shifts.' These included the universalisation of literacy and numeracy, but also the agronomy. 'As a result, people became acquainted not only with new fields of knowledge but also with *new motives for action.*' These developments produced new forms of consciousness, in which 'abstract' rather than 'situational' thinking came to predominate, on the basis of new state capitalist social relations rather than those associated with those of petty commodity production. As Luria notes:

...sociohistorical shifts not only introduce new content into the mental world of human beings; they also create new forms of activity and new structures of cognitive functioning. They advance human consciousness to new levels. We now see the inaccuracy of the centuries-old notions in accordance with which the basic structures of perception, representation, reasoning, deduction, imagination, and self-awareness are fixed forms of spiritual life and remain unchanged under differing social conditions. The basic categories of human mental life can be understood as products of social history – they are subject to change when the basic forms of social practice are altered and are thus social in nature.[56]

The second great influence on the forms of human mental life is the process of urbanisation which, in most cases, accompanies industrialisation. Here I simply want to quote from George Simmel, writing in Germany before the First World War, as he describes the influence of urbanism in an evocative passage from his great essay, 'The Metropolis and Mental Life':

> The psychological foundation, upon which the metropolitan individuality is erected, is the intensification of emotional life due to the swift and continuous shift of external and internal stimuli. Man is a creature whose existence is dependent on differences, i.e., his mind is stimulated by the difference between present impressions and those which have preceded. Lasting impressions, the slightness in their differences, the habituated regularity of their course and contrasts between them, consume, so to speak, less mental energy than the rapid telescoping of changing images, pronounced differences within what is grasped at a single glance, and the unexpectedness of violent stimuli. To the extent that the metropolis creates these psychological conditions – with every crossing of the street, with the tempo and multiplicity of economic, occupational and social life – it creates in the sensory foundations of mental life, and in the degree of awareness necessitated by our organisation as creatures dependent on differences, a deep contrast with the slower, more habitual, more smoothly flowing rhythm of the sensory-mental phase of small town and rural existence.[57]

In short, industrialisation and urbanisation, particularly when combined into one process, develop new structural capacities, new modes of experience and new psychological needs in the people who have to work in the factories and live in the cities. Tom Nairn has argued for the 'functionality' of nationalism in meeting the new needs created by these two processes:

> Nationalism could only have worked, in this sense, because it actually did provide the masses with something real and important – something that class consciousness postulated in a narrowly intellectualist mode could never have furnished, a culture which however deplorable was larger, more accessible, and more relevant to mass realities than the rationalism of our Enlightenment inheritance. If this is so then it cannot be true that nationalism is just false consciousness. It must have had a functionality in modern development, perhaps one more important than that of class consciousness and formation within the individual nation-states of this period.[58]

It is this need for some collective sense of belonging with which to overcome the effects of alienation, the need for psychic compensation for the injuries sustained at the hands of capitalist society, that nationalism *provides in the absence of revolutionary class consciousness, but in conjunction with reformist class consciousness.* One might say that the origins of national consciousness see the emergence of an identity-ensemble adequate to the historical conditions of generalised alienation. The initial experience of peasants and rural labourers plucked from their communities and dropped into the urban hells of Glasgow, Manchester, Berlin, Turin or Petrograd, is clearly relevant to the period under discussion here, but the needs produced by capitalist industrialisation are permanent. As Kerevan writes, 'if individuals only face one another in the market connected by money relations; then their social unity as individuals is reflected in only one all-embracing unit of civil society – the nation.'[59]

There are obvious similarities between what Marx himself said about religion and what I am saying here about nationalism. The former has of course long been subjected to both careless and deliberate misrepresentation. The point of the passage containing the reference to 'the opium of the people', is not that religion is a drug administered by a ruling class to dull the senses of the people, but that it is manufactured by the people themselves to fill the void created by what the later Marx would call their alienation: '*Religious* suffering is at one and the same time the expression of real suffering and a protest against real *suffering.*' [60] In this sense nationalism is the modern form of religion, with the state (or forces seeking to establish a new state) occupying the organisational role once played by the church.

The ideological role played by the ruling class in reinforcing nationalism is therefore only possible because nationalism already provides one possible means of meeting the psychic needs created by capitalism. Nevertheless, any suggestion that nationalism is ultimately linked to the ideological defence of capitalism is however one which many critics of Marxism find hard to accept. Gellner once claimed that in Marxist theory nationalism is simply 'a conscious distraction of populations from the real underlying conflict between classes, the obfuscation perpetuated in the interests of ruling classes, having much to fear from class consciousness, and much to gain from the encouragement of a spurious national consciousness'.[61] Breuilly certainly assumes that this is the Marxist position and has argued that nationalism is 'too pervasive to be reduced to the ideology and politics of this or that class or set of classes' and 'too complex and varied to be understood as a reaction to a particular type of economic relationship or disparity'.[62] These writers, who are by no means the most unsympathetic to Marxism, protest too much.

Once a capitalist nation state has been established, those who control the apparatus always seek to consolidate the hold of nationalism among the people who inhabit its territory. As Nigel Harris puts it:

> Once the boundary is beaten back and troops posted around the perimeter, the State undertakes to colonise all within, to drill all the inhabitants who find themselves behind the fence with an invented common inheritance, supposedly to a common culture or way of life, but in practice to a particular state.[63]

States need conscripts for their armies, citizens to pay taxes, workers to accept that they have more in common with those who exploit them at home than they do with their fellow-exploited abroad. The latter was particularly important in the early years of the nation state, since there is some evidence to suggest that members of what Peter Linebaugh and Marcus Rediker call the 'Atlantic working class' of the eighteenth century before industrialisation were not primarily national in their consciousness:

> At its most dynamic the eighteenth-century proletariat was often ahead of any fixed consciousness. The changes of geography, language, climate, and relations of family and production were so volatile and sudden that consciousness had to be characterised by a celerity of thought that may be difficult to comprehend to those whose experience has been steadier.[64]

This made it imperative that loyalty to a state be secured, and the nation was the *means*. Since the eighteenth century British workers have often been asked to accept rises in interest rates, cuts in wages and services, or participation in imperialist wars, but never for the benefit of British capitalism, always for the benefit of the British nation, for 'the national interest'. But it is not only the state which makes such appeals. The organisations of the working class themselves reinforce reformist class consciousness within a national context. At the most elementary level this is because such organisations are unwilling to challenge the nationalism within which political discourse is conducted, for fear of being labelled unpatriotic. More importantly, however, it is because they seek either to influence or determine policy within the confines of the existing nation state.

Typically, therefore, nationalism is invested with the contradictory character of the reformist world view. As Voloshinov notes: 'The ruling class strives to lend the ideological sign a supraclass, external character, to extinguish or exhaust the struggle of class relations that obtains within it, to make it the expression of only one, solid and immutable view.'[65] It cannot do so:

Existence in the sign is not merely reflected but refracted. How is this refraction of existence in the ideological sign determined? By an intersecting of differently orientated social interests within one and the same sign community, i.e. *by the class struggle*. Class does not coincide with the sign community, i.e. with the community which is the totality of users of the same set of signs for ideological communication. Thus various different classes will use one and the same language. As a result, differently orientated accents intersect in every ideological sign. Sign becomes an arena of the class struggle.[66]

Linda Colley provides us with a concrete example from our period in which the relevant sign, or word, is 'Britons'. She notes of one man rioting against increases to the cost of bread during the Jubilee of George III: 'The "Old Price" rioter at Covent Garden, who was seen on jubilee day 1809 carrying a placard "Be Britons on the 25th but riot on the 26th" was admitting that his protest was a partial one as well as accepting that patriotism necessarily involved celebration of the monarchy.'[67] 'Be Britons, but riot' sums up with admirable brevity the contradictions, but also the limits, of working class nationalism as an element of reformist consciousness.

Britain was the first state in which the entire process of nation-building – from the initial psychological formation among sections of the bourgeoisie through to social diffusion among the mass of the working class – was completed. This process had very nearly run its course by 1809, but the rioter quoted above was, one assumes, English, in addition to being a 'Briton'. Where does Scotland, a component part of the British state since 1707, fit into the historical trajectory outlined in this chapter? Angus Calder has written that: 'A Scottish "nation" exists insofar as many Scots believe that it exists.'[68] When did they come to believe this?

Was There a Scottish Nation Before 1707?

There is an obvious difficulty in situating Scotland within the trajectory of national development outlined in the previous chapter. If national consciousness only became general in Europe and North America in the latter half of the eighteenth century, then either Scotland constitutes an exception to the general rule or the Scottish nation is of rather more recent origin than is generally supposed, only emerging *after* Scotland ceased to exist as a state in 1707. National consciousness had developed earlier than the eighteenth century in England and (to a much lesser extent) in the United Netherlands. Even in these cases, however, the decisive period lay in the nearby seventeenth century; the origins of Scottish nationhood are usually located in the far-off Middle Ages. '[The Scots] were...the first people in all of Europe to set themselves apart as a nation', asserted one nationalist text in 1960.[1] More recently, the same idea has been rendered in academic language by the historian, John Foster:

> Most historians...agree that by the eleventh to the thirteenth centuries at least four...groupings had fused themselves into a nation that identified itself as Scottish; long before any moves towards modernisation and at a time when Scots society was anything but civil.[2]

Although Foster is a Marxist, the near consensus to which he approvingly refers is that of historians of Scotland opposed to the classical Marxist view that there is a necessary connection between nationalism and the rise of capitalism, as he recognises in his somewhat arch references to 'modernisation' and 'civil society'. His conclusion, made more explicit in an earlier essay, is that: 'Unlike the Welsh and Irish (whose independent development ended at a pre-feudal stage) the Scottish nation seems to have been an almost entirely feudal creation.'[3] It is worth noting that if this is true, then far from Scotland being 'the first nation in

Europe', it could equally be argued that *all* of the major nations in Europe arose at this time.[4] Comparable elements to those which are supposed to confirm the existence of the Scottish nation in the fourteenth century can easily be assembled for other modern nations: for the Scottish victory at Bannockburn in 1314, the Serbian defeat at Kosovo in 1389; for the martyrdom of the Scottish hero William Wallace in 1305, the martyrdom of the French heroine Joan of Arc in 1431; for the Scottish Declaration of Arbroath of 1320, the English Magna Carta of 1214. This is a position that many modern historians would be happy to endorse, although as I pointed out in the previous chapter it rests on a misunderstanding of what the term 'nation' meant in the Middle Ages. Since reference to the Declaration of Arbroath is unavoidable at this point in the discussion, let us use it to illustrate that meaning in the Scottish context.

The Declaration, according to Christopher Smout, 'expresses all the fierce nationalism of the fourteenth century'.[5] For Geoffrey Barrow there is both 'no clearer statement of Scottish nationalism and patriotism in the fourteenth century' and 'no finer statement of a claim to national independence...produced in this period anywhere in western Europe'.[6] The sonorous wording of the Declaration is in fact a clear statement of, among other things, the fact that the feudal ruling class still considered themselves to be a nation in the racial rather than the modern sense. The Declaration is a letter to Pope John XXII, from the leading Scottish nobles 'and the other barons and freeholders and the whole community of the realm of Scotland', asking him to intervene diplomatically with Edward II on behalf of peace between Scotland and England, who had been inter-mittently at war since 1296. It seems probable that the contents were agreed at an assembly of nobles at Newbattle Abbey in Midlothian during March 1320, and that the final text was prepared and sent by Bernard of Linton, the Chancellor of Scotland and Abbot of Arbroath, where the letter was dated on 6 April.[7]

Who were the 'community of the realm' to whom the Declaration refers? According to Barrow, they were:

> ..neither the feudal baronage on the one hand nor the common people on the other. It meant, rather, the totality of the king's free subjects, but also something more than this: it meant the political entity in which they and the king were comprehended. It was in fact the nearest approach to the later concept of a nation or a national state that was possible in an age when, according to older and still deeply-entrenched belief, a kingdom was, first and foremost, a feudal entity, the fief – and therefore in a sense, the property – of its king.[8]

'The nearest approach to the later concept of a nation' does not in this case mean 'very near'. The preamble to the Declaration does indeed trace the wanderings of the 'Scots nation' from 'Greater Sythia' to Scotland, celebrates Scottish triumphs over Britons and Picts, and survival from attack by 'Norwegians, Danes and English'.[9] Those who believe these statements prove the existence of a primordial Scottish nation must logically also accept the existence of primordial 'British' and 'Pictish' nations, but leaving that aside, two points arise even from the few short sentences summarised here.

The first is that they express a view of 'the Scots' as a racial or ethnic group who happen to have settled in 'the places which it now holds' – 'Scotland', in other words, is the territory currently occupied by the Scots. The second is that, even in these terms, the signatories are unlikely to have believed that their origin myth represented the literal truth. According to Susan Reynolds:

> The Scots claimed that the threefold division of Britain between the three brothers [i.e. of Brutus the Trojan] justified Scottish independence. Alternatively, they sometimes based their claim to autonomy on their descent from Pharaoh's daughter [i.e. Scota], whose people had either conquered Albany from the British, or had come there long before Brutus. Sometimes they simply stressed their continuous independence from the time of their travels from Greater Sythia and through the Pillars of Hercules.[10]

More prosaically, the names of Roger Mowbray and Ingram Umfraville suggest descent from Anglo-Norman settlers who were invited to settle in Scotland during the reign of David I (1124–1153), who were in turn descended from earlier invaders of England from Normandy, who were in their turn descended from even earlier Viking invaders of what is now France from what is now Norway – a place somewhat removed from Greater Sythia.

The Declaration has also been portrayed as the prototype for popular nationalism on account of a passage that states:

> Yet if he [i.e. Robert the Bruce] shall give up what he has begun, seeking to make us or our kingdom subject to the king of England or to the English, we would strive at once to drive him out as our enemy and a subverter of his own rights and ours, and we would make some other man who was able to defend us our king; for, as long as a hundred of us remain alive, we will never on any conditions be subjected to the lordship of the English. For we fight not glory, nor riches, nor honours, but for freedom alone, which no good man gives up without his life.[11]

Edward Cowan believes that this admittedly superb example of medieval prose represents 'the first national or governmental articulation, in all of Europe, of the principle of the contractual theory of monarchy which lies at the heart of modern constitutionalism'.[12] In fact, it evokes the role of the noble estate as defender of the kingdom against the claims of the individual monarch in a way that was entirely typical of pre-absolutist Europe. Indeed, according to Reynolds, the Declaration is 'the most eloquent statement of regnal solidarity to come out of the middle ages'.[13] In the context of 1320 the specific content of the Declaration can be interpreted as carrying two indirect messages. One was to Edward II, indicating that there was no point in attempting to depose and replace Robert with a more pliant king, since the remainder of the aristocracy would continue to resist. The other was to Robert, indicating that they would not tolerate his jeopardising their interests – which would of course include their 'right' to the unimpeded exploitation of their tenants – by making concessions to the English crown. The latter message can be seen as a pre-emptive Scottish version of the Magna Carta imposed on King John by the English barons 100 years earlier.

Reynolds has noted the 'anachronistic enthusiasm' that the Declaration aroused, but insists that this should not make us completely disregard its content:

> Even if the rhetoric of the letter were empty and disingenuous it would be fallacious to assume that it would have been used if it had not appealed to values and emotions current at that time. Arguments to the contrary spring from that curious historical cynicism – almost a sort of inverted naivety – which is determined not to take any statement of feeling or principle at its face value.[14]

Reynolds is right. There is no reason to doubt the *sincerity* of the beliefs of those who wrote or signed the Declaration. But to apply the term 'nationalism' to these beliefs does not simply obscure their real motives, but establishes a false identity, or at least a false continuity, between the forms of consciousness available to them and those – almost inconceivably different – available to modern Scots. Use of this term confers legitimacy on a key element in nationalist ideology, namely the primordial continuity of 'the nation' throughout history.[15]

It might be useful at this point to broaden the discussion out from the Declaration itself to the period in which it was drafted. Participation by the peasantry and urban plebeians in the Wars of Independence is often cited, particularly on the Left, as proving the existence of national consciousness in the middle ages wider than that of the ruling class. In response to his own question concerning who was responsible for the defeat of the English army in 1314, Thomas Johnston replied: 'They were the working class, and it was the their charge on the field that won the battle of Bannockburn.'[16] In fact 'mass participation' (as Finlay calls it) appears to have had no discernible effect on the outcome at

Bannockburn, although it did at the earlier Battle of Stirling Bridge in 1297.[17] What is not evident is why this participation *in itself* demonstrates the existence of national consciousness, since popular movements – or, at any rate, popular mobilisations in support of rival elites – have been traced as far back as the Greek city-states. We would surely have to know *why* the masses participated before judging them to have done so in defence of a national idea. We have some evidence, including the Declaration itself, which suggests that the 'community of the realm' regarded itself – in common with similar groups across Europe – as a regnal group based on racial identity, but we have no direct evidence whatsoever concerning how those outside 'the community' regarded themselves. Nevertheless, as Kerevan writes, in my view with justified ferocity: 'The notion that illiterate peasants, who lived and died their short brutal lives within a few hundred yards of their village had a conception of nationalism beyond a gut xenophobia for everyone beyond the next village is stretching the imagination.'[18]

It can more plausibly be argued that English attempts in 1296 to raise the level of taxation and even seize individuals to fight with the English forces on the European mainland provoked the 'middle folk' into claiming a role in politics that they had previously been denied.[19] These people were however still a minority of the population. The role of the majority was to continue, silently in the background, pumping out the surplus which sustained the feudal lords who signed the Declaration: it would take until 1648 for peasants to play a political role independent of (and opposed to) the classes above them. Furthermore, the expansion of 'the community of the realm' did not mean that the regnal solidarity on which it was based had changed.

In the four centuries which followed, the 'middle folk' would gradually mutate, first into the 'middling sort' and then into a 'middle class', or more precisely, a bourgeoisie. I argued in the previous chapter that this class – understood in the broadest sense – was the first to conceive of itself in terms of modern nationhood. How far had it done so in Scotland by 1707?

The 'Holy Trinity'

Most historians who accept that the Scottish national consciousness existed before the Union also take the view that it was maintained afterwards through the various institutions preserved in the Treaty, the so-called 'holy trinity' of Scottish nationhood. Richard Finlay outlines the orthodoxy: 'For most of the eighteenth century, Scottish identity focussed on the three institutions of the Kirk, the education system and the law, all of which had survived the Union of 1707 with England.'[20] Some writers want to go even further. When Graham Morton writes that: 'Chanting the mantra which is the "holy trinity" of kirk, law and education is not enough', it is not because he questions their significance, but because he wants to extend the source of continuing nationhood to civil society as a whole.[21] Clearly, the view that national consciousness was carried forward into the Union by these means is incompatible with my claim that it was only at the preliminary stage in 1707. However, the argument for institutional nationhood is considerably weaker than is commonly supposed. Because there is considerable evidence to show the strength of Scottish national consciousness around, say, 1815, and since it is axiomatic that there was a Scottish nation to be preserved after the dissolution of the state in 1707, proponents of this thesis must argue that continuity was preserved by those social institutions which survived. In other words, it assumes precisely what must be proved. The alternative argument is of course that national formation was not complete by 1707, that the 'holy trinity' consequently could not have been the bearers of national identity and that, since the origins of the Scottish nation lie within the Union itself, there is therefore a greater need to search for change in Scotland after 1707 rather than continuity. There are four general problems with the claim for institutional continuity.

First, it is rarely made clear *what* is supposed to have performed the role of preserving national identity. Was it the *content* of the kirk sermons, the court decisions and classroom lessons? The *structure* of the clerical, legal and teaching professions? The *political influence* of the General Assembly of the Church of Scotland and the Faculty of Advocates? All of the above? This lack of clarity obscures the agency by which continuity is supposed to have been achieved.

Second, if these institutions (however defined) are to play the role ascribed to them, then they must have acquired their social significance in the period before 1707. This may seem obvious, but the examples which are often cited as demonstrating their importance are from a later period, particularly in the case of education.

Third, as this suggests, it is assumed that these institutions all played an equivalent role, but while religion still touched every aspect of social life in 1707, can it seriously be contended that education did the same? Most Scots would have had no experience of the latter beyond the parish schoolroom, which was in many respects simply an extension of the kirk. Law falls between these extremes, since the profession in Scotland was demarcated from that of England by the existence of Scots Law, but while there was an increasingly large number of lawyers in Scotland throughout the eighteenth century, they were still a tiny minority of the population. What impact did the existence of Scots Law as a set of institutes, or the Faculty of Advocates as a pressure group, have on the identity of other Scots? There is a lack of discrimination between the three institutions, each of which carried a quite different weight within Scottish society.

Fourth, in order to feel distinct from other national groups (or other social groups more generally) one group must be aware of the differences between them. Indeed, the entire basis of any identity (to be identical to) depends on such differences (to be different from). Even if we assume that most Scots had more contact with these institutions than appears to be the case, how many could have said why these institutions were distinct from those of the English? Education and law were simply the part of the existing order of things. Institutions tend to become the focus for national identification where they are suppressed and those of another nation imposed in their place (think of the Catholic Church in Ireland after 1690); but precisely because this did not happen in Scotland, the majority of Scots would never have had reason to make them the focus of their identity in this way. Of the 'holy trinity', only religion – the local version of the Calvinist belief system, the presbyterian form of church government and the state-within-a-state that was the Church of Scotland – played a major role in the lives of most Scots.

It is worth examining the case of education in more detail before proceeding. David McCrone claims that 'education has been and still is vital to the sense of Scottishness', but goes on to note much of this vitality is dependent on a series of myths.[22] One of these myths is, precisely, the length of time during which Scottish education has been significant for national identity. Lindsay Patterson, for example, writes that; 'education has always been a Scottish icon: its autonomy having been preserved by the Union Treaty in 1707, it has been seen as a main bastion of Scottish independence.'[23] This is a common misconception. Education was not 'preserved by the Union Treaty' and, unlike law or religion, is not mentioned in either the Act of Union or the related legislation. Indeed, there is some evidence that the importance of education in this respect went unrecognised until well into the nineteenth century, which in turn suggests that perhaps it was not important. As late as the ninth edition of the *Encyclopaedia Britannia* in 1875, the entry on Scotland (by Aeneas MacKay, Sheriff of Fife) opined that: 'Whilst it would be incorrect to say that Scotland has had no independent history since the Union, that history must be chiefly read in the annals of its church, its law *and its literature*.'[24] Robert Anderson has argued that the two most important achievements of Scottish education were 'the early arrival of universal or near-universal literacy, and a precociously developed university system; on these was founded the "democratic" myth of Scottish education'. Yet as Anderson himself points out with regard to the first: 'For all the virtues of the rural parish school, the chief features of modern Scottish education were created in the few decades following the Education (Scotland) Act 1872.'[25] Nor are the particular qualities of the Scottish universities relevant here, for these only became apparent in the latter half of the eighteenth century, earlier than the school system but, once again, far too late for the connections being claimed with the pre-Union period.[26]

Outside the kirk then, even if we substitute burghal government for education, only a minority of Scots – even if a large or socially pivotal minority – were regularly or significantly involved with the social institutions carried over from before the Union. There is, however, a deeper problem. The very idea that national identity *can* be preserved 'institutionally' has been rightly criticised by Tom Nairn, who argues that rather than an *institutional* identity being preserved after 1707, it was a *bureaucratic* identity, which was inevitably undemocratic. Nairn notes that, when asked to define their identity, 'no [Scot] has ever responded...with a short lecture on the beauties of the sheriff system, the merits of the Scottish generalist education or the advantages of not having one's own politics.'[27] And, although Nairn does not pursue the issue, the point is, fairly obviously, that the reason behind maintaining these institutions was not to preserve the identity of the Scottish *nation* but to preserve the functions of the Scottish *state*. Nationalism involves at the very least some level of identification of the 'people' with the state, but identification with the state (as opposed to certain aspects of Scottish society) was impossible for the vast majority of Lowland Scots. Consequently, the only groups who felt any loyalty to these continuing aspects of the state were the cadres who ran the professions, but these men were the most Unionist of all in their politics.

The Missing Components of National Consciousness

The existence of the 'holy trinity' itself proves nothing about the extent of the psychological formation of national consciousness in Scotland before 1707. In what follows, I will examine, in relation to Scotland, the four elements which by the mid-seventeenth century had combined to produce national consciousness among the English bourgeoisie: the creation of a territorially bounded market in which production was increasingly organised on a capitalist basis; the spread of a vernacular language within these territorial bounds in which the business of both civil society and the state was conducted; the establishment of the absolutist state which both incubates capitalist production and institutionalises the vernacular language; and the organisation of a section of the territorial social group into a community of religious belief. These separate elements will be presented in the same order as in Chapter 2. It is in this context that the Scottish 'holy trinity' will be discussed, or not, as the case may be. As I have already noted, religion is by far the most important and will be considered individually. Law is less significant and will be incorporated into my discussion of absolutism. Education, as I indicated above, is of no consequence whatsoever in this context, except insofar as it was an aspect of religion, and will consequently not be discussed at all beyond this point.

Scotland had one of the lowest levels of *capitalist development* in western Europe. When Sir James Steuart wrote in 1767 that Scotland could still be compared to fourteenth century Europe, he was exaggerating (and by 1767 grossly exaggerating), but a hundred years previously his remarks would not have been so misleading.[28] There have been several recent attempts, by both academic historians and nationalist writers, to demonstrate that seventeenth century Scotland was not as backward as had previously been believed. In both cases the objective is to minimise the speed and extent of economic transformation during the later eighteenth century. The former are attempting to prove that economic development was a prolonged, gradual process and did not in any way resemble a revolution.[29] The latter, that backwardness is an ideological construction to justify the civilising role of England and to disguise the fact that the Union was unnecessary for economic development.[30] The evidence to support such claims largely rests on the existence of various Acts of Parliament passed by the Covenanting regimes of the 1640s and by the Revolution Parliament in the 1690s. But while these may reveal the *aspirations* of the most commercially orientated section of the Scottish ruling class at the time, those aspirations largely remained unfulfilled.[31] The events of the 1690s tend to cast doubt on the claim that Scotland was on the verge of take-off at the end of the seventeenth century. The subsistence crisis which claimed between 50,000 and 150,000 lives (or between 5 and 15 per cent of the population) was obviously not a typical occurrence, but it nevertheless demonstrated the consequences of failing to transform Scottish agriculture. Other European countries suffered equally or worse, the only two exceptions being England, which had broken through the Malthusian barriers to agricultural production and the United Netherlands, which could at least afford to buy grain with the profits of merchant capital. Equally, the failure of the attempt to establish a colony at Darien demonstrated that neither the Scottish state nor civil society had the wherewithal to carry such a venture through to success.[32]

The issue is in any case not so much the *extent* of the Scottish economy immediately prior to 1707 (how much it produced) as its *nature* (what were the social relationships on which production was based). It remained feudal in the sense that the main source of ruling class income was extracted, in the form of rent, from the surplus produced by the peasantry, and that this was made possible by the threat or actual application of force, exercised through the territorial jurisdictions through which landowners could bring tenants to their own court. The implications of this were twofold. First, although the feudal lords retained a form of regnal solidarity with the idea of the Scottish crown, this took second place to their own local, particular interests. It is no accident that one of the concessions made by the English parliament during the treaty negotiations was to include an article (20) explicitly retaining the heritable jurisdictions through which the Lords exercised power over their tenants. Second, an integrated economy connecting all regions within the state territory was absent. As Johnston long ago noted: 'Scotland was not a nation: it was a loose aggregation of small but practically self-supporting communities, and scanty supplies and high prices at Aberdeen may quite well have been coincident with plenty and comparatively low prices in Dundee and Glasgow.'[33] In these circumstances even the bourgeois elements in Scottish society retained what Gramsci calls a 'corporate', sectional identity – literally so in the case of the burghs – rather than a national one.[34]

Nor did *language* help nationhood develop. The inhabitants of Scotland were not united by language but divided by it into Gaelic and English speakers. There has never been a 'Scots' language other than Gaelic, so that even Lowland Scots could not distinguish themselves from the English by these means. The vast majority of Scots, even in 1688, spoke what was originally the dialect of English spoken in Northumbria and brought from there to the Lothians and beyond by trade and conquest from the tenth century onwards, long before the border was established. It was this that eventually superseded Gaelic, but only after dividing into countless regional sub-dialects in the process. The myth of 'Scots' as a separate language is based on two misunderstandings.

The first misunderstanding is over the nature of the English language. Scottish nationalists often assume that to deny the existence of Scots is to accept the dominance of what one calls 'Standard English with a Home Counties accent'.[35] But this is precisely to concede the point that standard English *is* 'correct' English. In fact, the English language consists of the totality of English as it is spoken and written in England, Scotland, Ireland, Wales, North America, the West Indies, Australasia, South Africa, south Asia and other more scattered areas of the world which were once part of the British Empire. Kenneth White, not a writer noted for denigrating Scottish writing or speech, once noted that he personally talked 'English with a Glasgow and West Coast accent – as Carlyle talked English with an Annandale accent, Burns with an Ayrshire accent, and MacDiarmid with a Borders accent.'[36]

The second misunderstanding is over the nature of Scots. The assumption can easily be made, on the basis of examining Scottish literature of the Renaissance that a fully developed language existed by the mid-sixteenth century. But Lallans, as we call the language in which these works were written, was simply one among many dialects, namely that spoken in the Lothians and the southeast more generally. The importance of Lallans lay in the fact that it was used at the royal court in Edinburgh, not because it was spoken by the majority of Scots. It is of course conceivable that Lallans *could* have become 'the Scottish language'. As Derrick McClure writes:

If the autonomy of the kingdom had been maintained, there is no reason to doubt that the subsequent stages would have occurred in Scotland as they were to do in France and England, leading to the establishment of a Scots language which today would have the same international status as Dutch or Portuguese.[37]

Instead, Lothian Scots reverted to being one among many Scottish dialects, and these in turn became merely several Scottish dialects of English. It is worth noting, however, that the poets who wrote in Lallans did not consider it to be distinct from English. In 'The Goldyn Targe', written in the early sixteenth century, William Dunbar acclaims Chaucer simultaneously as the finest of British authors and as one of the Makars – the contemporary Scottish poets first given this name by Dunbar. Most important in this context, however, is his assumption that they share the same language: 'Were you not the light of our English language, surmounting every terrestrial tongue as a May morning does midnight?' ('Was thou noucht of oure Inglisch all the lycht/Surmounting eviry tong terrestial/Alls fer as Mayis morow dois mydnycht?')[38] In any event, as White notes:

> Nobody in contemporary Scotland speaks consistent Lallans – that is part of our historical linguistic situation. What we speak is English with local accents and intonations, and sprinkled with elements of Lallans, and indeed of Gaelic, which have come down to us.[39]

This process began before the Union of the Crowns in 1603 and the departure of James VI and his court to London. In particular, the use in Scotland of the English vernacular bible from the Reformation onwards, and of the authorised version after 1611, was probably more important in thwarting the emergence of Scots as a separate language than the regal Union itself. David Murison has argued that English came to be 'the language of solemnity and abstract thought, of theological and philosophical disputation', leaving Scots 'the language of ordinary life, of the domestic, sentimental and comic'.[40] But substitute the words 'Scouse', 'Geordie' or 'Cockney' for 'Scots' in the passage quoted immediately above and it remains true, while no longer carrying the implication that Scotland was victim to some special form of cultural imperialism.[41] In fact, for both Scotland and England, English replaced *Latin* as the language of theology and philosophy, and *Norman French* as the language of administration. The majority of people in both countries spoke English, but would equally have found the emergent 'Standard English' separate from the English they used in either a domestic setting or their local communities. Language did not hold the Lowland Scots and the English apart, nor did it define them as protonations.

Absolutism too remained weak in Scotland. The social upheavals which might have pushed the Scottish lords into supporting and strengthening the monarchy instead of exploiting its weakness never emerged, but since peasant revolts were unknown in Scotland, at least until 1648, there was no need for a more highly centralised state to suppress the direct producers. The weakness of the urban sector meant that there was no burghal support system for rural insurrection, even had one been set in motion by the peasant masses. But if the peasantry was largely quiescent until after 1660, the individual lords retained a local weight unparalleled elsewhere in western Europe. It is unsurprising, therefore, that the attention of the monarchy was fixed less on suppressing the direct producers than on subduing their noble masters. The Stuarts did, in fact, attempt on seven different occasions between 1455 and 1662 to legislate out of existence the jurisdictions on which noble power rested. Had they succeeded in doing so it would, in the short term, have massively increased the authority of the state, and their failure is in itself eloquent testimony to the real balance of power between the nobility and the crown. Instead of creating a centralised authority to control the nobility, the crown strategy became one of supporting particular territorial lordships, such as those of Gordon in the northeast and of Argyll in the southwest, in order to maintain local stability and act as counterweights to each other. The effect was, however, to help create the alternatives to royal power which it was intended to avoid. In this respect the territorial expansion of the Earls of Argyll, both as feudal superiors and as Chiefs of Clan Campbell, is only the most extreme example of a general process.

If internal pressure towards absolutism was missing, however, external pressure was not. From the invasion of 1296 that began the Wars of Independence, down to the beginning of the Reformation in 1559, this threat had always been from the most obvious source: England. The result of the English threat was not, however, the emergence of a native absolutism but reliance by the Scottish monarchy on that of another: France. The 'Auld Alliance' between Scotland and France meant, above all, that the strength of the French state was employed, at various crucial points in the long struggle with England, as a substitute for absent Scottish military might and diplomatic influence. The Scottish state might therefore be described as a *dependent absolutism* – the powers and relationships which characterised the state in France and England only developed beyond embryonic stage in Scotland through the influence of external powers; but as a consequence of this dependency the Scottish feudal state seemed destined for incorporation into one or the other of these contending powers. The first attempt to achieve this incorporation, by the French state during the 1550s, was ultimately thwarted by English intervention during the Reformation.

Had the Stuart dynasty remained in Scotland, Scottish protonational consciousness might have developed around the local absolutist monarchy, if only in reaction to the increasingly self-confident English protonationalism characteristic of the Tudor period. The departure of James VI and I to England in 1603 meant, however, that his family would be unable to play this role. Subsequent attempts to exercise remote control over Scotland had the effect of heightening still further suspicion of English intentions – the assumption being that James had 'gone native', as it were – although he was not obeying the dictates of an adopted English identity but those of the international fraternity of absolutist monarchs. The absolutist innovations in the state introduced by James and his three successors acted to incubate English national consciousness, not that of the Scots. The combined events of 1649 and 1688 demonstrated that the incubation period was over. Thereafter, the only way the Stuart dynasty could have regained power anywhere in the three kingdoms would have been by reliance on the power of the French absolutist state – the very antithesis of a national project. When Andrew Scott writes of the first Jacobite rising of 1689 that, 'with Claverhouse's death, and the disintegration of King James' hopes, the Scottish nation ceased to be', he is identifying 'the Scottish nation' precisely with the forces of feudal absolutism most hostile to modern nationhood.[42]

It is in the framework of the absolutist state that the law is significant. 'After 1707', writes Harvie, 'law was, certainly, not just a national possession, but – in the absence of a Parliament – a critical institution of nationality.'[43] What stage of development had the law reached before 1707? In 1681 Sir James Dalrymple, 1st Viscount Stair, published *The Institutions Of The Law Of Scotland* (although there is evidence to suggest that it was completed by 1664).[44] This is indeed a major landmark in the development of Scots Law. John Cairns has noted that: 'The tendency for institutional writings frequently to be composed in the vernacular connects them with nascent national consciousness, the differentiation of the European *ius commune* and, ultimately, the ideals of the Enlightenment.'[45] Dalrymple did not, however, write his own work in the Scots vernacular, but in English. Leaving that aside, how far did his writing represent a 'nascent national consciousness'? In the dedication to Charles II which opens *The Institutions Of The Law Of Scotland* Stair refers to the nation several different times. Yet what does he mean by it?

We do not pretend to be among the great and rich kingdoms of the earth; yet we know not who can claim preference in antiquity and integrity, being of one blood and lineage, without mixture of any other people and have continued for above two thousand years; during all which no foreign power was ever able to settle the dominion of a

strange Lord over us, or make us forsake our allegiance to your
Majesty's royal ancestors, our native and kindly kings; whereas most
other kingdoms are compounds of divers nations, and have been
subjugated to princes of different and opposite families and oftentimes
foreigners.[46]

The claim that the Scots were an endogamous people is completely
false. Take the 'Dark Ages' between 400 and 1057. 'The period has, with
justice, been called "an age of migrations"', writes Michael Lynch, 'when
the different tribal peoples – Picts, Scots, Angles, Britons and
Scandinavians – who inhabited the mainland of modern-day Scotland
moved, fought, displaced and intermarried with each other.'[47] And to
these, of course, could be added the Norman English like Roger Mowbray
and Ingram Umfraville. But inaccuracy is less the issue here than the fact
that Stair considers the nation in virtually the same racial terms as
Mowbray and Umfraville and the other signatories to the Declaration of
Arbroath.

As this would lead us to expect, the actual content of Scots Law at this
time was similarly geared to governing the economic relationships
typical of society at that time. In *Institutions* he writes of juridical serfdom
that:

> there remain some vestiges in colliers and salters, who are astricted to
> those services by law, though there be no paction or engagement,
> which is introduced upon the common interest, these services being
> so necessary for the kingdom, where the fuel of coal is in most parts
> necessary at home and very profitable abroad; and seeing we have no
> salt of our own, but that which is made by the boiling of salt water,
> salters are also so astricted: so that colliers and salters, while they live,
> must continue in these services.[48]

There is not a hint of criticism in this learned account of how these
'necessary and profitable' activities are organised. Dalrymple reminds
us, by his very acceptance of the cruelties of his age, that the subject of
his great work was not 'the law' in some abstract sense, but the feudal
law by whose provisions the colliers and salters had been enserfed. And
the defining aspect of feudal law was the system of local heritable jurisdictions by which the lords ran their baronies and regalities, and which
were specifically preserved under Article 20 of the Treaty of Union. In
short, the most distinctive aspects of Scots Law during the relevant period
were those supportive of the feudal particularism which was the greatest
obstacle to the formation of national consciousness. Those which
remained distinctive after the abolition of the heritable jurisdictions in
1747 were precisely the most backward, pre-bourgeois elements which

prevented the Scots attaining even the level of individual liberty enjoyed by the English. The demand of Scottish reformers during the later half of the eighteenth century was not to preserve the juridical remnants of Scottish feudalism, but for them to be abolished. Nicholas Phillipson summarises their demands:

> In effect [they] meant that the principles of civil liberty which were enshrined in key English institutions should be extended to Scotland and that political reform should be directed towards the establishment of such institutions as a reformed electoral system, a new system of government, a reformed legal system based on civil jury trial and a system of criminal prosecution and jury procedure less like that of France and more like that of England.[49]

Consequently it was left to *religion* to incubate a protonational consciousness in place of the absent monarchy. While there is no doubt that the Church of Scotland had a 'popular' character, it is also important to understand the limitations of this. A religious community that excluded Catholics and – more importantly in a Scottish context – Episcopalians was always going to be limited in its inclusiveness. Even among Presbyterians the extent of national consciousness should not be exaggerated. As Arthur Williamson has pointed out, many of the kirk ideologues regarded the nobility as the true defenders of Scottish independence, precisely because their ownership of land gave them an 'interest' denied to the bishops, who were the dependants of royalty: 'The king may set them up and cast them down, give them and take from them, put them in and out at his pleasure.'[50] This is far from seeing the 'people' as the basis of the nation, although 'the people' themselves may have begun to do so.

In 1700 the Church of Scotland contained perhaps 95 per cent of church-goers, at a time when virtually everyone was a church-goer.[51] Nevertheless, as soon as one probes beneath the surface of these figures, the monolith appears less substantial. As Callum Brown notes:

> On the threshold of the agricultural and industrial revolutions, Scotland was not homogenous in religion. In the central and southern Lowlands there were significant differences in the cultural interpretation of presbyterianism, between the urban professional and business groups and the rural peasantry. In the Lowlands north of the River Tay episcopacy was strong and resisted presbyterian invasion. In the isolated Highlands and Hebrides, presbyterianism was weak and even episcopacy and Catholicism were enveloped within a popular religious culture of superstition.[52]

The Limits of Psychological Formation

The effect of the Darien tragedy was to raise popular hostility both to the supposed English source of national humiliation and to those among the Scottish elite who appeared insufficiently supportive of the endeavour. These were feelings which were maintained and heightened still further during the negotiations over the Treaty of Union, for there were material reasons for the widespread suspicion of the Union. The inhabitants of the Scottish Lowlands were indeed beginning to develop a sense of national *consciousness*, but the transformation of this form of consciousness into a political national*ism* was never fully achieved while the Scottish state was in existence.[53] The crowds who rioted outside the Parliament during the ratification of the Treaty were provoked, not by concern for the Scottish state which had failed them so badly, but by a concern for the Scottish *society* in which they experienced not only oppression, but also the things that made their lives halfway bearable. Their 'nationalism' was a reaction to the specific ways in which the Treaty threatened to weaken the social fabric (through undermining the kirk – the only institution over which the plebeians exercised any democratic control) and worsen their material conditions (through increasing the cost of salt, ale and so on). For the classes below the nobility and the merchant elite the Union offered, above all else, higher taxation and although it was not mentioned in the Treaty, it was quite clear that a more rigorous customs and excise regime on the English model was to be imposed for the purpose of thwarting the smuggling operations which provided illegal employment for many inhabitants of the east coast and access to cheap goods, especially wine, elsewhere. Yet many of these concerns were dealt with by amendments to the relevant Articles before the Treaty was ratified as a whole. In fact, the vote of 20 December 1706 on Article 8, dealing with Scottish exemption from English salt taxes, was the only serious defeat suffered by the Court throughout the entire ratification process. If taxes on Scottish salt were kept lower than on English or other imported salt, then it would remain affordable to the mass of the population, for whom it was a necessity, both to preserve food during winter and to render their regular diet more edible throughout the year.[54] It would be inadvisable to dismiss these as merely base material concerns. Given the highly circumscribed lives of most people at this time, a worsening of their material conditions in these areas was a serious matter.

The formative state of Scottish national consciousness on the eve of Union can be encapsulated by two passages from James Hodges, one of the pamphleteers who opposed what he saw as the surrender of Scottish sovereignty. In one he discusses the difference between Scottish and English church organisation, writing that, '*Scotland* hath a Distinct Constitution of Ecclesiastic Government from that of *England*, which none of the Kingdoms or Governments mention'd had from those, with whom they united in an *Incorporating Union*.' Hodges is here distinguishing between kingdoms like France, Spain or England itself, which became unified states through the incorporation of many different kingdoms, all of which shared the same religion forms, and the proposed British state, which would not. These remarks clearly point towards some sense of national identity based on cultural and social distinctions. On the same page, however, Hodges talks about the Scottish nation in precisely the ahistorical, racial terms with which we are familiar from both the Declaration of Arbroath and Stair's *Institutions*:

> ...whereas England hath been four times conquer'd, to wit, by the *Romans*, the *Saxons*, the *Danes*, and the *Normans*; the *Scots* are the only People of Europe whom, tho' none more violently assaulted, yet neither *Romans*, who conquer'd all the rest, nor any other Nation, have ever been able to conquer; since the first Settling of their Government; ...they have been able to defend, and preserve from conquest their National Freedom and Independency, for several Centuries of Years; above the one third of the World's Age from the Creation.[55]

Until this point in the discussion I have explained the limited extent to which national consciousness had developed in Scotland with reference to the absence or weakness of certain indispensable factors in national formation. There was however, another factor, unique to Scotland, which was neither absent nor weak, but present and growing stronger throughout the period up to 1707: the Highland/Lowland divide.

Lowland Perceptions of Highland Society

The type of division embodied in the Highland/Lowland divide was not unique in Europe. Indeed, definitions *of* Europe have themselves embodied such distinctions. These have been political, not least because, in strictly geographical terms, Europe is simply a western extension of mainland Asia.[56] These definitions have not merely been over which geographical territories (Russia east of the Urals) or nations (Turkey) are to be considered part of Europe; they have also been about demarcating Europe itself into distinct regions, particularly those of east and west. Hence the extraordinary efforts by dissident intellectuals in the Stalinist states before 1989 to redefine their respective countries as belonging to *central* (or even *east*central) Europe rather than eastern Europe, usually as a prelude to demonstrating that this region would have shared the same pattern of development as western Europe, had it not been artificially diverted, first by the Ottoman conquests of the fifteenth century, then by the hegemony of the Russian Empire, in both its Tsarist and Stalinist guises.[57] To argue in this way is to participate in perpetuation of a myth about the difference between east and west. As Norman Davis argues, it is one that rests on four assumptions:

> The first maintains that West and East, however defined, have little or nothing in common. The second implies that the division of Europe is justified by natural, unbridgeable differences; the third that the West is superior; the fourth that the West alone deserves the name of Europe.[58]

The same type of assumption is present, in miniature, in presentations of the Scottish Highland/Lowland divide. Indeed, if, in the passage quoted above, the word 'Scotland' is substituted for 'Europe', 'Lowland' for 'West' and 'Highland' for 'East' the parallels are almost exact. Geographical situation certainly has an important influence on human affairs, but not an all-determining one, and whenever differences between human societies are expressed in geographical terms, the likelihood is that some form of mystification is at work. Edward Said writes of the western conception of the Orient that it is 'a constituted reality', not merely an inaccurate representation of reality. As Said notes, 'the notion that there are geographical spaces with indigenous, radically "different" inhabitants who can be defined on the basis of some religion, culture, or racial essence proper to that geographical space is...a highly debatable idea.'[59] Which factors were involved in the construction of the 'constituted reality' that was the Lowland view of the Scottish Highlands? David Cannadine writes, correctly, that the division between the Highlands and the Lowlands was 'not just a function of geography, but also of culture'. He also writes, incorrectly, that on the Highland side these cultural divisions were the result of 'clans, Catholicism and Gaelic'.[60] There were indeed three factors involved in distinguishing the Highlands in Lowland eyes, but only one of them – Gaelic – is referred to in this list.

The first factor was identified in the earliest recorded reference to the existence of the Highlanders as a distinct group. This account, written by the chronicler John of Fordun in the last quarter of the fourteenth century, contains no mention of clans, but highlights the absence of law and order:

> The Highlanders and people of the islands...are a savage and untamed nation, rude and independent, given to rapine, easy-living, of a docile and warm disposition, comely in person but unsightly in dress, hostile to the English people and language and owing to diversity of speech, even to their own nation, and exceedingly cruel.[61]

In *A History Of Greater Britain*, first published in 1521, John Mair refers to 'two different ways of life and conduct' among the Scots: 'For some are born in the forests and mountains of the north, and these we call men of the Highland, but the others men of the Lowland.' Interestingly, Mair records that 'foreigners' refer to the former as 'wild Scots' and the latter as 'householding [i.e., domesticated] Scots', although it is clear that he shares the low opinion of the Highlanders which these terms imply.[62] Interestingly, given the status which the Makars are given as representing the early modern Scottish nation, poems by William Dunbar from the early decades of the sixteenth century like 'The Flyting of Dunbar and Kennedie' contain a level of abuse towards the Highlanders which suggests that they were not part of it.[63] As Patricia Bawcutt writes: 'In this poem Dunbar is not so much venting personal spite as voicing received Lowland opinion of the Highlanders: treacherous, thieving and murderous; not domesticated (like hens), but wild (like foxes).'[64] Hector Boece, the only important figure in Renaissance Scotland to argue that the austere regime of military discipline which supposedly prevailed in the Highlands might be a model for Lowland society, was, in this respect at least, ignored by his contemporaries.[65] Indeed, subsequent commentators added finer distinctions to the picture of Highland disorder. James VI, in his 1598 manual for aspiring absolutists, *Basilicon Doron*, divided the Highlanders into 'two sorts of people': 'the one, that dwelleth in our mainland, that are barbarous for the main part, and yet mixed with some show of civility: the other, that dwelleth in the Isles, and are utterly barbarous, without any show of civility.'[66] Such 'lack of civility' was often put down to the Highland environment. Samuel Johnston, touring the Highlands in 1773, shortly after order had finally been imposed, noted:

Mountaineers are warlike, because by their feuds and competitions they consider themselves as surrounded with enemies, and are always prepared to repel incursions, or to make them. ... Mountaineers are thievish, because they are poor, and having neither manufactures or commerce, can grow richer only by robbery. ... Mountainous regions are so remote from the seat of government, and so difficult to access, that they are very little under the influence of the sovereign, or within the reach of national justice.[67]

Fletcher of Saltoun provided the answer to Johnsonian environmental determinism in 1698, noting that the nature of Highland society cannot be the result of geography alone, since the Alps provided an example of a country which, although in many ways even less naturally endowed, was the very model of civilised industriousness:

...but they had no lords to hinder them from being civilised, to discourage industry, encourage thieving, and to keep them beggars that they might be more dependent; or when they had any that oppressed them, as in that part of the mountains that belongs to the Swiss, they knocked them on the head.[68]

These comments point towards an explanation of Highland criminality that rests on their social relationships rather than their surroundings. The poverty to which Fletcher refers provided an incentive for some of the warriors to engage in large-scale plundering, particularly of cattle, from the more settled Lowland communities. These onslaughts resembled more the lordly marauding typical of the feudal system in its formative years than the normal condition of the late medieval or early modern period. Nevertheless, two qualifications need to be made to this assessment.

One is that these raids were not directed solely at the Lowlands, but also at other Highland communities. They would have been committed not by lordly dependants (i.e., the tacksmen), who maintained their standard of living through collection of rent from the tenantry, but mainly by bands of 'broken men' who were *outside* the structure of Highland society. The Lowland Perthshire peasant, watching his herd being driven off by armed clansmen was, however, unlikely to give this fact consideration. The other is that the level of Highland disorder had reduced by the second half of the seventeenth century in keeping with the greater stability of the country as a whole. Between 1661 and 1674, Highlanders were involved in less than 30 per cent of crimes of aggression against persons and crimes against property brought before the Lords Commissioners of Justiciary. Indeed, the greatest source of disorder came not from the Highlands at all but from the political and religious revolt of the Lowland peasantry, 1,000 of whom fought in the Pentland Rising of 1666, 4,000 of whom fought at Bothwell Bridge in 1679 and between 3,000 and 14,000 of whom were involved in illegal armed religious assemblies during the 1670s.[69] If the twentieth century has shown us anything, however, it is that groups can be scapegoated as the cause of social ills on the most spurious of grounds. Although less sophisticated than modern ruling classes in the manipulation of such techniques, the Scottish ruling class certainly applied them to the Highlanders. A semi-official history of the revolution of 1688, published in 1690 says:

> The Highlanders of Scotland are a sort of wretches that have no other consideration of honour, friendship, obedience, or government, than as, by any alteration of affairs or revolution in the Government, they can improve to themselves an opportunity of Robbing and plundering their bordering Neighbours.[70]

The identification of the Highlanders as a pariah group was made easier by a second factor: the distinctiveness of their language. Gaelic was originally the language of the majority of the population within the territory of present-day Scotland. The Scots, one of the tribes who went on to form the Scottish people, originally came from present-day Ireland, and had by the sixth century established their own kingdom called Dalriada in present-day Argyll. William Ferguson has forcefully stated the case for the centrality of the Scots in the formation of Scotland:

> The origin of the Scottish nation is not in any detectable measure Pictish, British, Anglian or Norse, as the Declaration of Arbroath makes very clear, Scottish identity clearly and evidently evolves from the Gaelic tradition of Ireland as received, developed and modified in Scotland.[71]

Leaving aside the notion that a Scottish 'nation' existed in the eleventh century and the reliability of the Declaration of Arbroath as an authority, the evidence which Ferguson assembles leaves little doubt that the kingdom was originally unified under Scottish leadership and that their cultural influence, most notably in the use of the Gaelic language, was dominant until the twelfth century at least. By the time of the Declaration of Arbroath in 1320 the Gaelic-speaking Scots of Dalriada were almost universally recognised as the group which had founded the kingdom and established the regnal line – a recognition not unconnected with the usefulness of Scottish ancestry for refuting Plantagenet claims of English sovereignty over Scotland. The functionality of Dalriadic origins is best demonstrated by the fact that during the same century in which they became accepted the first literary distinctions were made between contemporary Gaelic speakers and the inhabitants of the Scottish kingdom.[72] Fordun writes that the inhabitants of Scotland spoke two languages, 'the Scottish [i.e., Gaelic] and the Teutonic [i.e., English]: the latter of which is the language of those who occupy the seaboard and plains, while the race of Scottish speech inhabits the highlands and outlying islands.'[73] Mair notes the same distinction between his 'wild' and 'householding' Scots: 'The Irish tongue is in use among the former, the English among the latter.'[74] What these comments reveal is the extent to which Gaelic, once the dominant language within the territory of the Scottish kingdom, had given ground since the eleventh century to its main rival, the Scots vernacular, which was at any rate *comprehensible* to those who spoke the English language of trade and administration. The first reference to the language spoken in the Lowlands as being *Scottis* or Scots is from 1494.[75] This may indicate the point at which the Gaelic had definitely ceased to be the language of the majority, or simply that the regnal solidarity of the ruling class required that they had their own language, separate from the English. Either way, from around this time a further layer of separation was formally interposed between the Highlanders and the other inhabitants of Scotland.[76]

The extent of the *Gaidhealtachd*, or geographical area in which Gaelic was spoken, at the end of the seventeenth century cannot be exactly defined, not least because of the way in which it shaded into areas on its south and eastern border where both Gaelic and Scots were spoken, often by the same people. Nevertheless, from the early eighteenth century onwards a number of attempts were made to map the boundary. From a study of these sources, Charles Withers has concluded that a working borderline can be established which, starting around the Clyde estuary in the southwest, follows 'a curving line from Dumbarton through central Perthshire and upland Aberdeenshire and Banffshire along the edge of the Grampians to a point at or near Nairn and thence along to the Easter Ross and Cromarty Lowlands.'[77] What is clear from this is that the *Gaidhealtachd* was increasingly synonymous with the geographical Highlands of Scotland. As James Walker noted in 1750: 'The Highlands is a very general name for a large tract of the kingdom, which appears to be the boundary of the Gaelic language.'[78] Gaelic was held to be a contributory factor to the supposed degradation of those on the Highland side of this line. An anonymous 'Highland gentleman', who had clearly assimilated Lowland attitudes towards his 'people', wrote in 1736:

Our poor People are from the Cradles trained up in Barbarity and Ignorance. Their very language is an everlasting Bar against all Instruction, but the barbarous Customs and Fashions they have from their Forefathers, of which they are most tenacious, and having no other languages, they are confirmed to their own miserable Homes.[79]

The two distinguishing features of the Highlanders continued to be reiterated down to and beyond the opening of our period: on the one hand, their disregard for the laws passed by the central state; on the other, their inability to communicate in the language spoken by most Scots in 1688. The supposed criminality of Highland social behaviour and the actual incomprehensibility of Highland language led the Lowlanders to compare their neighbours, not to themselves, but to the native Irish and the settlers who had over the centuries been assimilated to that culture. For although the Scots version of Gaelic is distinct from the Irish, it contains enough similarities for the former to be described as 'Erse' or simply 'Irish' by non-Gaelic speakers in Scotland. Around 1746 Duncan Forbes of Culloden, himself a Highlander, wrote: 'What is properly called the *Highlands of Scotland*, is that large tract of mountainous ground to the Northward of the Forth and the Tay, where the natives speak the Irish Language.'[80] The comparison between Highlanders and the Irish was not itself new. Fordun himself refers to 'The Scottish nation [i.e., the Highlanders]...is that which was once in Ireland, and resembles the Irish in all things – in language, manners and character.'[81] Yet without a third and final factor, which had not yet been introduced into Scottish society when Fordun or even Mair wrote their accounts, it is unlikely that the hostility between Lowland and Highland would have reached the extent that it did or that the identification of Highlander and Irish would have been so close.

This final factor was religion. Lowland kirk ministers constantly complained of the failure of the Reformation to make permanent inroads beyond the Highland line. The 'Highland gentleman' quoted earlier was in fact primarily concerned that perpetuation of the Gaelic language was preventing the Highlanders from being converted to the Calvinist version of Christianity practised by the Church of Scotland. He was not the first commentator to link their continued cultural backwardness to the lack of religious direction. The semi-official history of the Revolution of 1688, quoted above, states: 'If there be any smack of religion amongst them, 'tis generally of the Roman Catholic persuasion.'[82] Although still widely believed (not least by David Cannadine), such observations were inaccurate, the majority of Highlanders in 1688 were Protestants, albeit Episcopalians, but we are dealing here with the effect of perceptions, not their relationship to reality. Hugh MacKay, son of General MacKay (himself a Highlander), wrote more generally of the religious condition while describing his father's campaigns in the Highlands during the same period that:

> ...in all the progresses and marches of the General benorth Tay, he testified to have remarked no true sense of the deliverance which God had sent them, except in a very few, and that the people in general were disposed to submit to and embrace the party which they judged most like to carry it, their zeal for the preservation of their goods going by them, far beyond the consideration religion and liberty, which he attributed to the gross ignorance occasioned by the negligence of their ministers, as well as the large extent of their parishes, which made most of them come seldom to church.[83]

One aspect of this negligence was an unseemly empathy on the part of local ministers for the Highland culture of their flock. In 1624 some Lowland ministers visiting the presbytery of Inverness were dismayed to find Highland ministers wearing the same type of bonnets and plaid as their parishioners, and instructed them to adopt a manner of dress more becoming to their station.[84] Another sign of negligence was the failure to suppress peasant superstitions. The second sight was an established aspect of Highland culture, which Gaelic-speaking ministers saw no reason to challenge. As Jane Dawson notes: 'The Gaelic clergy took a similar relaxed attitude towards the fairy culture of Gaeldom.' This attitude was sustainable because of the separation that existed between the world of 'elves, fawns and fairies' and the Catholic world of saints,

angels and devils: 'The clergy could therefore accept the fairies and yet
attack all those practices associated with Catholic worship and reverence
for the saints.'[85] The Lowland ministers were not so much concerned
with substituting reason in the place of superstition, as with imposing
the particular superstitions sanctioned by the King James Bible ('thou
shalt not suffer a witch to live') in place of those which were part of the
peasant tradition. Anyone claiming to have the gift of second sight or
admitting to a belief in fairies in the Lowlands was likely to find himself
or herself accused of witchcraft. Toleration of such abominations in the
sight of the Lord introduced a further degree of separation between
Highland and Lowland. The four great witch-hunts that blighted early
modern Scotland in 1590–7, 1629–30, 1649 and 1661–2 were almost
exclusively Lowland affairs. 'In the Highlands,' writes Christina Larner,
'especially those parts outside the Kirk sessions system and within the
dominion of the clans there was no witch hunting, or none that reached
the records.'[86]

Relative stability *versus* endemic disorder. The English language *versus*
the Gaelic. Calvinism *versus* Catholicism and Episcopalianism. Can we
discern two separate *societies* here? Michael Mann has argued against
treating societies either as coincident with the boundaries of a local state
('Scottish society'), or, at the opposite extreme, as components of a global
system ('feudal society'). The first assumes the correspondence of state
and society, the second the homogeneity of societies formed by the same
economic process; but societies are neither confined by states nor
identical with systems.[87] The Highlands and the Lowlands can be
considered as two distinct societies, but it is possible to go further, and
many Lowlanders did, treating the 'other' to their own society: not the
Highlands alone, but the Highlands and Catholic Ireland together.

As we have seen, from the fourteenth century onwards the behaviour,
language and, in a minority of cases, religion of the Highlanders led to
them being described as 'Irish'. In particular, all the negative characteristics which the Lowland mind identified with the Highlands appeared
to be confirmed by the close links which existed between Ulster and the
western Highlands (which, it will be recalled, James VI identified as
lacking in all 'civility'). The political implications of these connections
were made clear during the civil wars. The British colonists in Ulster who
came under attack in the Irish rising of 1641 largely consisted of
Protestant Scots from the Lowlands. In Scotland itself some of the clans,
led by the royalist commander James Graham, Marquis of Montrose,
leagued with the Irish Confederacy, led by Alasdair MacColla, in support
of Charles I: the Scottish MacDonalds fighting alongside the Irish
MacDonnells. In fear for relatives in Ireland and in reaction to the
violence of royalist supporters in Scotland it became easy to ascribe such
behaviour to all Highlanders, and to explain it as arising from their

nature. The massacre of the local population after the battle of Aberdeen on 13 September 1644 is perhaps the most notorious example of such violence.

John Spalding, who lived through these events, describes the conduct of the Irish and Highland troops after entering the burgh, which Montrose had 'promised to them the plundering of the town for their good service':

> The Lieutenant [i.e., Montrose] followed the chase on to Aberdeen, his men hewing and cutting down all manner of men they could overtake (within the town, upon the streets, or in their houses, and round about the town as our men were fleeing) with broad swords but [no] mercy or remedy. The cruel Irish, seeing a man well clad, would first strip him and save the clothes unspoiled, and then kill the man. ... And nothing could be heard but pitiful howling, crying, weeping, mourning, through all the streets.
>
> Thus the Irish continued Friday, Saturday, Sunday, [and] Monday. Some women they seized to deflower, and others they took perforce to serve them in the camp. It is lamentable to hear how the Irish who had the spoil of the town did abuse the same. The men that they killed they would not suffer to be buried, but took from them their clothes and left their naked bodies lying on the ground. The wife dared not cry nor weep at her husband's slaughter before her eyes, nor the mother for the son, nor the daughter for the father; for if they had done so, they would presently have been slain also.

It is important to understand that the author of this passage was both a Royalist in political sympathy and an Episcopalian in religious belief, but in this context the fact that he was a Lowlander was of far greater significance.[88]

No individual event did more than the massacre at Aberdeen to fuse the Highlander and the Catholic Irish in the Lowland mind not simply as alien, but as murderously alien, even though the Irish were far more heavily involved. The extent of civilian losses was not great by the contemporary European standards of the Thirty Years' War – perhaps 100 non-combatants were killed. Indeed, far greater numbers had been slain in Argyllshire by the troops of MacColla and Montrose before the sack of Aberdeen and still more were to fall between 1644 and 1647. These victims were themselves Highlanders, however, notwithstanding the adherence of Argyll and Clan Campbell to the Covenant: Aberdeen saw the first major *Lowland* civilian losses of the war in Scotland, in a burgh which had a record of support for the King, and moreover they were perpetrated by troops who were already supposed to have committed atrocities upon Protestants in Ulster – imaginary events which nevertheless appeared to receive confirmation with this new and verifiable atrocity. 'The double standard that allowed and even encouraged atrocities in Ireland [i.e., against Catholics] but expressed revulsion at atrocities in Great Britain might be hypocritical,' writes Stevenson, 'but it was a double standard that was generally accepted.'[89] It is in this context that the hatred brought into focus by an event like the descent of the 'Highland Host' must be understood.

Highland Perceptions of Lowland Society

The divisions that opened up between the Highlands and the Lowlands in the late fourteenth century continued to widen until and beyond 1688. As Barrow writes:

> To Boswell of Auchinleck, born in Edinburgh in 1740 and brought up in Ayrshire, much more than to Robert Bruce, born at Turnberry in 1274, the Highlands were a foreign country, alien in language, in religion, in dress, in traditions, alien even in their own particular varieties of hospitality and of poverty.[90]

Those Scots who were beginning to acquire a protonational con-sciousness through hostility to the English state and identification with their native Church were exclusively in the Lowlands. The divisions between Highland and Lowland prevented its extension across the entire territory of the Scottish state, Highlanders still thinking of themselves as Scots only in the sense of being notionally subject to the Scottish crown.[91] Indeed, Highlanders would have seen more similarities between the Lowland Scots and the English than between Lowland Scots and themselves. The word 'sassenach', usually taken to be an abusive Scottish term for the English, is in fact derived from the Gaelic word ('*sasunnach*') for Saxon, and was originally used by Highlanders to describe all non-Gaelic speakers, Lowlanders as much as the English. 'In Highland eyes,' writes Linda Colley, 'these two peoples were virtually indistinguishable, and both were equally alien.'[92] The difficulty for the historian is that the voice of the Highland peasant is even less audible than that of their Lowland counterparts. Only in the period after 1746, when Highland society was collapsing round about them, can the songs, memoirs and protests of the peasants be distinguished from those of their lords, or, more precisely, from those of the clan poets and mythologists who served the lords. A late example, from the work of Highland Jacobite poet, Alexander MacDonald, asserts that the Gaelic speakers *were* the true representatives of the Scottish 'race', as opposed to the

Lowlanders who had abandoned their original linguistic traditions. He writes of the Gaelic:

> She still survives
> and her glory will not be lost
> in spite of the deceit
> and great ill-will of the Lowlander
> She is the speech of Scotland
> and of the Lowlanders themselves
> of our nobles, princes
> and dukes without exception.[93]

Nor was language the only reason for hostility towards the *sassunachs*. In 1724, shortly after taking up his position as Commander in Chief of the British army in Scotland, George Wade – himself an Irishman – attempted to explain Highland attitudes in a report to George I:

> *They have still more extensive adherence one to another as Highlanders in opposition to the people who Inhabit the Low Countries whom they hold in the utmost Contempt*, imagining them inferior to themselves in Courage, Resolution, and the use of Arms, and accuse them of being Proud, Avaricious, and Breakers of their Word. They have also a tradition that the Lowlands were in Ancient Times, the Inheritance of their Ancestors, and therefore believe that they have a right to commit Depredations, wherever it is in their power to put them in Execution.[94]

But if Highlanders felt no affinity with the Lowlanders, neither did they look across the Irish Sea for an alternative. Scottish clan poets of the seventeenth century occasionally invoked pan-Celtic solidarity between the native Irish and the Highlanders. Ian Lom MacDonald, celebrating the royalist massacre of Clan Campbell at the Battle of Inverlochy in 1645, gives high praise to the Irish leader Alasdair MacColla:

> Alasdair, son of handsome Colla,
> skilled hand at cleaving castles,
> you put to flight the Lowland pale-face:
> what kale they had taken came out again.[95]

As Allan MacInnes has pointed out: 'The poet felt an immediate hostility towards the Campbells who, as the main upholders of the Covenanting Movement among the clans, were promoting cultural assimilation with the racially inferior Lowlander, the *Gall*.'[96] But no general movement of solidarity among the two Gaelic peoples was present in the Scottish Highlands, at any rate beyond the MacDonald strongholds on the western seaboard. Indeed, even the links which did exist between the western clans and those in Antrim should not be taken to mean that the former regarded themselves as more 'Irish' than 'Scottish' – that would simply be to adopt the ideological framework through which the Lowlanders viewed them. Neither the Scottish nor Irish clans – or more precisely their respective nobilities – would have recognised the concept of the nation as having any significance to their way of life. As late as 1617 the 'Irish' MacDonnells came out best in a dispute with the 'Scottish' Campbells over which had the superior claim over Rathlin Island off the coast of Antrim.[97] Such a dispute could only be resolved without bloodshed – as happened in this case – where the debatable land was not felt to belong to a national territory which must be defended at all costs.

Nor did the absence of national consciousness mean that the inhabitants of the Highlands and the Lowlands assimilated themselves to other nations instead. In the case of the Highlanders, there was no 'Irish' nation to which they could become assimilated, the Irish clans having equally little conception of themselves as a national grouping. In the case of the Lowlanders, although an English nation existed by this time (and indeed has some claim to being the *only* nation in existence at this time) the mutual hostility of the populations acted as a barrier to any assimilation taking place, even after the Union of Crowns. Some opportunistic blurring of identities took place at the territorial margins: an English Border official, Thomas Musgrave, Captain of Bewcastle, wrote in the early seventeenth century of 'lawless people' on both sides of the Border who were 'Scottish when they will, and English at their pleasure'.[98] In general, however, the situation remained as described by *The Complaynt Of Scotland* in 1546: 'There are no two nations under the firmament as different from each other as England and Scotland, although they are neighbours within the same island and speak the same language.'[99] And by 1707 they were also subjects of the same state. As we shall see in the next chapter, there remained many obstacles preventing the formation of both Scottishness and Britishness among people in Scotland after that date.

4

Highland *versus* Lowland, Scotland *versus* England

The name of Scotland concealed the existence of two regions whose inhabitants had been antagonistic to each other for centuries. With neither region able to agree that the other was Scottish, how liable were they to subsume themselves jointly into a new British national identity? Edward Burt, an English officer serving in the Highlands during the 1720s, reminds us of the degree of separation which still existed between Highland and Lowland nearly 20 years after the Union:

> The Highlands are but little known even to the Inhabitants of the low country of Scotland, for they ever dreaded the Difficulties and Dangers of Travelling among the Mountains; and when some extraordinary occasion has obliged any one of them to make such a Progress, he has, generally speaking, made his Testament before he set out, as though he were entering upon a long and dangerous Sea Voyage, wherein it was very doubtful he should ever return.[1]

What little the Lowlanders did know of the Highlanders was scarcely liable to encourage feelings of common nationhood. Since the Highlanders were first identified as a distinct group in the fourteenth century, Lowlanders had not only been contemptuous of them, but fearful, seeing their region as one outwith the constraints of state authority, the English language and the Protestant – or at any rate Presbyterian – religion. Jacobitism attempted to integrate the Highlanders into a shared Scottish identity, but on what basis? To argue that the Highlanders were the most loyal subjects of an absolutist monarchy that the majority of Scots rejected, was never likely to be convincing, even if the restoration of the Stuarts had been achieved.

Neither were the English eager to merge themselves into a new British identity with the Scots.

On the one hand, like many Lowland Scots, the English were deeply ignorant of the Highlanders. Burt considered that:

> ...to the people of England, excepting some of the Soldiery, the Highlands are hardly known at all: for there has been less that I know of written on the Subject, than of either of the Indies; and that little which has been said, conveys no Idea of what a Traveller almost continually sees and meets with in passing among the Mountains; nor does it communicate any notion of the Temper of the Natives, while they remain in their own country.[2]

One of the letters written by Jonathan Swift to his beloved Esther Johnston demonstrates the truth of this observation: 'I dined today with [the] Lord Treasurer and two gentlemen of the Highlands of Scotland, yet very polite men'.[3] Thus, in 1711, the author of *Gulliver's Travels* – a naturalised Englishman in this respect – records his astonishment at finding two Highlanders actually acquainted with table manners.

On the other hand, English knowledge of the Lowland Scots was scarcely any greater than their knowledge of the Highlanders. Burt was not exaggerating when he wrote during the 1720s:

> The verbal Misrepresentations that have been made of the Lowlands are very extraordinary; and though good Part of it be greatly superior in Quality of the soil to the North of England, and in some Parts equal to the best of the South, Yet there are some among our Countrymen who are so prejudiced that they will not allow (or not own) there is any Thing good on this Side of the Tweed.[4]

In 1710, at another of the dinners which feature so regularly in the *Journal To Stella*, Swift again confirms these generalisations: 'I dined today with Dr Cockburn, but will not do so again in haste, he has generally such a parcel of Scots with him.'[5]

Nor was this hostility confined to the British Isles, but was carried over to the American colonies. Disputes between Scottish and English settlers in New Jersey occurred from the 1690s onwards, leading by the early 1700s to intercommunity riots and electoral campaigns explicitly conducted on national lines. The basis for these conflicts was ultimately the different systems of landownership which had been transferred to the New World with the colonists. Territories settled by the English tended to be divided into small freeholds whereas those settled by the Scots consisted of large holdings where tenant farmers were dominated by a few proprietors. The central issue was the type of tenure which would prevail in the as-yet-unsettled territories beyond the existing settlements. In 1702 one English campaigner for local office denounced the Scottish proprietors, saying: 'We will not go to North Britain for

Justice, No Turkish Government, No French Government, No Arbitrary Government'.[6]

The identification of Scotland with absolutism contained in the slogans of the English settlers was heightened in Britain itself by the outbreak of the last counter-revolutionary Jacobite rising in 1745, which gave the already high level of English xenophobia towards the Scots a harder political edge. Andrew Mitchell, Under Secretary to the Marquis of Tweedale, wrote regretfully from London to Forbes of Culloden in 1745, shortly after the Jacobites had taken the Scottish capital without resistance:

> I need not describe to you the Effects of the surrender of Edinburgh, and the progress the Rebels made, upon the country. I wish I could say that they were confined to the lower sort of people, but I must fairly own, that their betters were as much touched as they. The reflections were national; and it was publicly said that all Scots were Jacobites...[7]

In a letter of 1753 James Wolfe, who had served with the Hanoverian army during the '45 and played a particularly brutal role in the aftermath of Culloden, went beyond politics into the very nature of the Scottish and English 'races': 'The English are clean and laborious, and the Scotch excessively lazy and dirty, though far short, indeed, of what we found out a greater distance from the borders.'[8] It was precisely in order to undermine these representations that an ideological counter-offensive was mounted by representatives of bourgeois Scotland, in which the Highlands were cast as the barbarian Other to Lowland civilisation. In a letter to Hugh, 3rd Earl of Marchmont, during the '45, one correspondent, a Mr George Carre of West Nisbet, Berwickshire, expresses his disgust at the actions of the Highlanders in supporting Charles: '*For though I have no other connection with the Highlanders than in the common appellation of Scotsman*, I blush this moment at the thought that these wretches are acting as Allies of France and Traitors to Great Britain.'[9]

The Highlanders were not, however, merely passive recipients of the hostility of others. The following passage appears in a song by Alexander MacDonald, written shortly after the '45, where the singer recollects how the Highland Jacobites defeated Sir John Cope at the Battle of Falkirk:

> I could relate the fear that mob
> Showed upon many a field
> If only we recount again
> What always did take place;
> One of them was Bannockburn
> Where we our valour showed,
> And Killiecrankie, too, where we
> Did knock them to the grass.[10]

Who is 'that mob' in this context? The enemy at Bannockburn was certainly English, but at Killiecrankie they were mainly Lowland Scots. At Falkirk both were present in the Hanoverian ranks. The Lowlanders and the English, united by nothing else, were still conjoined as *sassunachs* in the minds of the Highlanders – particularly in the minds of those committed to the Jacobite cause.

How could this triangular field of hostility between Highlander, Lowlander and the English be overcome sufficiently for the first two to consider themselves as Scots, and for all three to consider themselves as Britons? The Union itself had failed to achieve either. The '45 had heightened still further existing differences between Highland and Lowland (within Scotland), and between Scotland and England (within Britain). Nevertheless, a Scottish national consciousness, embracing both the Highlands and the Lowlands, did come into existence for the first time between 1746 and 1820. And it did not come into existence alone.

The creation of a new, unified, national ruling class from the elements of different pre-existing formations is not unique to Britain. In particular there are parallels among the 'revolutions from above' of the 1860s. Gramsci wrote of Italian Unification that it involved 'the formation of an ever more extensive ruling class': 'The formation of this class involved the gradual but continuous absorption, achieved by methods which varied in their effectiveness, of the active elements produced by allied groups – and even those which came from antagonistic groups and seemed irreconcilably hostile.'[11] The distinctive nature of the British experience lay in two aspects. On the one hand it was the first capitalist ruling class to be formed in this way. On the other hand, unlike the different regional groupings which combined to form the Italian (or German) ruling classes, the Scottish component retained the separate national consciousness it had so recently acquired and, despite being numerically the smaller of the two ruling classes involved, it was the most insistent that integration take place.

At the centre of this project were the Scottish bourgeoisie themselves. By 1746 the capitalist hard core of this class were groups such as the capitalist landlords (with great magnates like Argyll at their head), the tobacco and sugar merchants, and the textile manufacturers. The 'social penumbra' of which Draper writes were professional groups such as Church of Scotland ministers and lawyers – the two groups to which the majority of Enlightenment theorists belonged – but also the Scottish component of the British military officer caste and – at the opposite extreme – the playwrights and poets who celebrated the new society emerging in Scotland. This bourgeoisie was the class in Scotland which had the clearest conception of what it was to be Scottish (although that was still to undergo a further transformation in relation to the position of the Highlands), but they were also the class most insistent on being recognised as British.

The First Modern Britons

The idea of Britain was not new. Since the appearance of *The History Of The Kings Of Britain* by Geoffrey of Monmouth in the twelfth century, the English ruling classes and their ideologues had tended to equate the kingdom of England with the territory of the entire island archipelago of Britain. In one sense the Wars of Independence had been a successful attempt by the Scottish nobility to establish their own state free of feudal superiority to the English crown. Not until John Mair published his carefully titled *A History Of Greater Britain As Well England As Scotland* in 1521 did the idea that the Scots and the English together might form one nation enter political discourse. Mair was concerned both to end the centuries of destructive warfare between Scotland and England, and to use the power of the more advanced English state to quell that of the Scottish nobility, but he wanted to do so from a position of equality between the two kingdoms. These positions were repeated during the 1540s by a minority of Scots, like the merchant James Henrisoun, who believed that the future lay in some form of union with England:

> And so much the better, when those hateful terms of Scots and Englishmen shall be abolished and blotted out for ever, and that we shall all agree in the only title and name of Britons (as verily we ought to do) and the same realm, being thereby reduced into the form of one sole Monarchy, shall be called Britain....[12]

The contemporary English regime of Protector Somerset remained set on subjugation rather than fusion, however, and the ideal of Britishness perished temporarily in the fires ignited during the 'Rough Wooing' of 1547.[13] The last attempt to resurrect the idea of Britain before 1707 came from James VI and I himself, who took to styling himself King of Great Britain shortly after his coronation in 1603. Once again the scheme foundered on the rocks of the English inability to consider the Scots as equals. 'An Anglo-Scottish union on the lines of the Anglo-Welsh one would have been entirely acceptable', writes Jenny Wormald, 'a union of equal partners was not.'[14] It was not until feudalism itself was eliminated from England that the notion of Scotland as a feudal dependency of England disappeared from English political discourse.[15]

At the Union of Parliaments in 1707 the Scottish people in general no more regarded themselves as British than they had at the Union of Crowns in 1603. Scots who also considered themselves to be Britons were exceptional and tended to be found among the most advanced sections of the bourgeoisie. William Paterson, inspiration for the Scottish Company Trading to Africa and the Indies and a founder of the Bank of England, was a rare exception. Sir Paul Rycaut, the English Resident at Hamburg, reported to his employers in February 1697 that 'Mr Paterson told me that he was always well effected to the English nation and looked on them as one people with theirs under one denomination of Britons'.[16] Acceptance of the 'denomination of Britons' did not at this stage necessarily involve accepting the need for a British state. It was only after the disastrous failure of the Company, however, that Paterson and others began to think in these terms.[17] In 1706, for example, shortly before the Treaty was ratified, George MacKenzie, 1st Earl of Cromarty, looked forward enthusiastically to the abolition of national differences between Scotland and England: 'May we be Britons, and down go the old ignominious names of Scotland, of England.'[18] This was by no means a universal shift in attitude. One opponent of the Treaty of Union, James Anderson, wrote in 1705 that his intended audience consisted, not only of 'all true SCOTS-MEN', but of 'all Sincere well-wishers, of the peace and quiet of Britain'.[19] Britain was still merely a territory and, although the inhabitants of that territory may all lay claim to the title of 'Britons', that was merely a descriptive term, rather than one which expressed deeper loyalties to the societies into which Britain was divided. When Duncan Forbes of Culloden wrote to Robert Walpole in 1716 that 'Britain receives still another distinction from the two different countries whereof it is composed', he was more far-seeing than most of his contemporaries.[20] Britain was not simply an expanded English nation state into which Scotland had been submerged, nor a 'state-nation' with no reality outside of its components, but an entirely new formation, a new nation state with its own attendant national consciousness.

Why then was it that the Scottish bourgeoisie become the principal advocates of Britishness? At bottom, the British state was far more important to them than it was to their English counterparts. Once it became clear that the Union was not to be undone (and acceptance of this fact seems to have become widespread by the 1730s) its advantages to a Scottish bourgeoisie, restricted in both numbers and influence, was becoming more apparent. 1746 was the decisive turning point in that it both opened up opportunities and necessities. On the one hand, the suppression of internal reaction against the new order and the block which the pacification of the Highlands placed on external invasion meant that risks could be taken, investments made without the fear that these would be lost through civil war or invasion. On the other hand, the military and juridical onslaught on the remains of Scottish feudalism meant that every landowner, no matter how brightly they shone in the firmament of the Scottish nobility, was now compelled to enter into fully commercial relations with their tenants.

In 1755, Alexander Wedderburn, editor of the first and as it turned out short-lived *Edinburgh Review*, sought to explain the bourgeois experience – *their* experience – since 1688:

At the Revolution, liberty was re-established, and property rendered secure, the uncertainty and rigour of the law were corrected and softened: but the insolence of parties was scarce abated, nor had industry taken place. What the Revolution had begun, the Union rendered more complete.[21]

Two years later in 1757, John Dalrymple, in his comparative study of feudalism in Scotland and England, followed an acute social and economic analysis of their political divergence with the necessary happy ending:

The revolution first brought other maxims into our government, and the union gave other rights to our part of the legislature, so that now, our lords and commons being incorporated with those of the English, the constitution of Scotland is settled upon that just poise betwixt monarchy, aristocracy and democracy, which has made the constitution of England the wonder of mankind.[22]

Another two years later in 1759, William Robertson – Principal of Edinburgh University, Moderator of the Church of Scotland and himself involved in the production of the *Edinburgh Review* – concluded his *History Of Scotland* with these words:

Another great event completed what the revolution had begun. The political power of the nobles, already broken by the Union of the two crowns, was almost annihilated by the union of the two kingdoms...the feudal aristocracy, which had subsisted so many ages, and with power so exorbitant, was overturned, and the Scottish nobles, having surrendered rights and pre-eminences peculiar to their order, reduced themselves to a condition which is no longer the terror and envy of other subjects. Since the union, the commons...have emerged into dignity; and being admitted into the privileges which the English had purchased at the expense of so much blood, must now be deemed a body not less considerable in the one kingdom, than in the other.[23]

The common theme here is that the Union both continued and brought to a conclusion the political process begun at the Revolution, and by doing so brought to an end the crisis of Scottish society. That process, it should be noted, is not only the absorption of Scotland into Britain, but the raising of Scottish political life to the level which had already been attained 'at the cost of so much blood' by England. (Robertson's phrase, which causes so much anguish among Scottish nationalists to this day, does not, of course, imply that Scots had not shed their blood – indeed his work surveys copious amounts being spilt – but that prior to 1688 this was not done to any rational purpose.)

It is in these texts that the ideological origins of British Unionism can be found. Scottish history before 1707 was from this perspective essentially meaningless, devoid of any pattern that might be incorporated into a Scottish history of liberty comparable to that enjoyed by England. If Scotland had escaped absolutism, it was not because the population had succeeded in overthrowing the state, as they had in England, but because the feudal barons had proved too powerful for such a state to be constructed in the first place, as was the case in Poland. As Colin Kidd writes: 'There was nothing of which a sociological whig might be proud in such a fortuitous avoidance of absolute monarchy.'[24] As Robert Wallace wrote, in a work first published anonymously in 1758:

> England is the land of liberty; London, the centre, from which this liberty flows to the rest of the island. The rays of liberty, like those of light, are denser when nearer the centre. The Scots are at a greater distance from it. The English are nearer it, and must have peculiar advantages.[25]

The same theme emerged, as is often the case, in culture before political theory. The Scottish poet James Thompson has the goddess in his poem *Liberty* (1735–6) cast Britain as the successor to the great civilisations of the past:

> Hence, Britain, learn; my best establish'd, last,
> And More than Greece, or Rome, my steady reign;
> The land where, King and people equal bound
> By guardian laws, my fullest blessings flow;
> And where my jealous unsubmitting soul,
> The dread of tyrants! Burns in every breast.

These sentiments, more famously expressed in his *Rule, Britannia* (1740), are not simply imperialist boasting. As Bonamy Dobree comments, the 'fullest blessings' which Liberty has caused to flow in Britannia are mainly those of 'peace, commerce, civic virtue and public works'. In his poem *The Seasons*, Thompson lists political and military figures like Drake, Hampden, Russell and Sidney, but also philosophers like Bacon, Shaftesbury, Newton and Locke, and poets like Chaucer, Shakespeare, Spenser and Milton – not a Scot among them.[26]

These effusions were not primarily designed for an English but a Scottish readership. The Scottish Enlightenment intellectuals were all too aware that many of their countrymen were not convinced of the advantages which had accrued to them either since the Revolution of 1688 or even the Union of 1707 (although – probably for patriotic reasons – the former event featured more frequently in their writings). Unlike many of his more renowned colleagues, Wallace was also prepared to argue that the English had also benefited, although in different ways from Scotland:

> Notwithstanding the arguments for proving that Scotland is much richer, than before the Revolution, such is the force of prejudice, that many in Scotland cannot be convinced of it. They will grant, indeed, what many among the English deny, that *England* has gained greatly by the union of the two kingdoms, but content earnestly, that *Scotland* has been undone by it. The case is otherwise. Both England and Scotland have gained greatly: England, by a more perfect peace and security; so that having nothing to fear in regard of those parts that lie nearest to Scotland, it can with safety cultivate them to great advantage: Scotland by a share of English trade, by a more speedy propagation of the English spirit for agriculture and manufactures, and by the happy progress, that has been made towards a complete rescue of the commons from that slavish dependence which was formerly so common, and still prevails too much, in North Britain.[27]

Why, in the face of this enthusiasm for all things English, were the English so unwilling to accept the Scots as co-partners? James Young has insisted it was because 'the English' were merely continuing to display their traditional xenophobia towards 'the Scots'. Young does not exclude those who participated in the radical movement of the 1760s from this accusation – indeed, he claims that the movement around John Wilkes was at the forefront. Wilkes himself is described as being 'an English chauvinist who hated Scotland and the Scots' and Edward Thompson is taken to task for ignoring 'the strong evidence of the English radical's contempt for the Scots', and remaining 'silent about Wilkes role in inhibiting a real British radicalism'.[28] There are three points to be made here.

First, Bute and the other Scottish favourites of George III, although not Jacobites, were certainly on the right of British political life in the epoch of the American Revolution. Consequently, the hostility directed at them was not only from Wilkesite sources. One anonymous letter to Bute read:

> We know that your friends Cob and Wall have made a fool of [us] to get an Order in Council against us poor journeymen[.] our masters can keep Country Houses while our poor families starve and we work hard, but know that it is resolved among us that if one Publican or one of us suffer we will revenge it on you in a dreadful manner, your royal Mr [i.e., George III] shall not prevent it remember and tremble[.]

Yet this epistle is signed by 'a Scotch journeyman Cabinet maker', suggesting a degree of class opposition to Wilkes which could scarcely be tainted by Scotophobia![29]

Second, Wilkes occupies a very ambiguous position in the pantheon of English radicalism, and cannot be taken as typical of English radical attitudes. He was simultaneously the most effective critic of the restricted democracy operative in Hanoverian England and a ruthless manipulator of popular prejudices in support of his cause – a combination only possible, as Thompson carefully explains, because of the political immaturity of the plebeians during the middle decades of the eighteenth century:

> For the London crowd of the 1760s and 1770s had scarcely begun to develop its own organisation or leaders; had little theory distinct from that of its 'managers'; and there is a sense in which it was manipulated and called out by Wilkes to 'operate on behalf of external interests' – the interests of the wealthy tradesmen, merchants, and manufacturers of the City who were his most influential supporters.[30]

It is only in the most naive versions of 'People's History' that Wilkes could appear as a principled figure, whose attitude to the Scots might indicate some serious division between radicals on different sides of the border.

Third, the agitation led by Wilkes, although seemingly directed at Scots in general, was in fact designed to discredit one group of Scots in particular, namely those who – from the Prime Minister Bute downwards – were occupying the leading offices of the British state in a way which barred the progress of Wilkes and his associates. As Henry Fox confessed in a private letter: 'Every man [i.e., Englishman] has at some time or other found a Scotchman in his way, and everybody has therefore damned the Scotch: and this hatred their excessive nationality has continually inflamed.'[31] So although Wilkes dredged up every prejudice against the Scots which had currency in the England of his day, notably the idea that they were 'natural Jacobites', the real reasons for English hostility to the Lowland Scots – although expressed in similar terms to those voiced during the '45 – had changed significantly within the subsequent two decades. *The Scots were no longer distrusted because they were seen by the English as reactionary opponents of the new capitalist order, but because they were seen as competitors with its existing beneficiaries from inside the system itself.*[32] Thus, as Colley points out, Wilkesite hostility to the Scots may have been 'deeply felt', but it was also 'profoundly ironic':

> So often interpreted at the time and since as evidence of the deep divisions between south and north Britain, in reality its extremism was testimony to the fact that the barriers between England and Scotland were coming down, savage proof that the Scots were acquiring power and influence within Great Britain to a degree previously unknown.[33]

Nevertheless, the campaign waged by Wilkes and the popular response which it produced, showed that the mere establishment of a British state was not enough to ensure the establishment of a British identity. What were the major external factors in finally 'bringing the barriers down'? Writing in 1988, Alexander Murdoch observed that 'It would take the loss of America, the expansion of British power in India, and the Napoleonic wars, before some sort of new British entity would evolve.' 'That process', he concluded, 'is not yet fully understood'.[34] Since 1992 attempts to understand it have been dominated by the arguments of Linda Colley.

The Colley Thesis

Colley argues that Britishness was constructed between 1707 and 1837 from four interconnected elements. The first was popular mobilisation behind the British state in the recurrent conflict with its French rival: 'From the Act of Union to the Battle of Waterloo in 1815, Great Britain was involved in successive, very dangerous wars with Catholic France.'[35] The second, as this quotation suggests, was the identification of the French as the Catholic 'other' to British Protestantism. Colley does not argue that the British-French wars were fought mainly for religious reasons, of course, but suggests instead that religion gave an ideological colouration to the competition for empire between these great powers. The third was the monarchy, adoration of which consolidated the other elements into an essentially conservative national identity. The fourth was the Empire.[36] The argument is intelligently presented and supported with a great deal of evidence. Yet, however convincing it may be as an explanation for the construction of Britishness across the archipelago as a whole (which can itself be disputed), it contains major weaknesses as an account of how the Scots came to be considered as Britons by the English.

War was a constant factor in British relations with France from 1688, not 1707, but between the former date and 1746 a significant section of the Scottish ruling class had looked to France as an ally in maintaining their position. War was scarcely a factor is consolidating *their* sense of Britishness. After 1789 and, more particularly, 1792, France was not opposed by the British ruling class because of its Catholicism, but because it represented the centre of European revolutionary republicanism – a title it retained in the mind of counter-revolutionaries even through imperial pretensions of the Napoleonic period. In short, Britain and France had exchanged positions on the scale of bourgeois development, and this had more contradictory effects on British national consciousness than Colley allows. Similarly, after 1789 a still larger section of the population, at the opposite end of the social scale, looked to France as an inspiration for their own democratic ideals: 'The success of the French

Democrats,' wrote one government informant during 1792, 'has had a most mischievous effect here.'[37] Indeed, as Henry Cockburn recounts in *Memorials Of His Time*: 'There was a short period, chiefly in 1793 and 1794, during which this imputation was provoked by a ridiculous aping of French forms and phraseology, and an offensive vaunting of the superior excellence of everything in that country.'[38] The Scottish plebeian radicals did not reject Britishness – indeed, as I argue in Chapter 10, most had by that date come to accept a form of dual national consciousness – but their conception of Britishness involved notions of radical democracy which were then being explored in France.

These comments obviously have implications for the significance of *Protestantism* in Colley's account, since it carries the greatest explanatory weight for her: 'It was their common investment in Protestantism that first allowed the English, the Welsh and the Scots to become fused together, and to remain so, despite their many cultural divergences.' Can we say so easily, however, that 'Protestantism lay at the core of British national identity'?[39] Even if we assume that religious belief can be an autonomous force in the action of states, it is clear that, apart from the anti-French alliance of convenience between the Lords of the Congregation and the Tudor state during the Scottish Reformation, Protestantism was not a factor in bringing Scotland and England closer together. The commanders of the English troops sent to assist the Lords of the Congregation in 1560 commented on the indifference, or even hostility, shown towards them by the people whom they had ostensibly come to liberate from the French Catholic yoke. Indeed, the variants of that religion adhered to by the respective majorities in each nation helped rather to enforce divisions, not least during the period of the Solemn League and Covenant, when the Scottish Estates and the English Parliament began their doomed experiment in Presbyterianism. France was no less Catholic in 1689, at the start of the War of the British and Irish Succession, than it was in 1759, at the start of the Seven Years War; yet Protestant Scots were divided in their attitude to France at the former date and united in opposition at the latter. As Ian Cowan writes:

> The Revolution of 1689 unexpectedly allowed the Scots to realise their aims [of establishing Protestantism] and with the divergence between the two churches extended thereafter to polity as well as worship, religious issues by the late seventeenth century were more likely to jeopardise than aid union negotiations.[40]

Even those who regarded the common Protestantism of Scotland and England positively were as likely to be opponents of the Union as supporters, taking the position that peaceful co-existence would be best served by each nation continuing to practice their versions of the faith independently. We noted in the previous chapter the insistence by James

Hodges that '*Scotland* hath a Distinct Constitution of Ecclesiastic Government from that of *England*'.[41] Similar arguments were put by James Anderson in the conclusion to his polemic against English claims of sovereignty over the Scottish crown, where he states that:

> ...a Good Understanding may be established between two Nations planted by nature in on[e] Isle, People of the same Language, linked by frequent Inter-marriages in Affinity and Consanguinity, and by the Blessings of Heaven already Engaged to one another, by the most Endearing ties of Religion.

Those who pressed English claims he supposed to be attempting 'to Foment and Create Misunderstandings between two Protestant Independent kingdoms, which I pray GOD may continue in Peace and Amity, while Sun and Moon endure'.[42]

Even after the tensions between the two nations had long since been overcome in the Union, Presbyterianism acted as a divisive factor in Anglo-Scottish relations, particularly in the colonies. The original Scottish settlers in New Jersey during the last quarter of the seventeenth century had included Quakers and were dominated by Episcopalians from the northeast, that is, the congregations 'in communion' with the Church of England. Yet by the middle of the eighteenth century the community had moved away from Episcopalianism and had largely been unified under Presbyterian leadership which often took positions close to the most radical of the post-Covenanting sects. There was, of course, a class element to this: the Presbyterian majority tended to be smaller landowners and tenants, while the large landowners retained the Episcopalianism for which they had provided the base of support back in Scotland. In one sense, then, the colony came to reproduce contemporary Scottish social structures to a greater extent in the period after the consolidation of Union than before. As Ned Landsman writes:

> The unification of Scottish settlers within Presbyterianism represented something more than a simple reproduction of Old World patterns, however, Scotsmen in their homeland had never been so united within their national church, and especially within the evangelical wing of that church, as they would prove to be in New Jersey.[43]

Between 1839 and 1851 Scottish assisted migrants comprised a minority of 11.6 per cent (3,638) of those arriving at Port Phillip in Australia.[44] For these settlers, the Church of Scotland was the main institution through which they maintained specifically Scottish aspects of their identity, in a society where the majority was English. The Anglican Church was seen to represent both 'Englishness' and, to a certain extent, the local Tory establishment. Scots seeking to climb the social ladder therefore tended to abandon Presbyterianism for Episcopacy: 'The opinion held by their fellow nationals and former co-religionists of these Scottish Presbyterians who deserted their church in this way was that they had renounced their national identity.'[45] In short, far from bringing the two nationalities closer together, Protestantism was virtually the only factor that continued to hold them apart.

Even anti-Catholicism was a source of division, rather than unity, among the Scots. The ruling class in Scotland fully intended to implement a measure of Catholic relief in 1778, along the lines of the Roman Catholic relief bills passed that year for England and Ireland in the British and Irish parliaments. Dundas himself announced his intention to do so in the House of Commons debate over the English bill, which permitted Catholics free access to the market in land and allowed them to teach, providing they took the oaths of allegiance and foreswore the temporal powers of the pope. The attempt was abandoned in February 1779 because of popular protest against even this modest measure to relieve the oppression of Catholics.[46] Leaving aside the question of how far the outcry represented a distorted form of class feeling (a claim more plausibly made about the contemporaneous Gordon Riots in London[47]), the participants play all the wrong roles for the Colley thesis. The politicians most anxious to complete the creation of a British identity – Henry Dundas and his supporters – proposed the lessening of anti-Catholic legislation. The institution which is most responsible for sustaining Scottish national consciousness – the Church of Scotland (and the secessionist sects which were satellites in its orbit) – was the most determined to oppose it.

Monarchy also plays an exaggerated role for Colley, largely because of her failure to consider it, like attitudes to France, in the context of class relations. In Part 2 of *The Rights Of Man*, published in 1792, Tom Paine wrote, among other observations on the monarchy, that: 'It takes some talents to be a common mechanic; but, to be a king, requires only the animal figure of a man – a sort of breathing automaton.'[48] As Edward Thompson points out, between 1791 and 1793, the various editions of the book may have sold as many as 200,000 copies in England, Wales and Scotland: 'Paine's book was found in Cornish tin-mines, in Mendip villages, in the Scottish Highlands, and a little later, in most parts of Ireland.'[49] Paine himself estimated, with his usual lack of modesty, that within ten years of the publication of Part 1 in 1790, as many as 500,000 copies had been sold. Assuming that this is near the truth, and that 4,000,000 British citizens were literate, nearly one reader in ten must have bought the book, and this does not account for the others who read it in pirate or serialised editions, or the illiterate who had it read aloud to them. As Paine's most recent biographer notes, these figures made *The Rights Of Man* 'the most widely read book of all time in any language', selling proportionally more copies than the publishing sensation of the next generation: Sir Walter Scott.[50] As we shall see below, the spectacle of the royal visit to Edinburgh in 1822 was important in fastening together Highlander and Lowlander within a Scottish identity, but the success of the monarchy in forging any broad popular appeal lay well beyond 1837, the date chosen by Colley to mark the point at which the British nation had been 'forged'. Support for this claim can be found in the work of David Cannadine, who notes widespread hostility to the monarchy continuing into the reign of Victoria: 'During this early period, the royal family was so unpopular, and the appeal of its ceremonial so limited, that it was not deemed worthy of large scale financial exploitation.'[51]

The factors discussed above were in reality either *obstacles* to the construction of Britishness (Protestantism) or the cause of *political divisions* within an already existing national framework (counter-revolutionary Francophobia, Monarchism), although the latter two factors were clearly important in making the dominant strain in British nationalism a reactionary one *after* 1789. One factor therefore remains for the period between the '45 and the French Revolution: the *Empire*.

Scotland After 1707: Oppressed or Oppressor Nation?

Before turning to the role played by the Empire in the formation of national consciousness in Scotland, I must first consider the role it did *not* play. There are several variations on the theme that the Scots, far from being willing participants in and beneficiaries of the imperial project, were themselves victims of it. None of these is remotely convincing – indeed, if what they claim were true, the trajectory of Scottish nationalism would be completely different from the one actually written into the historical record – but their inadequacy must be demonstrated rather than asserted. What position then did Scotland really occupy within Britain after 1707, and after 1746 in particular?

Angus Calder once described the commercialisation of Scottish agriculture as 'a movement for self-colonisation'.[1] The phrase gives a misleading impression of the forces involved, for does not every indigenous ruling class 'colonise' the subordinate classes? Most applications of the term 'colonialism' to Scotland have, more conventionally, argued that it was a colony, not of its own ruling class, but of England. The implication here, especially when it is taken in conjunction with the notion of national oppression, is that Scotland has been subject to English imperialism. But what do the terms 'oppression' and 'imperialism' mean in this context?

'Oppression' is relatively straightforward. I take it to mean systematic discrimination by one social group against another on the grounds of characteristics either inherited (skin colour, gender) or socially acquired (religious belief, sexual orientation). The experience of oppression cuts across class lines, although that experience is more or less severe depending on where its victims are placed within the class structure. Some forms, like the oppression of women, have persisted throughout the existence of class society, while others, like racism, are specific to capitalism alone. Sometimes the reasons, or pretexts, for the oppression of a group may change over time. During the feudal era, for example, Jewish people were persecuted for their religious beliefs, but as capitalism developed persecution increasingly took place on the grounds of their supposed race. Whatever the reason or pretext, however, ruling classes throughout history have instigated or endorsed the oppression of different groups in order to maintain or create divisions amongst those over whom they rule. *National* oppression does not, however, simply involve subjugation by a stronger group backed or encouraged by the state, but subjugation by the stronger state itself. This has been the common experience of nations that have suffered imperialist rule.

'Imperialism' is unfortunately far from being straightforward. On the contrary, it is one of the most ill-defined terms in political thought. As Alex Callinicos points out, it has had at least three meanings: a general one referring to the process by which some states throughout history have come to dominate others, either for military-territorial advantage, or economic gain, or both; a specific one referring to the expansionist colonial policy of the European powers between 1871 and 1918; and the classical Marxist definition, which defines imperialism as a specific *stage* in capitalist development characterised by the concentration and centralisation of capital, the fusion of capital with the state, but also, paradoxically, of capital breaking outwith the boundaries of the nation state.[2]

Are any of these conceptions of imperialism relevant to Scotland? It would be difficult (though not impossible, as we shall see) to argue that Scotland has suffered from anything resembling the latter two; consequently, it is imperialism in the generic sense which is most frequently evoked in these discussions, and even then, the term is often softened by a qualifying adjective, as in *internal* colonialism and *cultural* imperialism. Let us examine these in turn.

Internal Colonialism?

The concept of internal colonialism was introduced to the debate on the Scottish question by the American sociologist Michael Hechter, in his study of the persistence of 'Celtic' nationalism in Scotland, Wales, Ireland and, to a lesser extent, Cornwall and the Isle of Man. Hechter discussed the UK in terms of 'core' and 'periphery', the latter zone (to which he assigned Scotland) being characterised by economic dependence, a retarded development geared to complement that of the 'core', specialised industrialisation for the export market and lower standards of living than those enjoyed in the 'core' areas: 'Internal colonialism, therefore arose out of the same systemic needs which later spawned its more notorious overseas cousin.'[3] The suggestion here is, of course, that Scotland's 'peripheral' status is merely a variant on the experience of those nations subject to 'classical' imperialism. According to Hechter, the English state first succeeded in making an internal colony of Scotland with the Union of Crowns in 1603 and continued in this role even after the Parliamentary Union of 1707 when, despite the formal dissolution of the existing states, the 'core'/'periphery' relationship was retained within Britain.

Hechter also noted, however, that of all the 'peripheral' nations, Scotland was least amenable to this type of categorisation. He later retreated still further from his original position, but too late to prevent it becoming a theoretical justification for Scottish nationalism.[4] James Young, for example, wrote that: 'Scottish society [was] pushed into a subordinate role [as] a victim of "internal colonisation" with an economy peripheral to the core of British capitalism, and with institutions dominated by the "conquering metropolitan elite"'.[5] Other writers, less committed to a nationalist perspective, or perhaps more aware of the dissimilarities between Scotland and, for example, India, have adopted less extreme formulations. According to Keith Burgess and his colleagues:

In relation to Britain as a whole, what was to emerge in Scotland [after the Union] were complementary rather than competitive forms of capitalism, their interdependence being regulated under the political dominance of Westminster. Such were the roots of the dependent or client status of the Scottish bourgeoisie.[6]

The difference between 'subordination' and 'dependence' is not particularly great. How valid are either of these terms? David McCrone has criticised the theoretical assumptions behind this analysis:

In what was perhaps the quintessential free market economy there is little need to import the notion that economic activity was managed by the state... Insofar as capital would flow into those sectors where profits were made, and capitalists would invest in areas on strictly economic terms, the notion of 'complementarity' (with its implication of explicit intervention in the working of the market) does not ring true. ... It is difficult to see what the mechanisms would be for permitting or forbidding such activity.[7]

The point can be demonstrated empirically by reviewing the progress of the leading industries in the three non-agricultural sectors of the Scottish economy – extraction, manufacturing and overseas trade.

The *coal* industry experienced the most spectacular expansion. Christopher Whatley has argued that, contrary to what has been assumed by most economic historians until recently, annual output during the 1690s was not of the order of 475,000 tons, but the considerably lower figure of 225,000 tons, and that it fell still further by the turn of the century. Rather than coal output in the eighteenth century rising to four times the 1700 level, as was previously thought, it may have risen by as much as eight or ten times – a rate nearly double that for Britain as a whole. The industry continued to use the most advanced forms of technology:

> For the [eighteenth] century as a whole, Scottish collieries accounted for 17 per cent of all steam pumping engines erected in Britain (including the improved and more efficient Boulton and Watt engines) – at a time when Scotland accounted for only 13.3 per cent of British coal production.[8]

By the last quarter of the eighteenth century the class position of the men operating this machinery had, however, undergone a decisive change: they were no longer legally bound as serfs to the coal they dug, but had become wage labourers.

Linen production was dominant within Scottish manufacturing as a whole, not merely in textiles: 'The amount of linen stamped for sale (after inspection by the stampmasters of the Board of Trade) rose from 3.7 million yards in 1730 to 7.6 million in 1750 and to 12.1 million in 1775.' Alistair Durie has argued that the majority of this output was for sale in the English and colonial markets, the scale of the latter in particular being obscured by the fact that perhaps as much as half of the linen exported from England was in fact of Scottish origin. On this assumption, 'after 1747 the percentage of Scottish-made linen production exported from Britain seldom dropped below 20%–30%, and on occasion reached 35%–40%'. Given that these figures relate only to linen which qualified for a 'bounty', if other linen is taken into account the total might have exceeded 50 per cent.[9]

Tobacco was the most successful Scottish import. According to Devine the 'heroic age' of this commodity began in the 1740s: 'In 1741 8 million lb were landed; by 1745 the figure had climbed to 13 million lb and, after a dramatic spurt, to 21 million lb in 1752.' By 1758 imports to Glasgow exceeded those of London, reaching their peak in 1771 when 47 million pounds were landed. The figures showing Scottish imports as a proportion of British imports are even more dramatic. Between 1721 and 1743 the Scottish overseas tobacco trade never accounted for more than 15 per cent of British imports. By the early 1760s the figure had risen to over 40 per cent of British imports. This remarkable increase was of particular importance since, of all components of the Scottish economy, tobacco was the most stimulated by access to previously restricted English home and overseas markets after 1707. As Devine writes: 'It is impossible to imagine the huge imports of tobacco in the middle decades of the eighteenth century without the Union.'[10]

Only if there had been no English coal, linen and tobacco industries would the notion of 'complementary' development have any relevance to Scotland, and this was far from the case. It is possible to draw further evidence from the nineteenth century. From early in the industrial revolution Scotland was pre-eminent in the major exporting trades, with early successes in tobacco, cotton and jute being overtaken by heavy industrial goods. Until the Second World War, Glasgow was the biggest exporter of steam locomotives in the world. By the 1850s Scotland accounted for 90 per cent of British pig iron exports and by 1885, when steel had begun to replace iron, Scotland turned out 42 per cent of all Siemens steel. Shipping was still more impressive. Shipbuilders along the Clyde alone produced 70 per cent of all British iron tonnage between 1851 and 1870, and in the latter year employed 20,000 out of a British workforce of 47,500. By the end of the nineteenth century the proportion of Scots employed in primary industry was one third higher than in England and Wales, and 11 per cent higher in heavy industry.[10]

Had Scotland been an independent centre of capital accumulation, it could be said to have 'caught up and overtaken' its one-time English rival by, at the latest, the end of the Napoleonic Wars in 1815. By that date there were no longer 'Scottish' and 'English' economies separate from that of Britain, except in the geographical sense which allows us to talk about 'the southeast of England' or 'the Midlands' as distinct economic regions. Nevertheless, abstracting 'Scotland' as an economic unit from Britain as a whole, these figures clearly indicate that, far from being 'peripheral' to the British economy, Scotland – or more precisely, the Lowlands – lay at its core. In terms of personnel too, there were no obstacles to the advance of the Scots, as can been seen in examples from both civil society and the state.

Take medicine, one of the professions that did not have a specifically national character in Scotland (i.e., unlike the law or the church). Qualified Scottish physicians moved to England in great numbers. In 1851, there were 511 physicians resident in Scotland, even though Edinburgh University Medical School *alone* graduated 40 every year throughout the 1830s. Over half of Scottish graduates moved to England to practice, and in some cases to become licentiates and even Fellows of the London College of Physicians, without either graduating from Oxford or becoming Anglicans – both obligatory for English physicians. There seems to have been no comparable movement of English physicians northwards to Scotland.[12] If Scotland was indeed an oppressed nation, would her trained professionals be allowed to enter the 'oppressor' nation, taking jobs away from English physicians in the process, without retaliation?

A similar pattern can be found among politicians. After 1746 there was an entirely new level of participation by Scots in political life, particularly outside Scotland. Between 1747 and 1753 only 8 of the 45 Scottish MPs held paid state office; by 1780 the number had risen to 23 or over half. What is more striking is the fact that between 1754 and 1790, 60 Scots had been elected as MPs in England and Wales. And in a situation comparable to that of the medical profession cited above, no English or Welsh MPs sat for Scottish constituencies. Between 1790 and 1820 the number of Scots representing seats in England and Wales rose to 130.[13] More recently, 'Campbell Bannerman, Asquith, Bonar Law, members of the Scottish legal banking and commercial dynasties, held the office of Prime Minister almost continuously for the first two decades of the twentieth century.'[14] And this continues down to the present; of the 23 Cabinet posts announced immediately after the General Election of 1 May 1997, six were held by Scots, including those of the Chancellor of the Exchequer, Foreign Secretary and Lord Chancellor.[15] As Keith Webb once noted, with commendable restraint: 'It is unusual for a colonised nation to provide the political leaders for the colonising nation.'[16]

Cultural Imperialism?

It is possible to accept all of the points made above and still cleave to the belief that Scotland is subject to a colonial relationship with England. The key notion here is *cultural imperialism*. For some writers the desire to assimilate Scottish to English history, displayed by the thinkers of the Scottish Enlightenment in particular, reveals this subjection: 'It was not the crude type of colonial relationship that English capitalism was imposing on large parts of Africa and Asia,' writes James Young:

> ...and the very *subtlety* of the mediating role of the indigenous elite of agrarian capitalists, merchants and intellectuals in assisting the English to impose cultural imperialism on the Scottish populace has obscured its importance in dictating cultural, political and economic developments down to 1820.[17]

William Robertson would presumably qualify as one of Young's 'indigenous intellectuals'. A passage in his *The History Of Scotland* (1759) suggests that a new British consciousness had been achieved:

> At length the Union having incorporated the two nations, and rendered them one people, the distinctions which had subsisted for many ages gradually wear away; peculiarities disappear; the same manners prevail in both parts of the island; the same authors are read and admired, the same entertainments are frequented by the elegant and polite; and the same standard of taste and purity of language, is established.[18]

Supporters of the cultural imperialism thesis could however claim that this was self-delusion on the part of Robertson and point to remarks made in 1797 by Robert Heron, an English traveller in Scotland, as being closer to reality, suggesting as they do that, far from English and Scottish identities having been dissolved into that of the British, the Scottish identity had been dissolved into that of the English:

> National prejudices are gradually losing ground on both sides; and the language, the dress and the manners, of the English, begin to gain the ascendancy. In short, the happy era seems not very distant, when the *English* and the *Scots* shall be, in every sense of the word, ONE NATION.[19]

According to Craig Beveridge and Ronald Turnbull, cultural imperialism has continued down to the present day. The problem they identify is that 'Nationalist philosophy must come to terms with the pervasive effect of Scotland's dependency in relation to England'. And how is this to be achieved? 'The concept of inferiorism developed by [Franz] Fanon in his account of the strategies and effects of external control in the Third World seems to us to yield valuable insights and perspectives on the Scottish predicament.'[20] Turning to Fanon's major work, we find the following description of the psychic aspects of 'external control': 'Every effort is made to bring the colonised person to admit the inferiority of his culture...the unreality of his "nation" and, in the last extreme, the uncivilised and imperfect character of his own biological nature.'[21] These observations, made by Fanon while he was involved in the eight-year struggle for Algerian independence, are an aid to understanding one aspect of Western imperialism during the period of colonial rule. What we are being asked to accept, however, is that they can help illuminate the relationship between Scotland and England. Beveridge and Turnbull are nationalists, but similar observations have been made in relation to Scotland by academics. According to Hechter:

> A defining characteristic of imperial expansion is that the centre must disparage the indigenous culture of peripheral groups. ... This insistence of cultural superiority on the part of the expanding metropolitan state is a characteristic of more recent imperialism as well.[22]

Nor are Beveridge and Turnbull alone in seeking parallels to the Scottish situation among the African liberation movements. Billy Kay, for example, writes that: 'Scottish culture has been suppressed or remained on the periphery for so long that the thought of giving it status provokes feelings of unease and insecurity'. Those who feel this way then become the denigrators of their native culture, the enemy within. But Scotland is not the first nation to have borne this affliction:

The Portuguese colonies in Africa gave the name 'assimilados' to the members of the native population who adopted not only the language and culture of the Portuguese but also the Portuguese contempt for the native culture. For some Scots Scotland is a country of assimilados with everyone educated here inheriting this ambivalence about the Scottish/English balance within themselves.[23]

One might think that present-day black nationalists would find ridiculous, even insulting, the suggestion that Scotland is comparable in any way to the nations of black Africa, but at least one important figure has endorsed just such a position. Cedric Robinson writes:

There are parallels between Scottish, African, and Black history...The exploitation of the Scottish people by the English ruling class, and its suppression by the English government, catalysed the development of Scottish consciousness...In short, the peoples of Scotland were subject to the same historical process, *mutatis mutandis*, under English colonialism which affected British Africa.[24]

Finally, Pat Kane has outlined a comparison that *is* in the developed capitalist world. Where might this be? Quebec? Wallonia? Unfortunately not: it is the black population of the United States: 'It would be impudent to claim that the task of reclaiming Scottish history was equal to the afro-centric agenda of intellectually refuting centuries of active racism...' So far, so good: '...but both projects serve the same nationalistic ends; the broadening of the meaning of one's national community into its true complex history out of the hands of the wilful mystifiers.'[25] In all of these extracts it is through the domain of culture that analogies with classical imperialism, impossible to sustain frontally, are readmitted through the back door, so to speak.

There are occasions when such claims appear to have a certain plausibility. Shortly before his death Alan Taylor reacted with anger to a suggestion by John Pocock that there might even *be* specifically British, as opposed to English, history or culture:

Everyone knows what we mean whether we call our subject English history or British history. It is a fuss over names, not things...The culture is and always has been exclusively English, with some contributions from the outposts that are on a very small scale. For instance, what has Scotland contributed to English culture? David Hume to some extent; Walter Scott certainly, although mainly as a matter of fancy dress; Burns as an element in English culture not at all. (Scotch [sic] ignorance of Burn's work suggests that he is also not much of an element in Scotch [sic] culture)... What does not make any sense is to imply that there is something called British history that is different from English history... British history starts only when the Scotch [sic] and Irish become English speakers, in other words, a variant of Englishmen.[26]

Taylor was on the Left; and indeed, among British post-war historians, was popularly regarded as the socialist alternative to the conservatism of Hugh Trevor-Roper. Unfortunately, this extract (which contains a level of English chauvinism that both he and his opponent normally reserved for the German people) shows that, far from being the mirror image of his conservative rival, he was all too often merely his echo. In addition to being offensive, however, these comments are also profoundly inaccurate, which might be thought a failing in a professional historian.

The extent to which it is wrong to say that 'the culture is and always has been exclusively English' can be demonstrated in a number of ways. Take, for example, one English cultural product from towards the end of our period: *Mansfield Park* (1814) by Jane Austen. What is interesting about this work in connection with our theme is the way in which the characters casually identify with Scottish culture; indeed, they treat it as an aspect of their own. In Chapter 9 we find two examples of this in quick succession. First, we find Fanny Price lamenting to Edmund Bertram that the chapel on the Sotherton estate has none of the romance she has come to expect in Walter Scott's *The Lay Of The Last Minstrel* ('No banners, cousin, "to be blown by the night winds of Heaven". No signs that "a Scottish monarch sleeps below"'). Second, we find Mary Crawford complaining to Edmund of the inadequacy of most clergymen compared to the Scottish minister Hugh Blair ('How can two sermons a week, even supposing them to be worth hearing, supposing the preacher to have the sense to prefer Blair's to his own, do all that you speak of? govern the conduct and fashion the manners of a large congregation for the rest of the week?').[27] Austen knew the people of whom she wrote, and since they were also her intended audience she was not in the habit of misrepresenting their tastes. These passages suggest that, far from Scotland being the subject of English cultural imperialism, the situation was in many ways reversed.

The suggestion is strengthened if we broaden the definition of culture from works of art to aspects of a 'way of life' more generally. Before the mid-eighteenth century anyone in Britain who wished to join the medical profession had to go to the European mainland for training, usually in Leiden or Paris. The first serious medical faculty in Britain was established in Edinburgh after 1750 and by the end of the century it had become the most important institution for the medical training of physicians in all of the four nations of the UK. Between 1830 and 1839 1,102 physicians graduated from Edinburgh, 389 Scots, 301 English, 292 Irish and 4 Welsh, and by then the capital had also been joined by a further school at Glasgow. In short, during the first half of the nineteenth century, most British medical practitioners had tended to receive at least part of their education in Scotland, typically at Edinburgh.[28] Who is culturally dominating whom in this situation?

Finally there is what David Morse calls a 'curious fact' about the construction of Englishness, namely that many of the people most responsible for it were in fact Scottish:

> It was Hume and Mackintosh who laid the modern foundations for a modern history of *England*. It was Adam Smith who elaborated an economic theory that could serve as a framework for England's destiny as a trading nation. It was James Mill who in his *History of British India* (1818) mapped out Britain's future as an imperial power and legislator for mankind. It was Sir Walter Scott who in *Ivanhoe* produced the definitive myth of a proud Saxon race indomitably struggling against the Norman yoke. It was Thomas Carlyle who extended and developed this into a philosophy of the English character and a critique of industrialisation, and while Macaulay, who was perhaps the one single writer to produce a view of England that was more influential than Carlyle's, was not himself Scottish, he was deeply influenced by the ideals of the Scottish Enlightenment, the foremost protégé of Francis Jeffrey at the *Edinburgh Review* from 1839 to 1847, and from 1852 to 1856 MP for Edinburgh itself.[29]

In fact, as Cairns Craig writes:

> As England was being transformed by the construction of a new British identity which had significant Scottish components – to which the likes of Hume were prime contributors – so Scotland was transformed by English elements of that same British identity, and both were resisting uniformity by discovering new ways of relating to their independent pasts.[30]

Why then does the myth that the Scots were culturally subjugated persist? The proof tends to be drawn from an exceptional episode in Scottish cultural history that is then treated as typical. A famous letter of 1764 by David Hume to Gilbert Elliot in 1764 is often considered in this connection. In it Hume writes of the English:

> Some hate me because I am not a Tory, some because I am not a Whig, some because I am not a Christian, and all because I am a Scotsman. Can you seriously talk of my continuing an Englishman? ... Am I, or are you, an Englishman? Will they allow us to be so?[31]

These comments, and his often expressed desire to purge his work of 'Scotticisms', shared with other Scottish writers like James Boswell and

Tobias Smollett, imply that Hume was concerned with remaking himself as English, rather than Scoto-British. There are four reasons why it would be wrong to infer this conclusion.

First, because they were historians, philosophers, biographers and novelists (and not poets) they were more concerned with comprehensibility to the greatest public, and English allowed this. As Paul Scott, who can scarcely be accused of anti-Scottish feeling, has written about Hume in particular: '[He] preferred English because it was already widely understood and was likely to endure: Scottish words and usages he thought of as an obstacle to understanding anywhere outside Scotland.'[32] For real examples of anti-Scottish ideology manifested in attacks on the language, it is necessary to cross the Irish sea to a genuinely colonial society. In 1792 we find one pseudo-anonymous contributor to the *Belfast Telegraph* writing about 'the disgusting gibberish of Scottish versification with which our eyes, our ears, our feelings, have been so much wounded', in response to the popularity of Burns with both Protestant and Catholic Irish poets:

> It is strange that, when so noble a language as the English can be had, any writer whatever in these countries should yet have recourse to a dialect absolutely barbarous, especially as the best authors among the Scots themselves have long since abandoned it for the elegant and expressive English. I do not think I am easily wrought upon by prejudice, but I acknowledge myself to be one of those who have an invincible aversion to the Scotch language and the Scotch accent; and I may say the same with regard to the Irish.[33]

Second, all of these writers attempted to build careers in England and, more specifically, in London, during or after the '45 when anti-Scottish prejudice was running high. During the Wilkesite insurgencies of the 1760s in particular, there was likely an element of self-defence in their attempts not to display Scottish traits in their writing. It is significant that the entire movement to eliminate literary Scoticisms had come to a halt by the 1770s, not only with the death of Hume and Smollett, but also with the fading of English Scotophobia.[34]

Third, as Cairns Craig has stressed, Hume does not, in his philosophy, represent 'an acceptance of English values' but rather acceptance of 'a set of *class* values' which are those of the English ruling class. And, although Craig does not make the point in his otherwise useful discussion, it may be that the reason Hume felt particularly drawn towards these values was precisely because they were so *underdeveloped* in a Scotland which was still emerging from feudalism, and would remain so until Hume and the other Enlightenment thinkers had completed their work. As Craig adds:

That 'London is the capital of my own country' for Hume is not a simple commitment to English culture: it is a commitment to the construction of a new British culture which works through the language of class as a common bond for its diverse national groups.[35]

Fourth, many leading Scottish figures were developing and implementing economic strategies which they saw as conducive to the betterment of Scotland at precisely the same time that they were removing Scoticisms from their writings: greater weight should perhaps be given to the former rather than the latter aspect of their activities. 'The ideology which triumphed in 1707 was not anti-Scottish', writes Christopher Harvie 'it was perfectly possible to be both a sincere nationalist and an advocate of the Union: it may even have been essential.'[36] These remarks are even more applicable to the period after 1746. The 10th Earl of Eglinmont, about to take part in a duel and anticipating his own death, sent a testament to his younger brother, concluding his advice on a pathetic but intensely practical note: 'Don't neglect horse-hoeing if you love Scotland.'[37] Lord Kames, as might be expected, put the matter more elegantly:

> Every gentleman farmer must of course be a patriot; for patriotism, like other virtues, is improved and fortified by exercise. In fact, if there be any remaining patriotism in a nation, it is found in that class of men.[38]

The identification of bourgeois with national interests suggested by these comments is reinforced by those of a non-Scot, one Eric Thomas Svedenstierna, a leading official in the Swedish Iron Bureau who visited Britain in 1802 to study the methods of production which the Swedes rightly treated as a threat to their own iron industry. One of the ironworks which Svedenstierna visited was at Wilsontown outside Edinburgh, owned by James Wilson, which, the Swede calculated, could not make a profit given the cost of production, particularly in transporting the refined iron ore to the nearest port over two miles away:

> However, Mr Wilson is a good patriot, and has sufficient steadfastness to follow a plan which, without paying in the first years, gives an almost certain hope of high returns for the future, and through which in any case a place of refuge is prepared for many people who, otherwise than in wartime, would have to seek their living in foreign parts.[39]

But perhaps the most vigorous defence of the Scottish element in Britishness can be found in one of the most important non-literary Enlightenment figures: James Watt.

Watt has sometimes been carelessly treated as an English figure. According to Gerald Newman, who discusses him as the successor to

'John Kay, perhaps the greatest English inventor of the preceding generation', Watt was 'the pioneer of English engineering'. Newman quotes Watt: 'If I merit it some of my countrymen, inspired by the *Amor Patriae* may say: "*Hoc a Scoto factum fuit*"' [i.e., 'This was made by a Scot'], but seems incapable of seeing what this means.[40] As Alexander Murdoch writes: 'The nationalism Newman perceives in Watt is his participation in the new modern construction of Britishness in a way which did not exclude his traditional national identity as a Scot.'[41] Leaving aside the notion that his Scottishness was or could have been 'traditional', this dual aspect has struck many historians, of whom Colley is perhaps the most eloquent:

> James Watt...remained throughout his career a Scottish patriot. Every invention he patented, every steam engine he pioneered, filled him with the glowing thought that in the future his own countrymen would be able to say: 'This was made by a Scot'. Yet when Catherine the Great tried to persuade him to come to Russia, Watt told her he could never leave his own nation which was Great Britain. ... Scots like Watt do not seem to have regarded themselves as stooges of English cultural hegemony. Far from succumbing helplessly to an alien identity imposed by others, in moving south they helped construct what being British was all about.[42]

The Highlands: an Exceptional Case?

The proposition that Scotland was an 'internal colony' of England or subject to 'cultural imperialism' at the hands of England is therefore impossible to sustain. There was, however, one part of Scotland where the term 'colony' might be used in the classic sense and without any qualifying adjectives: the Highlands. But who were the colonists?

Perhaps the most widely read historian of events in the Highlands between the Massacre of Glencoe and the Clearances is the Scottish-Canadian writer John Prebble. He draws an explicit comparison with the colonial world: 'The exploitation of the country during the next hundred years was within the same pattern of colonial development – new economies introduced for the greater wealth of the few, and the unproductive obstacle of a native population killed or forcibly removed.' There is, however, a problem for those who seek to establish the presence of English colonialism, as Prebble himself makes clear: 'At Culloden, and during the military occupation of the glens, the *British* government first defeated a tribal uprising and then destroyed the society that made it possible.'[43] This is the only context in which the 'self-colonisation' of which Calder writes has any relevance.

Unfortunately, mere facts have not deterred writers from confusing the issue, as the following remarks by the New Zealand socialist Keith Buchanan demonstrate. His discussion of the Highlands begins with a reference to the British Empire similar to that made by Prebble: 'It was the pattern of exploitation subsequently repeated by Britain in her overseas colonies suited to settlers of British stock...'. By the end of this sentence, however, the protagonists have been transformed: '...in a more sophisticated form it is this process of exploitative development that still governs the relationship between Scotland and her more powerful southern neighbour.'[44] In a far more serious historical contribution, Charles Withers begins an assessment of the decline of Gaelic as a language with these fundamentally accurate observations:

What made these changes possible was the incorporation of the Scottish and Highland gentry and elite into a British ascendancy, the increased career opportunities for men of ability and the patronage to be procured amongst men of wealth and influence as Scotland turned away from the native traditions and embraced the British scene.

By the next sentence, he too has changed the protagonists:

It remains as a final part of setting Gaelic's place within the move towards an English way of life to show how, in combination with these processes, the adoption of English cultural norms as the yardstick of cultural status had an important bearing on the Gaelic language and on the these Gaelic cultural forms that were the vehicle for the language.[45]

The almost imperceptible slide in both examples, from the Highlands and Britain to Scotland and England, encapsulates the way in which the fate of the Highlands is made to act as a surrogate for the Scottish condition. James Campbell made this explicit in his record of a journey through Scotland in the early 1980s. He renders events after 1746 as involving 'the completion of the process begun at Culloden to undermine the Highlanders way of life and the ways he had of interpreting it: his customs and his culture.' Pausing only to note the startling absence of women in the Highlands, we then come to this remarkable passage:

That is why the Highland Clearances is Scotland's most forceful, clear and *valuable* myth. Throughout the country there is a sense that what took place in the Highlands during the earlier part of last [nineteenth] century is a clue to what has happened to modern Scotland.[46]

I take this to mean that, even if the experience of the great majority of Scots has been quite different from that of the Highlanders, the Scots must nevertheless act as if it has been the same. Consider, for example, the claim by Berresford Ellis and Mac a' Ghobhainn, 'the English' defeated 'the Scots' at Culloden 'and began one of the worst persecutions of a nation known to history'.[47] The object, at least in the hands of Scottish nationalist ideologues like these, is to shift attention from class divisions within Scotland, on to a supposedly external national oppression. Claims of this nature are unsustainable.

Who committed the worst atrocities during the pacification of the Highlands after Culloden? In almost every instance it was the Lowland Scottish officers, rather than their English counterparts. Prebble presents us with a grim identity parade:

'All the officers of Blakeney's regiment except three...were extremely cruel, but none exceeded Captain Dunlop.' Dunlop, a Scot, was an interrogation officer, and any prisoner who thought that his part in the interrogation meant saying anything more than Yes or No soon found himself gagged by a drum stick. Late in the year, when the prisons of Inverness were full and the Highlands were rimed with frost, Dunlop ordered that no fires and no candles were to be lit in the goals. Major Lockhart of Chomondeley's [regiment], Captain Caroline Scott of Guise's and Captain John Fergusson of the Royal Navy, three more Lowland Scots, also earned reputations that would not have been out of place in a mess of the *Schutzstaffeln* two centuries later.[48]

It could be argued, of course, that these officers had internalised English attitudes towards their fellow-countrymen, but such claims must ignore the evidence presented in the two previous chapters that Lowland Scots felt a deep hostility towards the Highlanders which stretched back centuries before the Union of the Crowns. Indeed, it might be argued that the English attitude towards the Highlanders was an extension of that held by the Lowland Scots, rather than the other way around.

The situation with respect to the Clearances is even plainer, for, with the exception of George Levison-Gower, Marquis of Stafford and later Duke of Sutherland, those responsible were not only Scottish but Highland Scots. The changing attitudes of the chiefs towards their tenants can be followed in the correspondence of the last two chiefs of Barra. Writing as late as 1816 to the parish minister, Angus MacDonald, about the emigrations then taking place, MacNeil of Barra states: 'It is no doubt distressing to my feelings that the people to whom I am so much attached should leave me: but if it was for their own good, I should regret it less.' Later in the same letter he writes: 'Were it agreeable, I would with pleasure do all that was possible to save the small means of these people, and so, let their situation be better, when they get to America.'[49] His son, Colonel Roderick MacNeil, took a somewhat different approach. Writing to the same clergyman, MacNeil makes his credo plain: 'Every man my good sir has the right to do the best he can for himself in his own affairs – if one set of servants (tenant at will are nothing else) won't do, the master must try others.' In one respect, however, MacNeil did continue an existing tradition; that of using the local minister to disseminate his instructions:

> Say to those who are about to emigrate that I sincerely wish them well through it, and assure those who have signed and repented that their repentance comes too late – So help me God, they shall go; at all events off my property – man, woman and child. Tell the people once for all, that I shall consider any act of inattention to the orders of my factor Mr Stewart as an impertinence to myself. Nor shall anyone who dares even to hesitate to obey him or Mr Parry (in both of whom I have the greatest confidence) remain on my property should his, or their, character have been even so good formerly.[50]

MacNeil made clear shortly after this outburst the reason for his attitude: 'From old Feudal feeling, I was desirous of effecting the objects I had in view, by means of the natives of these islands'. Regrettably, however, their unaccountable refusal to obey his every command had made him realise the futility of this approach; consequently: 'I shall now look to my own interests without any further regard to obsolete prejudices.'[51] Here is the authentic voice of nineteenth century political economy in what might be called its practical aspect. The issue is surely not national identity but class position.

The British state certainly has much to apologise for, since it endorsed and supported what occurred in the Highlands, but the Clearances were carried out at the behest of Scottish landowners, organised by their Scottish factors and, where necessary, enforced by Scottish police or Scottish regiments. Unless one supposes that the Highlands was a separate nation during this period the charge of colonialism is as empty for that region as it is for Scotland as a whole, and since for supporters of the 'internal colonisation' thesis take the Highlands to represent Scotland as a whole, this is a position which they cannot adopt. The inhabitants of the Highlands suffered terrible oppression, as did peasantries across Europe in the transition to capitalism, but they no more suffered *colonial* oppression than did the English peasants who were dispossessed nearly 400 hundred years before the Clearances began. Many of the Highlanders forced to emigrate by the likes of MacNeil of Barra were, however, themselves playing a colonial role in their new homelands.

The native Americans, to whom the Highlanders were so frequently and inaccurately compared, might have expected different treatment at their hands than was generally dispensed by settlers from elsewhere in the British Isles. Alas, this was not the case. There were individual examples of inter-marriage, or even of Highlanders adopting native

American lifestyles, but as James Hunter writes: 'Most North American Indian native peoples...would have been hard pressed to distinguish between the behaviour of Scottish Highlanders or any other of the various types of European with whom they came in contact.' In some cases this behaviour contained some particularly bitter ironies:

> Emigrants to Cape Breton Island, many of them refugees from clearances of the sort organised by Patrick Sellar, showed not the slightest scruple about displacing the area's traditional inhabitants, the Micmac, from territories the latter had occupied for much longer than there had been Gaelic-speaking Scots in Scotland.[52]

The Highlanders were forced from their homes by the operation of an indigenous capitalism. As a result, some went on to establish their own colonial dominion over the natives of another land, for the benefit of the same capitalist interests. There is tragedy enough here, surely, without inventing a wholly fictitious colonisation of the Scots, either by the English or themselves.

Imperial Caledonia?

As the example of the Highland colonists suggests, it is possible to go further than simply denying that the concept of colonialism is valid in any sense in relation to Scotland. Far from being in any sense a victim of imperialism, Scotland was, as an integral part of the British state, a major component of one.[53] As Colley remarks, 'at no time have [the English] customarily referred to an *English* Empire'.[54] David McCrone has remarked that the notion of Scotland as a colony, although still a vital component of political polemic, has largely been abandoned by academics for 'the view that Scotland was not a colony of England but a successful junior partner in the wider process of British imperial colonialism'.[55] Although not a manifest absurdity like the 'colonial' thesis, the 'junior partner' also contains its own difficulties. To say that Scotland behaved in certain ways is to direct attention away from the unity of the British state and to lend support to Unionist arguments that elements of the Scottish state survived the events of 1707 to operate externally in partnership with that of England. To talk of the 'the Scots' being 'junior partners' with the English would – even if one forgets to ask *which* Scots and *which* English – be theoretically acceptable, but unfortunately it would also be empirically false, for in many cases the Scots were in the senior position, and not the junior. Here, the 'junior partner' thesis can be used to evade responsibility for the nature of the British Empire.

Certain classes of Scot were central to conquering and running the Empire, but it is important to get the sequence of events in their proper order, in particular the conjunctural aspects of Scottish imperial involvement. 'The architects of the Union did not design it as the Scots consolation prize for their abandoned emporium,' writes David Armitage, 'nor did the Scots join it hoping to gather the fruits of empire.'[56] Indeed, far from being any form of compensation, the Empire – such as it was in 1707 – did not enter into the calculations of either set of negotiators, nor, insofar as their private correspondence is any guide, was Scottish participation even one of the unspoken assumptions underlying their discussions. A minority of Scots attempted to exploit the opportunities of empire from almost as soon as the Treaty of Union was ratified. In 1708 one Captain Samuel Vetch, son of a Covenanting Minister and a survivor of Darien, made a proposal to the Board of Trade that he be empowered to make an attempt on the French colony of Acadia, which had once been the Scottish Colony of Nova Scotia. Vetch hoped to reinstate Scottish rule (with himself as Governor) but in order to 'infinitely advance the commerce of Britain' and to 'make Canada a noble colony, exactly calculate for the constitutions and genius of the most Northern of the North Britons.'[57]

Vetch was exceptional in his enthusiasm for personally adding to British overseas territory. The most important opportunity provided to Scots by the Empire was not for displays of derring-do, but for the expansion of the key Scottish export: tobacco. The Glaswegian tobacco merchants were finally able to expand legally into territories in the West Indies and North America, from which they would certainly have been completely excluded without the Union – as they would had the French subsequently taken control of the Atlantic Empire. In this case there is a definite causal link between Union and the expansion of the Scottish economy which was felt far beyond Greenock and Port Glasgow where the tobacco was landed: 'Merchants founded a series of industries from brewing to linen, from coal to iron in Glasgow and the immediate neighbourhood in order to ensure cheaper and more reliable supplies for their planter customers in the colonies.'[58] One Scottish owner of Chesapeake (Maryland and Virginia) tobacco and West Indian sugar plantations, Richard Oswald, began to invest his profits in Scotland in 1763, purchasing 5,614 acres outright and mortgaging another 9,056. In 1773 his property increased five times over and, at its peak in 1782, he owned 102,679 acres, all in Ayrshire.[59] This new breed of landowners immediately fell to improving their estates in the manner that had already become established while they were making their fortunes in the Americas.[60] In order to exploit their estates to the full, however, the merchants also found it necessary, not only to implement the informal programme of the Improvers, but to organise the digging of canals, the setting up of turnpike roads and local communications networks more generally. Oswald, for example, lobbied for a private act to be passed in parliament in 1766, the first in Scotland to establish a 'public' turnpike trust in which decision-making power was vested in a committee of local landowners:

> The result was a complete transformation of Ayr's transportation infrastructure: old roads on which coal could not have been carried more than two miles in 1763 were fully traversable in 1784, and four new roads, 100 miles in all, which did not exist when [Oswald] bought [his estate in Ayr], were by his death major arteries connecting various parts of the county to its centre.[61]

The impact of such developments went beyond easing the access of crops and minerals to regional markets for their initiators: they were to provide one of the foundations of the coming industrial revolution.

Both the Chesapeake tobacco production and the West Indian sugar production that made Oswald his fortune took place on the basis of slave labour. In Jamaica between 1673 and 1774 the white population doubled, but the slave population increased 25 fold. Indeed, the disproportion between whites and slaves grew so extreme that the latter half of the eighteenth century saw the passing of the so-called 'deficiency laws', which required all plantations to employ a minimum number of white workers, usually one for every ten slaves. Despite the fact that fines were imposed for failure to comply, many plantation owners refused to do so, finding it cheaper to be penalised than to tilt the balance even marginally further towards non-slave labour. In 1817, ten years after the abolition of the slave trade, the Scots in Jamaica still held more slaves than the average white. The slave registration returns for that year show that, in the parishes sampled, Scots comprised 23.5 per cent of the white population, but owned 32.4 per cent of the slaves.[62]

Not all Scots approved of slavery, in spite of its extent and profitability. Scottish immigrants to Georgia had raised a petition as early as 1739 protesting at a plan to abrogate a standing ban on the introduction of slaves to the colony, at least some of the grounds of their complaint being the treatment of the slaves. Several prominent figures in the Enlightenment – including Hutcheson, Smith and Millar – also criticised slavery, but often from the perspective of political economy, drawing particular attention to the greater productivity of free labour.[63] Smith in particular insisted that 'the work done by freemen comes cheaper in the end than work performed by slaves'.[64] He acknowledged that profits on the sugar and – to a lesser extent – tobacco plantations were high enough for the issue not to impinge on the owners, but tended to regard this as an exception, and consequently never integrated the institution of systemic slavery into his view of capitalist development.[65] In this respect at least, his work suffers from a confusion between the model of 'commercial society' which he personally favoured and the reality of 'actually existing capitalism'.

Other American colonists were hostile to the Scots. On 29 April 1776, Ezra Stiles, the future president of Yale University, recorded in his diary his belief that the conflict between Britain and the American colonies was because 'The Scotch Influence blinds the Parliament and Nation':

Scotch Policy transfused through the collective Body of the Ruling Powers in Great Britain: and their violent oppressive and haughty Measures have weaned and alienated the affections of three Millions of people and dismembered them from a once beloved Parent State. Cursed be that arbitrary policy![66]

Like many Americans, Stiles believed that, if the Scots, with their supposed propensity for absolutist tyranny, could be removed from the government, the policy of George III towards the colony would be reversed. They were right in their estimation of Scottish influence over government policy, but wrong to imagine that it was in any way contrary to the wishes of the majority of their English compatriots. Indeed, insofar as Americans felt any sense of national belonging before the formation of their own state, it was to England, not Britain.[67] Ironically, although this identification was for the same reasons as the Scottish Enlightenment intellectuals – a desire to be assimilated to the tradition of English liberty – the Scots were excluded. Some even felt that the term 'Great Britain' itself was a Scoticism. The Virginian William Lee wrote in 1774: 'What chance can England or America have for a continuance of their liberty or independence when not only the principles, but the phraseology of that accursed country is prevalent every where?'[68] Of course, the hostility felt by the American colonists to the Scots did not mean that they had no use for the ideas of the Scottish Enlightenment (any more than the hostility felt by the Scottish Lowlanders to the Highlanders meant that they rejected the Dalriadic origins of the state). On the contrary, those who framed the American Constitution drew heavily on the Scottish theorists.[69]

From their initial point of entry in the Americas the Scottish bourgeoisie spread themselves outwards, and indeed they were forced to do so. The liberation of the American colonies in 1783 meant that it was in India that the greatest opportunities were to be found for relatively impoverished Lowland landowners – or at any rate, their younger sons – to elevate themselves. As Walter Scott complained in 1821: 'Our younger children are as naturally exported to India as our black cattle were sent to England before the Southron [i.e., the English] renounced eating roast-beef, which seems to be the case this year.'[70] Indeed, one might hypothesise that, because of the more established patterns of capital accumulation which prevailed in England, the uncertainties involved in subduing and exploiting North America or South Asia held considerably less appeal there than they did for the Scots, for whom these territories might have provided the only possibilities of speedy advancement. The field was therefore open to Scots on the make in a way that would be closed once the boundaries of Empire became more established and the typical British ruler became the imperial bureaucrat – the 'box-wallah' later disdained by Rudyard Kipling – rather than the merchant adventurer.

By the mid-eighteenth century 60 per cent of British imports regularly came from Bengal. Trade was controlled by a small number of merchant agencies. At their height, in 1803, there were only 23 based in the regional capital of Calcutta, of whom the six most important were dominated by Scots. 'In Bombay an even smaller oligarchy of agencies had by the end of the century gained a stranglehold over the economy.' Of the five agencies involved 'at least three' were Scottish and these also exercised a degree of political power unknown to their colleagues in Calcutta – not least because of their willingness to supply funds to the ruling East India Company in times of crisis.[71] The Company itself, which had successfully campaigned to prevent the Scots from establishing their own colony at Darien, now found themselves subverted from within: 'In 1772 Scots in the company represented one in nine of its civil servants, one in eleven of its common soldiers, and, already, one in three of its officers'.[72] The most important economic consequence of the Scottish presence in India was the investment in Scotland of the wealth accumulated by the nabobs upon their return. In this respect, as one historian of their presence writes: 'India had an impact upon eighteenth-century Scotland out of proportion to the number of Scots who went there.'[73]

One might also say that Scotland had an impact on India out of proportion to the number of Scots who went there, although this is an impact the Indians might well have done without. We are fortunate to have an excellent description of imperial rule in the Asian subcontinent by James Callender, a Scottish radical active during the 1780s and 1790s:

> In Bengal only, we destroyed or expelled within the short period of six years, no less than five millions of industrious and harmless people; and as we have been sovereigns in that country for about thirty-five years, it may be reasonably computed that we have strewn the plains of Indostan with fifteen or twenty millions of carcasses. ... The persons positively destroyed must, in whole, have exceeded twenty millions, or two thousand...acts of homicide *per annum*. These victims have been sacrificed to the balance of power, and the balance of trade, the honour of the British flag...[74]

Who was responsible for this havoc? James Young, who rightly admires Callender, writes of 'the crude type of colonial relationship that English capitalism was imposing on large parts of Africa and Asia', but

Callender is far more acute than his contemporary admirer.[75] It was not 'English capitalism' which caused the bones of countless Bengalis to bleach in the sun, but a fully integrated *British* capitalism in which the Scots played a leading role. Indeed, the capitalist class in Scotland was at the forefront, not only of colonial expansion, but also of the overseas investment characteristic of the imperialist stage of capitalism. 'It was a commonplace of late Victorian comment', writes Bruce Lenman, 'that Scotland invested abroad on a scale per head with no parallel among the other nations of the United Kingdom.'[76]

On the threshold of the nineteenth century, the Scottish bourgeoisie could legitimately have cried: yesterday, America; today, India; tomorrow, the world. By 1858, with *Pax Britannica* – or perhaps one should say *Pax Caledonia* – at its height, William Burns, a tireless campaigner against real or imagined English slights to Scotland, compiled a comprehensive account of how much the Empire owed to his native land:

> Allow us to ask. What portion of our present colonial possessions belonged to England prior to her union with Scotland? We know of none, except one or two West Indian islands – very profitable appendages they are! – and some narrow strips on the sea-board of Hindustan. Our Indian empire has risen under the joint energies of Scot, Irishman and Englishman; as the names of such men as Munro, Malcolm, Wellington, Dundas, Stewart, Burness, Napier, Dalhousie, and the recorded exploits of Scottish soldiers assure us. Australia, New Zealand, the Cape, Malta, Gibraltar, our Chinese establishments, are all in the same position. The remark, however, applies particularly to Canada, Nova Scotia, and our other North American possessions. Canada was conquered by Scotsmen; Scotsmen were the pioneers of all our operations, and now form the staple of society in that great country.[77]

If, as I have argued here, Scotland was indeed an imperial nation within the context of the British state, then we can now return to the question that we left unanswered at the close of the previous chapter: how did the Empire help to develop the dual national consciousness of Scottish people?

6

British Imperialism and National Consciousness in Scotland

The function of the British Empire in the construction of national consciousness is frequently misunderstood, even by those who are aware of its significance. Michael Lynch, for example, writes of 'the rapturous embrace made by the Scots, not of Britain, but of the British Empire, which opened up in the 1780s and disappeared after 1945.'[1] There are a number of problems with this perspective.

First (as we saw in Chapter 4), a minority of the Lowland bourgeoisie embraced a British identity even before the Union was an established fact, notably the profoundly ambiguous figure of William Paterson. Thereafter, the Scottish bourgeoisie, of all social classes in the British Isles, were the most enthusiastic for constructing a British nation long before the decade of the 1780s that Lynch identifies as decisive.

Second, although the Empire certainly brought material benefit to members of this class (as we saw in Chapter 5), they also used it as a means of demonstrating their Britishness, of proving the validity of the British nation to their English counterparts. During the 1780s we find John Knox writing, in a book called *A View Of The British Empire*:

> Upon the whole the interest of Scotland is in every possible respect the interest of England. Both Kingdoms are inseparably united by nature, and they will rise or fall together. All local distinctions ought therefore to cease, and all persons who endeavour to sow, or keep up a flame of discord, should be considered as enemies of their country, by destroying that harmony which constitutes our strength, security and reciprocal benefit.[2]

The 'Britishness' of the Lowland bourgeoisie was therefore merely heightened, not brought into being, by the possibilities of the British Empire. Indeed, it could be argued against Lynch that the function of Empire was not only to give Scottish capitalism an additional reason for loyalty to the British state, but also to provide an opportunity to demonstrate their *existing* loyalty, since it was hard for one-time English rivals to regard the Scots as partners rather than competitors – the immediate stimulus for Wilkes to begin his campaign was, after all, his failure to win the post of Governor of Quebec in the face of competition from a Scot, Brigadier James Murray.

Third, as this suggests, British national consciousness (as opposed to the British state) did not have a separate existence that the Scots refused to embrace until the Empire made it profitable to do so. In fact, it was Scottish participation in the Empire that helped bring the British nation into being. The social and commercial connections of the Scottish merchants, particularly in the Indian subcontinent, were important in contributing 'to the assimilation of the Scottish upper classes to the pre-dominantly South-of-England elites who ran the United Kingdom', but these merchants were a small minority of the population.[3] The formation of a new national consciousness below elite level was to come from a rather more unexpected source.

Graham Walker has noted 'the extent to which *Scottishness* was promoted and enhanced within the Empire': 'Far from being eclipsed by her larger neighbour Scotland used the opportunity structure offered by the Empire to demonstrate what Scots quite immodestly considered the superiority of their nation's cultural and moral distinctiveness.' This is correct, but one-sided. Far from only a means which Scots used to 'enhance Scottish institutions and assert their differences with England', the Empire was also the principle means by which the Scottish and English identities were transcended in a new sense of Britishness.[4]

Scots and the British Empire

The actual term, 'British Empire' was first used by propagandists for Henry VIII and the regents of Edward VI during the renewal of Anglo-Scottish conflict in the 1540s. It referred not to overseas colonial possessions, however, but the imperial territory situated on the 'mainland' of the British Isles on which the English state aspired to the same sovereignty over Scotland as it already possessed over Wales. The first example of the British Empire as a territory external to the main island of the archipelago was in connection with the Ulster plantation. From 1607 James VI and I authorised Scottish and English colonists to settle in Ulster, the first 162,500 acres parcelled out being divided equally between both nationalities. These were jointly referred to as 'British undertakers' or 'British tenants', the distinction being between them and the native Irish, or indeed the Scottish Highlanders, who were categorised as 'Gaels'. It can be argued that Ulster was not only the first territory to be identified as British, but the first place where the colonial inhabitants displayed a consciousness of being so, certainly before Britain came into existence in 1707. It was this consciousness which developed in Scotland and England in step with the expansion of the Atlantic Empire between 1707 and 1746, and which is best encapsulated in the song 'Rule, Britannia', written by the Scot James Thomson in 1740.[5]

Chronology is important here, since there is an influential view that the Empire became a significant component of Scottish national identity only in the mid-nineteenth century. Richard Finlay has argued that 'the Scots used the opportunities afforded by the growth of British imperialism as a stage upon which they could vindicate and assert the romantic notions associated with mid and late nineteenth-century European nationalism' as part of a three-pronged strategy to reinvent themselves after the 'holy trinity' ceased effectively to embody their identity.[6] Leaving aside the fact that the 'holy trinity' was considerably less significant for Scottish identity than is usually supposed, I have two difficulties with this analysis. The first is that Finlay separates out 'Scottishness' from 'Britishness' in a way that I am arguing is untenable. The second is that the inpact of Empire on both identities began at least a century earlier than Finlay's starting date of 1850.

In fact, it was first demonstrated soon after the Union in the paper proposing the conquest of Canada that Samuel Vetch read to the Board of Trade in 1708. Within the first paragraph, the connection, already formulating in the minds of Scots on the make, is established between Britain, the Empire and trade:

It cannot but be wondered at by all thinking men who know the valuableness of the *British Monarchy* in America, both with regard to their power and trade, that a nation so powerful in shipping, so numerous in subjects, and otherwise so wisely jealous of their trade, should sit and so tamely allow such a troublesome neighbour as the French, not only to sit peaceably down beside them, but with a handful of people vastly dispersed to possess a country of above 4,000 miles extent, quite encompassing and hemming in betwixt them and the sea, all the *British Empire* upon the said Continent of America, by which they have already so mightily obstructed the *British trade*...

Vetch may have been the first person to use the term 'British Empire' in its modern sense. He was astute enough to realise that he had to raise the spectre of Darien for this audience, if only to exorcise it as a comparison irrelevant to this project ('how infinitely more agreeable this climate would be to our Northern constitution than Darien'). He was subtle enough to hint to them that the troops who would now no longer be required in Scotland could, however, be used to rout the French ('there would need no more than two battalions of regular Troops from Great Britain, who would cost the Crown no more expense, excepting their provision and transportation than they now do in Scotland, where they are idle').[7]

Although an attempt to put his plan into effect failed in the short term, this early association of being British with possession of the Empire anticipated what was to follow. For it was the North American colonies, the main component of the Empire down to the 1780s, which were the proving ground on which the Scots showed their commitment to a British nation. It was in the struggle to conquer and hold North America, first against the French state during the Seven Years War (1756–1763), then against the colonists during the American War of Independence (1776–1784), that the first approximation of Britishness was achieved. Some Scots, of whom Hume was the most outspoken, sympathised with the American rebels in their struggle for political power after 1776. Smith proposed a federal solution which would have allowed colonial representatives to sit in the British parliament (thus removing the basis for the demand of 'no taxation without representation'); this clearly drew on the experience of the Anglo-Scottish Union, but the practical difficulties in this case were much greater. Other Enlightenment thinkers were supportive of the colonists up to the point at which they began to demand secession, William Robertson arguing that as 'a subject of Great Britain' the colonies should be physically prevented from leaving British control.[8]

Most Scots, however, saw it as an opportunity to prove once and for all their loyalty to the British state and British Empire. Indeed, the more outspoken ridiculed the English for their inability to govern the Empire effectively, as revealed by their failure to retain control of the American colonies. 'Rarely', writes John Dwyer:

> ...did they take quite so strong a form as that presented to the *Caledonian Mercury* by NORTH BRITON in 1778, who referred to the English as 'ye unregenerate race' and claimed their 'gaudy glitter' and 'profuse expenses' had rendered them quite 'incapable to support the dignity of the British Empire'.[9]

Recollection of the Wilkesite abuse of the 1760s no doubt gave these sentiments a harder edge than they might otherwise have possessed, particularly as many Scots blamed Wilkesite radicalism for causing the war, both by encouraging the Americans to rebel abroad and by undermining the authority of the government at home.[10] It is ironic, however, that the most significant role in the external construction of Britishness and Scottishness was not played by the Lowland bourgeoisie who had the most to gain from it, but by former Jacobites and Highland

Scots, the two groups who had previously been the most politically and socially alien, both to them and their English counterparts.

As in so many other aspects of Scottish life, the catalyst in provoking change was the suppression of the '45, or more precisely, what followed: the elimination of Jacobitism as a political movement, the abolition of feudal landowning and – at a slightly greater distance in time – the clearing of the Highland estates. The section of the Scottish ruling class which had once given its allegiance to the Stuarts now transferred their loyalties to the Hanoverian dynasty and were anxious to prove that the reconciliation was genuine – as anxious as the ministers of state were to have it proved. Opposition to radicalism at home and republicanism abroad allowed them to reaffirm their fidelity to the monarchical principle – even the insipid constitutional monarchy of George III – against republicanism.[11] In 1775, one Hector Stuart of Lochaber, who claimed to have fought on the Jacobite side in both the '15 and the '45, wrote a letter to the *Dundee Weekly Magazine* attacking Wilkes: 'Admitting that his own generation had been deluded into believing in the *jus divinum* of the House of Stuart, the writer pointed out that "we were for *some* King, but erred in our choice; you and your Myrmidons are enemies to *Monarchy* – to a regular and mild establishment, and to civil society."'[12] Such adherence to the most reactionary position available at the time was bound to impress the English section of the British ruling class favourably. The Empire provided the perfect set of opportunities for proof of Jacobite conversion to be offered. Admirers of absolutist monarchy in politics and themselves recently monarchs-in-miniature in their superiorities, they found that their authoritarian propensities could be given full expression as imperial administrators or military commanders. Of far greater significance numerically than the ex-Jacobites were the Highland peasants who were forced to leave their homes, not to take their place among the ruling class, but because that class was busily destroying the only society they had ever known. For peasants displaced by rationalisation or outright clearance, the Empire provided a way out, a means to a livelihood increasingly denied to them in the home country itself. Whether the Empire was considered as a proving ground or an escape route, two roles were particularly important for both Jacobites and Highlanders; one as the soldiers responsible for conquering new territories and defending old possessions, the other as the settlers responsible for colonising them.

Warriors

The main function of the British army, at least until the radical movements of the 1790s required their domestic presence in greater numbers, was to conquer new territories for the Empire and to defend those which already existed. The Scots played a disproportionately large role in this endeavour. Some writers have doubted the significance of the Scottish regiments in developing national consciousness:

> Their actual careers make it difficult to sustain the view that they were vehicles of Highlandism and national identity. Most of the regiments raised for the Seven Years War and the American War were soon disbanded and, if not, they were soon consigned to remote imperial garrisons.[13]

Yet this severely underestimates their impact. Even before 1707 the armed forces provided the most important institutional basis for Anglo-Scottish integration at the level of the ruling class and the Union merely accelerated the growth of the Scottish presence: 'During the first half of the eighteenth century 25 per cent of all regimental offices in the British army went to Scots, and the Scots captured 20 per cent of all colonelcies between 1714 and the end of the Seven Years War.'[14]

For these, mainly Lowland officers, dual nationhood had never posed a problem, as can be seen from the diary of John Peebles of Irvine in Ayrshire, who served as a Captain in the grenadier company of the Black Watch during the American War between 1776 and 1782. There is little that is specifically Scottish about his commentary. He makes a passing reference to attending a Presbyterian church with the Company of Guards. The festivities during St. Andrew's Day, which was officially celebrated by the British army along with the other national saint's days, are recorded ('a very good dinner with Several Scotch dishes such as Sheep's head broth, cockaleekie, a Haggis, etc., the Band of Music and the Pipes of the 42nd [i.e., the Black Watch] played alternately, and the little Prince being highly pleased with the Piper gave him a bumper after every tune'). Peebles devotes equal attention to such British occasions as George III's birthday, during which, after the Royal Salute, he sadly notes 'no illuminations at night – these things are out of fashion in this Country now.'[15] Although Peebles makes no secret about his affection for his native Ayrshire, finally buying himself out and returning there to marry, there is not the slightest sense of conflict between the Scottish and British aspects of his identity.

The sections of the Scottish bourgeoisie and nobility which accommodated themselves to the Hanoverian regime before 1746 had therefore already begun to make inroads into all-British institutions, but the Scottish presence increased markedly after 1746 when the previously Jacobite faction changed allegiance to that of their former adversaries. It was for this section of the Scottish ruling class – which, it bears repeating, was by no means based entirely in the Highlands – that the army was most important. And their incorporation took place with remarkable speed. Simon Fraser of Lovat, had, rather unwillingly, joined his father in rebellion in the '45. Unlike him, he was spared the executioner's axe and, within ten years of Culloden, was given command over the first two regiments to be raised in North America to fight the French.[16] Less than 30 years after Culloden even the symbols of Jacobitism were grudgingly tolerated in the struggle against the French: 'Allan Maclean, who fought at Culloden and was subsequently a colonel in the British Army, used to lead his men into action in Canada in the 1770's wearing a white cockade, to the disgust of his superiors.'[17]

Nor was this penetration of the armed forces restricted to the officer class. One correspondent to the *Scots Magazine* during 1760 claimed that as many as 42,700 Scots, or one in four of the male population of military age, were serving in the army or navy, their absence on duty abroad leaving Scotland exposed to French attack.[18] Highland Scots in particular were dominant among the rank and file. From being vilified as a threat to the British state, the male inhabitants of the Highlands were increasingly central to its military apparatus. The recruitment figures are staggering:

> In addition to the Black Watch (operative from 1740), twenty-three regiments of the line and twenty-six fencibles, in excess of 48,300 men were recruited from Scottish Gaeldom following the outbreak of the Seven Year's War in 1756 until the conclusion of the Napoleonic Wars in 1815.[19]

During the entire period from 1792 to 1815, 75,000 men out of a total population of only 300,000 – 25 per cent – may have served in one military capacity or another.[20] The point of citing these figures is not to denigrate men who were, in their vast majority, forced to enlist as the only means of escaping the destruction of their society. It is rather to emphasise that a region once considered 'naturally' productive of traitors, was now thought a suitable – indeed *the* most suitable – source of combatants to kill and be killed under the British flag.

The transformation did not happen overnight. While posted in Banff during 1753 James Wolfe wrote a famous letter to a fellow officer in Nova Scotia with some recommendations:

> I should imagine that two or three Independent Highland Companies might be of use; they are hardy, intrepid, used to a rough country and no great mischief if they fall. How can you better employ a secret enemy than by making his end conducive to the common good?[21]

Yet by the time Wolfe himself landed at Halifax in Nova Scotia in 1758, *en route* to a glorious death on the Plains of Abraham, his own attitude had begun to change. Writing to his former Commander, Lord George Halifax, he enthused that:

[Simon] Fraser's and Brigadier Lawrence's Battalions are here, and both in goodly condition. The Highlanders are very useful serviceable soldiers, and commanded by the most manly corps of officers I ever saw.[22]

An anonymous pamphleteer of 1773 listed the triumphs down to that date: 'The reduction of Louisburgh, Quebec, Crown Point, Montreal, Niagara, and Fort du Quesne, the taking of Guadaloupe, the conquest of Martinico, and the Havana, the plains of Germany and our conquests in India, will all tell what assistance the government received from the Scots Highlanders.'[23] Scottish propagandists were especially eager to point out their effectiveness in battle against the Auld Ally. 'The French trembled at the sight of them,' boasted John Knox, 'calling out, *the English lions!*'[24] Scottish readers will no doubt forgive the French soldiers this appalling lapse, particularly when they learn from David Stewart that they soon recognised their error in mistaking the Scots for English: 'the French had formed the most frightful and absurd notions of the "*Sauvages d'Ecosse*"; they believed that they would neither take nor give quarter'.[25] The adaptation of Scottish martial traditions to the service of British imperialism helped overcome remaining popular hostility, both to the Highlanders in the Lowlands and to the Scots in England. 'Long dreaded by many of their Lowland compatriots as semi-savage denizens of an internal border region,' writes Bruce Lenman:

> ...they were, once their capacity to harm was broken, incorporated into the Scottish national self-image in the same way that Americans to some extent build their self-image on the safely dead savages of their own bigger frontier.[26]

It was perhaps more that their capacity to harm was redirected outwards. The qualities of bravery, endurance and military skill, despised by upright burghers trying to turn an honest profit, now became admirable when their descendants discovered new markets overseas, and relied on military force to prise them open.

Within decades of Culloden, therefore, Highlanders were considered by Lowlanders to be an integral part of the Scottish nation. Consider this entry in the diary kept by James Boswell during his sojourn in London. The scene is the Covent Garden opera house late in 1762:

> Just before the overture began to be played, two Highland officers came in. The mob in the upper gallery roared out, "No Scots! No Scots! Out with them!", hissed and pelted them with apples. *My heart warmed to my countrymen*, my Scotch blood boiled with indignation. I jumped up on the benches, roared out, "Damn you, you rascals!", hissed and was in the greatest rage. ... I hated the English; I wished from my soul that

the Union was broke and that we might give them another battle of Bannockburn.[27]

What is remarkable about this passage is not, as is so often said, his nationalist outrage as such, but the fact that it is being expressed on behalf of a group of Highlanders who, less than 20 years earlier, might have been among those instilling fear into his class. As John Telfer Dunbar writes, 'the Highlanders were no longer clansmen, they were the Scottish Nation'.[28] Ten years later, after recording his tears upon listening to an eye-witness account of Culloden, Boswell wrote:

> The very Highland names, or the sound of a bagpipe, will stir my blood, and fill me with a mixture of melancholy and respect for courage; with pity for an unfortunate and superstitious regard for antiquity, and thoughtless inclination for war; in short, with a crowd of sensations with which sober rationality has nothing to do.[29]

This was not a one-way process. The Scottish identity offered to the Highland soldiery was accepted by them in return. One officer in Fraser's Highlanders, captured with other members of his regiment at the opening of the American War of Independence, has left an account of their treatment at the hands of the rebel population as they were taken across country by foot. The writer recounts the mainly verbal abuse which he and his comrades received: '*But what vexed me most was their continual slandering of our country (Scotland)*, on which they threw the most infamous invectives'.[30] Thirty years before, he would have been as unlikely to identify his country as Scotland, as Boswell to have his blood stirred by the sound of the bagpipes.

Qualities could now be admired which were once feared; most importantly, their supposed military prowess – even though the abilities of the Highland warrior were, except in very specific circumstances, largely mythical. It took incorporation into the British military apparatus to transform the majority of one-time clan members into the skilled professional killers subsequently celebrated in Unionist ideology. Once *that* transformation had been achieved the commendations began to flow from the highest levels of the state. Secretary at War Barrington justified the policy of Scottish military recruitment in terms as notable for the date they were expressed as the sentiments themselves:

> I am for having always in our army as many Scottish soldiers as possible; not that I think them more brave than those of any other country we can recruit from, but because they are generally more hardy and less mutinous: and of all Scottish soldiers I should choose to have and keep as many Highlanders as possible.[31]

This was said in 1751 when large sections of the Highlands were under military occupation – which perhaps indicates that not all sections of the British state were as convinced of the natural affinities between Highland birth and Jacobitism as some affected to believe. The most powerful of Scottish politicians, Lord Advocate Dundas, made the same point still more forcibly in a letter to the Under Secretary of State, William Eden, during 1775. Affirming his retrospective support for those who subdued the Highlands after Culloden, he writes of his opposition to retaining the same level of repression 'now that the reason for it has totally vanished':

...I say vanished, for it is to talk like children to talk of any danger from disaffection from the North. There is no such thing and it ought to be the object of every wise ruler in this country, to cherish and make proper use of the Highlanders of Scotland. ... If you ask me what these purposes are, I readily answer that the Highlanders were born to be soldiers and the Highlanders ought to be considered as a nursery of strength and security to the Kingdom.[32]

Finally, in this connection, is the famous speech by Pitt the Younger to the House of Commons on 14 July 1776:

I have no local attachments; it is indifferent to me whether a man was rocked in his cradle on this side or that side of the Tweed. I sought for merit wherever it was to be found: it is my boast that I was the first minister who looked for it; and I found it in the mountains of the north. I called forth and drew into your service a hardy and intrepid race of men; men who, when left by your jealousy, became prey to the artifices of your enemies, and had nigh gone high to have overturned the State in the war before last [i.e., the War of the Austrian Succession]. These men, in the last war [i.e., the Seven Years War] were brought to combat on your side: they served with fidelity as fought with valour, and conquered for you in every part of the world: detested be the national reflections against them![33]

Nor was it only abroad that the Highland soldier was regarded as the first line of defence for the existing order. During the first radical stirrings of the 1790s, the Highlanders were specifically commended for the resistance to revolutionary doctrines emanating from France. In February 1797 the Duke of York proposed that 16,000 men be raised for a Highland Corps composed of different clan brigades. Aside from the fact that overpopulation in the Highlands meant that men could be removed from the land without harming production, the Duke believed that:

...they may be justly considered, the only considerable Body of Men, in the whole Kingdom, who are as yet absolutely Strangers to the levelling and dangerous principles of the present age, and therefore may be safely trusted indiscriminately with the knowledge and use of arms.[34]

During the second wave of radicalism, which rose after the end of the Napoleonic Wars in 1815, Sir Walter Scott assumed that the Highland chiefs-turned-landowners would offer their services to the state against the threat from below.[35] He was also sure that their tenants would allow themselves to be used for this purpose: 'They have no common sympathy with the insurgents and could be better trusted than any new forces that could be levied'.[36] Whether the latter would have been as willing to lend themselves to suppressing their rebellious Lowland cousins is open to question. The point is, however, that representative figures among the ruling class and its ideologues believed that they would. National acceptance can go little further than willingness to put a gun in the hand of those who had once been considered the Other. The wars against revolutionary and Napoleonic France completed the process by which the Highlander was incorporated into British and Scottish society, but also saw the identification of Scotland with militarism taken to a new level, not least because, for the first time since the Union, the organisation of national defence was left to the Scots themselves. The number of Scots who were mobilised for both wars was proportionally greater than the English throughout: at the end of the Revolutionary War there were 25,000 volunteers; at the end of the Napoleonic Wars there were 50,000.[37]

Colonists

It is often the case that in the colonial extensions of an imperial society the new national consciousness is forged and, indeed, can be manifested in the most chemically pure form. The case of North America, site of the most important British colonies for most of the eighteenth century, is of crucial importance in this respect: in many ways it represents a more extensive development of the 'colonial' Britishness first encountered in Ulster. Fry has argued that the Scots did not behave in the same way as the English in America. For the former, the colonies were temporary bases from which to construct an empire of commerce before returning to Scotland with their wealth. For the latter, the colonies were places of permanent settlement in which they intended to remain. After the War of Independence concluded in 1776, the Scots mainly chose to return to Scotland or to migrate north to Canada, the English tended to stay and participate in building the new state.[38] The implications of this are most important for the national consciousness of both groups. The Scots went to America and became Britons (or, if they were Highlanders, became Scots and Britons); the English went to America and became Americans.

The scale of the Scottish emigration must first of all be understood. The entire number of Scots settling in America during the seventeenth century was 7,000, but during the eighteenth century to 1780 alone it was 75,000. Together with 115,000 settlers from Ireland the latter figure represented 70 per cent of the total British emigration between 1700 and 1780, a clear shift from the English dominated emigration of the previous century.[39] The crucial decades for the Scots were the 1760s and 1770s. The total number departing Britain between 1763 and 1775 may have been as high as 25,000, the overwhelming majority heading either for the West Indies or – more usually – North America.[40]

Nevertheless, the Highland and Lowland components of the Scottish emigration to North America initially tended to remain as geographically and culturally separate as they were in their homeland. The first Highlanders to arrive in significant numbers were those transported in the aftermath of the '15 and the '45. The first mass voluntary emigration was during the 1770s when several thousands arrived in North Carolina, which along with New York was the most common destination prior to Independence. This was not entirely a movement inspired by the need to escape economic hardship or the loss of land – that would come later. 'In the present eagerness of emigration', wrote Samuel Johnson in 1775, 'families, and almost whole communities, go away together.' At their head were the relatively prosperous tacksmen strata, whose military and administrative functions were no longer required in the increasingly commercial Highlands, but who saw the prospect of becoming landowners in their own right. 'Those who were considered as prosperous and wealthy sell their stock and carry away the money.'[41]

The Highland immigrants tended to remain within the clan formations which had left Scotland, and were easily distinguished by their continuing to speak Gaelic, wear Highland dress and carry the weapons they were forbidden to in Scotland – for in some colonies, Georgia, for example, the crown required settlers to act as a line of defence against imperial rivals, in this case the Spanish enclave in Florida: 'In February, 1736, Governor Oglethorpe of Georgia paid a visit to the Highlanders at Darien [i.e., Darien in Georgia, not the long-defunct colony on the Panamanian Isthmus] and found them in their tartan plaids, armed after the fashion of their country with broad swords, small round shields, and muskets.'[42] Lowlanders, on the other hand, tended to arrive as individual families, and were often distinguishable from Englishmen by nothing but their accents.

What attitude would the Scots take to the Crown, faced with the open opposition to His Britannic Majesty displayed by their fellow colonists? The British authorities certainly anticipated the Highlanders taking a rebel stand. The Lord Advocate halted all emigration after 1775 (although paradoxically the other reason given for the ban was to maintain the supply of recruits for the British army), but his fears were misplaced. The '45 was the last occasion in which the British state was in danger from forces representing economic retrogression. As soon as it came under threat from rebellious American colonists who were at the same stage of economic development, but more advanced in political terms, many of the transplanted Highlanders threw themselves into the defence of the Hanoverian monarchy which they had previously worked to overthrow. Why?

Highlanders had been settling along the Cape Fear River in North Carolina since the 1730s, and by the outbreak of the revolutionary war in 1776 maybe as many as 12,000 had done so, most of them in that decade, but as Duane Meyer writes: 'The loyalty of the Highlanders to the king [i.e., George] was by no means an immediate, automatic or unanimous response.'[43] In June 1775 Donald McLeod, a recent immigrant and one-time tacksman, petitioned Congress twice for the authority to raise a regiment of 100 men, either from unemployed Highlanders already resident in New York or their compatriots then in the process of arriving. His only condition for performing this service to the revolutionary cause was that the men be dressed in Highland costume which was still banned in Britain, but not in the colonies.[44] The majority of these were Argyllshire Campbell Presbyterians whose leaders had always been committed to the Hanoverian cause, but this was no guarantee that their followers would continue to be so. Furthermore, the settlement also included wealthy Jacobites such as Allan and Flora MacDonald, who owned a plantation of 475 acres, and might have been expected to continue their opposition to the Hanoverian monarchy. They had arrived bedecked in Jacobite paraphernalia:

> When Allan Macdonald of Kingsburgh landed in the province [i.e., of North Carolina] in 1774, with his wife Flora, the famous preserver of Prince Charlie, he wore a tartan plaid over his shoulder, a large blue bonnet with a cockade of black ribbon, a tartan waistcoat with gold buttons, and tartan hose.[45]

Meyer has suggested four principle reasons why the majority of these Highlanders remained – or perhaps *became* – loyal to the crown.[46] First, the fear of reprisals, for people who had lived through the aftermath of Culloden, would have done much to prevent support for the rebel cause, but in order to mobilise support for the crown required more positive incentives. Second, the acceptance of Highland troops by the British ruling elite assured the settlers that there was a place for them in the Empire. Third, Governor Martin made land grants of 200 acres to every head of family who enlisted, with a further 50 acres for every additional family member. Fourth, and finally, the leadership of the ex-Jacobite, now Hanoverian, tacksmen over the settler groups. Far from opposing the Hanoverian monarchy, Allan MacDonald was particularly active in mobilising support for the King among the Highland settlers. In February 1776, '13,000 tartan-clad men mustered to the sound of the pibroch' before marching off to resounding defeat at the hands of the rebel militia.[47] This particular Loyalist manifestation demonstrates the continuing influence which tacksmen continued to exert over their erstwhile tenants, even in this new environment. The contrast with the behaviour of another identifiable national group – the Scots Irish – could not be more dramatic.

The decisive battle in the Southern campaign of the Revolutionary War was the Battle of King's Mountain in 1780, in which the largely Presbyterian Highland Scots of North Carolina were pitched against an army of equally Presbyterian Ulster Scots. One historian of the Scottish presence in America notes that, 'nothing, perhaps, better illustrates the divergent roles of Highland Scot and Ulster Scot in the American revolution.'[48] And nothing, perhaps, better illustrates the divergent roles of Ireland and Scotland within the British Empire, respectively that of colony and coloniser, than the attitude of these groups. The Ulster Scots were not, of course, British Loyalists but small-holding Presbyterian radicals who left Ireland to escape the destruction of their wool-growing and cloth-manufacturing industries at the hands of the British Parliament and their exclusion from all public office – the same class who formed the Protestant element of the United Irishmen in 1798. Transplantation to America had not altered their attitude of opposition to the British state, merely changed the context in which it occurred. The Highland Scots, on the other hand, despite their recent experience of oppression at the hands of the British state, had embraced the defence of its overseas extension:

> In Ireland, the Irish nation was irrevocably opposed to the English, while in Scotland, the Highlander and Lowlander were coming to see themselves as members of a single nation, in equal partnership under the flag of the United Kingdom. In Scotland the first two Georges were no more or less foreign than in England. In Ireland they represented the alien and super-imposed rule of the English.[49]

Would Lowland Scots display the same attitudes as the Highlanders? One (non-Scottish) rebel wrote to a friend in London during 1776 that despite 'many reflections on the Scotch in the English papers', they were 'the very warmest advocates for liberty'. The English papers who attacked the Scots for threatening the British state with their Jacobitism would scarcely have congratulated them for now threatening the British Empire with their Republicanism. Even leaving such naivety aside, however, our writer acknowledges that there were exceptions, namely, 'a few tattered

Scotch Highlanders...whose ignorant attachment *to names* keep them servile and wholly at the beck of their Chiefs.' These Highlanders could be found in familiar company: 'Is it to be supposed that 50,000 men, composed of German mercenaries, Scottish Jacobites, Irish Papists and the produce of your jails, are to conquer America?'[50] In fact, not only did the Highlanders prove ultra-loyal and prepared to fight for the overseas extension of the Hanoverian regime, so too did the majority of their Lowland compatriots. The correspondent cited above had in fact drastically over-estimated the level of support for the rebellion among the Lowland settlers. South of the Highlanders mustering in North Carolina, the Lowlanders in Virginia were also taking up arms for George III. Adjacent to loyal Highland communities in New York, were equally loyal Lowland communities in New England.[51] The American revolutionaries themselves had little doubt on this score. The House of Assembly in Savannah, Georgia, passed the following act on 5 August 1782:

Whereas the people of Scotland have in general manifested a devoted inimicability to the Civil Liberties of America and have contributed principally to promote and continue a Ruinous War, for the Purpose of Subjugating this and the other Confederated states – be it therefore enacted by the Authority aforesaid that no Person a Native of Scotland, shall be permitted or allowed to emigrate into this State with intent to Settle within the same, or to carry on Commerce or other trade, Profession or business, but every such Person, being a Native of Scotland shall be within three days after his arrival within this State be apprehended and Committed to Gaol there to remain without bail or main prize until an opportunity offers of shipping or Transporting him to some part of the English [sic] King's Dominion.[52]

Before the American War of Independence there had been an attempt by English ideologues of Empire to bypass the specific Scottish component of Britishness, by extending the notion to everyone within the imperial territory. As Arthur Young wrote in 1772:

The British dominions consist of Great Britain and Ireland, divers colonies and settlements in all parts of the world and there appears not any just reason for considering these countries in any other light than as part of a whole ... The clearest method is to consider all as forming one nation, united under one sovereign, speaking the same language and enjoying the same liberty, but living in different parts of the world.[53]

After 1784 and the detachment of the biggest component of the Empire to whose inhabitants the notion of Britishness could seriously be extended, this was no longer possible. The Scots may therefore have the

Americans to thank, at least in part, for inadvertently assisting them to adopt the British identity that the Americans had wished to deny them.

If Scottish participation in the Empire was the key external factor in constructing both forms of national consciousness, there was, however, another, internal factor of significance: the changing perceptions of the Highlanders within Britain itself.

Scottish History and Highland Mythology

The Czech historian Miroslav Hroch once argued that the development of any national movement involves three distinct stages.

> During the initial phase, which I have called Phase A, the energies of the activists were above all devoted to scholarly enquiry into and dissemination of an awareness of the linguistic, cultural, social, and sometimes historical attributes of the non-dominant group – but without, on the whole, pressing specifically national demands to remedy deficits (some did not even believe their group could develop into a nation).

Even where the process went no further than this, however, certain 'resources' were retained which, in some cases, could contribute to the reactivation of the national movement at a higher phase. In this connection Hroch specifically identifies three factors; 'relics of an earlier political autonomy', '"memory" of former independence or statehood' and 'a medieval written language'.[1] Insofar as this pattern can be found in Scotland, Phase A was only consciously undertaken after 1746. The 'relics of political autonomy' are easily identifiable in the continuation of the Scots Law, the Church of Scotland – a state church for a stateless nation – and the educational system. The other two factors, however, are at first sight more elusive. The '"memory" of former independence and statehood' was precisely what the Scottish Historical School was seeking to escape. If Scots can indeed be considered a separate 'medieval written language', and not a component of English, then it had been in retreat since the publication of the English translations of the Bible which accompanied the Reformation. Yet two substitutes *were* found for both 'memory' and 'language'. It is one of the many ironies of Scottish history that they should be found in a region that had previously been seen, however inaccurately, as the source of Scottish backwardness: the Highlands.

The adoption of Highland symbols and cultural artefacts by the Scottish people as a whole was a complex process. For these symbols were by no means the authentic products of a traditional culture, but had been significantly modified in order to make their adoption possible. Nevertheless, the fact that they *were* adopted was important in the formation of a Scottish identity that was not simply that of the Lowlands writ large. Malcolm Chapman argues that Gaelic culture was subjected to 'symbolic appropriation' at the hands of the majority culture: 'The majority society has used Gaelic culture as a symbolic element in a process of defining itself, and consequently Gaelic culture is only present in English literary discourse in a shape that has been imposed upon it from without.'[2] The discovery – or perhaps it would be better to say, part recovery, part production – of a Gaelic literary heritage provided the emergent Lowland literati with a culture which could be celebrated as a source of pride rather than disavowed as a source of shame.

During the 1760s James MacPherson, a Gaelic-speaking Highlander with a Jacobite family background from Ruthven in Badenoch in Inverness-shire, claimed to have discovered, during visits to the Western Isles, poems written in the third century by a blind harper known as Ossian. William Ferguson has argued that the Ossianic poems were compiled by Macpherson from a mixture of genuine Scottish Gaelic ballads and prose which he had collected during his own field work in the Highlands, medieval Irish sources done into Scottish, and his own writings, rendered in the Homeric form that his Lowland admirers expected this national epic to take.[3] The Irish component, dealing with the eighth century Viking invasions, was transposed *en bloc* to a Highland setting where, for example, the character of Finn MacCumhal appears as Fingal. The publication by Macpherson of the Ossianic poems – *Fragments Of Ancient Poetry Collected In The Highlands Of Scotland* (1760), *Fingal* (1761) and *Temora* (1763) – meant that the Highlands had seemingly provided Scotland with a national literary epic which was to win them Europe-wide admiration: Napoleon was supposed to carry a copy of *Fingal* with him on campaign; Madame de Stael to have declared Ossian the equal of Homer.

The poems are in fact important, if 'inauthentic', works of literature. The opposition to the Scots extended to the cultural productions of the Scots in Scotland, like the Ossianic poems, which were regarded as 'an upstart attempt to gain favour at court through a new literary pedigree: an ancient epic couched in biblical language with all the trappings of serious scholarship.' And one derived without acknowledgement from Irish sources: 'What is *Fingal* but genuine Erse?' wrote Wilkes in the November 1762 issue of the *North Briton*.[4] Acceptance of the authenticity of the Ossianic poems, which led most Scots to defend Macpherson's 'discoveries' against the hostility of Wilkes, Samuel Johnston and – almost uniquely among the Scots themselves – David

Hume, was not however based solely on their quality, or the credit which they consequently reflected on contemporary Scotland. The moment when the rehabilitation of pre-'45 Highland society began can be traced to the publication in the *Scots Magazine* of the 'Introduction' to *Ossian's Poems Of Fingal* by Hugh Blair in 1763. The 'barbarism' which the Enlightenment thinkers had seen embodied in the Highland clans was not now simply characterised by backwardness, but by the possession of qualities of nobility and bravery which, alas, had no place in 'commercial society' – as of course clan members had recently discovered for themselves. MacPherson himself wrote much more explicitly of the unsullied nobility of Highland society, 'free of intermixture with foreigners' in his Introduction to *Temora*: 'Their language is pure and original, and their manners are those of an ancient and unmixed race of men. Conscious of their own antiquity, they long despised others as a new and mixed people'.[5]

Having apparently preserved this world from extinction, MacPherson had to be defended. In 1760 a rumour circulated that a young member of the Aberdeen Philosophical Society, James Beattie (1735–1803), was writing a work on the Ossianic poems, not casting doubt on their authenticity, but criticising their quality. This was enough to produce a letter from no less a person than Kames, effectively warning Beattie against setting such views down in print. Beattie stood his ground, but here we can already see the claims of science bow before the needs of ideology.[6] Only Smith refused to endorse the revised view of the clans that his colleagues were propounding, maintaining, in *The Theory Of Moral Sentiments*, that they were merely sentimentalising the harsh reality of social relations within the clan.[7]

The two enthusiasms of the Enlightenment thinkers embroiled them in an unresolved ideological tension. On the one hand, Scottish history is dismissed because of the failure to overthrow feudalism through resources internal to the nation. On the other, the literature associated with feudal society is celebrated precisely because it is the most – perhaps the only – distinctively Scottish culture capable of commanding international respect. The first is a realistic historical assessment pointing towards 'Britishness'. The second a romantic mythology emphasising 'Scottishness'. *Douglas*, the play by John Home first performed in Edinburgh during 1756, goes some way to rehabilitating the Scottish martial tradition, but the hero was by no means identified with the Highlands in particular and, as John Robertson has pointed out, the enemies against whom he struggles were the Danes, not the English: 'Celebration of the martial values of the Scots was evidently now subject to the qualification that anglophobia be denied.'[8] Perhaps the clearest expression of the Highland embrace of both Scottishness and Britishness is given in a poem of 1758 by MacPherson who, it is important to note in this context, was aware from personal experience of the atrocities which followed Culloden. His patriotic epic *The Highlander* (1758) is remarkable both for making the hero, Alpin – the young warrior who rouses the Scots against the Viking enemy – a Highlander, and for its appeal for unity between the Scots and the English:

> See Scot and Saxon, coalesced in one,
> Support the glory of the common crown,
> Britain no more shall shake with national storms,
> but o'er the trembling nations lift her arms.[9]

It was only very late in the post-revolutionary period that this tension was completely resolved. The person most responsible was Sir Walter Scott.

Scott was by no means dismissive of the Ossianic poems. In the very article in which he pointed out their historical inaccuracies, he concluded that:

> ...while we are compelled to renounce the pleasing idea, 'that Fingal lived and that Ossian sung', our national vanity may be equally flattered by the fact that a remote, and almost a barbarous corner of Scotland, produced, in the 18th century, a bard, capable not only of making an enthusiastic impression on every mind susceptible to beauty, but of giving a new tone to poetry throughout Europe.[10]

His own work, however, would not take refuge in myths set during antiquity. In a series of poems, beginning with *The Lay Of The Last Minstrel* (1805) and novels, beginning with *Waverley* (1814), Scott deployed an interpretation of Scottish history which finally allowed the tension between realism and romanticism to be resolved. The adoration of the British state achieves perhaps its perfect literary incarnation in *Marmion* (1808), where Scott is at his most effusive:

> What powerful call shall bid arise
> The buried warlike and the wise;
> The mind that thought for Britain's weal,
> The hand that grasped the victor's steel?
> Even on the meanest flower that blows;
> But vainly, vainly may he shine,
> Where glory weeps o'er NELSON's shrine;
> And vainly pierce the solemn gloom,
> That shrouds, O PITT, thy hallowed tomb!
>
> Deep graved in every British heart,
> O never let those names depart!
> Say to your sons, – Lo, here his grave,
> Who victor died on Gadite wave.[11]

The last reference is again to Nelson, but later in the poem we encounter the author, reliving the stories of Scottish history which he heard as a boy:

> Of Wallace wight and Bruce the bold;
> Of later fields of feud and fight,
> When, pouring from their Highland height
> The Scottish clans, in headlong sway,
> Had swept the scarlet ranks away.
> While stretched at full length upon the floor,
> Again I fought each combat o'er
> Pebbles and shells, in order laid,
> The mimic ranks of war display'd;
> And onward still the Scottish lion bore,
> And still the scattered Southron fled before.[12]

At the same time that Scottish history was being dismissed as of no consequence, it was also being mythologised, but there is no paradox here. 'Sir Walter Scott,' writes Colin Kidd:

> ...despite his public image as a maker of national myths, subscribed to the Anglo-British interpretation of the history of liberty, and can be reliably identified as a continuator of the eighteenth-century tradition of sociological whiggism.[13]

It is in his novels, however, that his achievement is most fully realised. Georg Lukacs wrote in *The Historical Novel* (1937) that Scott was attempting to reveal two aspects of British history in his work. First, that Scottish and English development was not a smooth upward ascent, but one punctuated by violent social upheavals. Second, that a middle way exists for these forces to resolve their differences:

> He finds in English history the consolation that the most violent vicissitudes of class struggle have always finally calmed down into a glorious 'middle way'. Thus out of the struggle of the Normans and the Saxons there arose the English nation, neither Saxon nor Norman...[14]

This is of course the theme of *Ivanhoe*, but the novel also works as an extended analogy for the creation of a British nation, with the Saxons and Normans standing in respectively for the Scots and the English. Scott's reading of the Scottish historical record was intended to convey the impression – which, as we shall see, Scott knew to be false – that internal division was a thing of the past. For although *national* reconciliation had indeed taken place, *class* divisions were opening up which he saw no possibility of overcoming. This is one reason why Scott almost never discusses the contemporary world in his novels. (*The Antiquary* is a partial exception.) He is only comfortable writing about historical situations that have already been resolved, and for that reason protagonists on both sides can be equally celebrated.[15] Tom Nairn has described him as a 'valedictory realist': his valediction is bestowed upon a heroic but vanquished feudal past; his realism forces him to acknowledge that it would be madness – even if it were possible – to counterpose that past to the unheroic but commercially successful present.[16] Nairn is wrong, however, to suggest that Scott does not use his vision of the Scottish past to construct a national myth. Unlike the German Romantics who followed and, to a large extent, were inspired by him, Scott had no interest in building a Scottish nationalist *movement* among his fellow-Scots, but he was certainly interested in developing a Scottish national *consciousness* among them. In 1527 Hector Boece had attempted to persuade his fellow-Lowlanders to look upon the Highlanders as models for their own conduct. Now, the virtues of their society could be acknowledged, if only in retrospect. In this sense Scott provided the ideological link between the contemporary deeds of the Highland soldiers and those of their clan ancestors.

Tourism and Tartanry

The mythic world of the Scottish past, envisaged first by MacPherson in the Ossianic poems, then by Scott in his poems and the *Waverley* novels, gained much of its conviction from two changing perceptions which took place in parallel: one of the Highlands as a geographical area; the other of its former inhabitants who were increasingly the backbone of the British Army.

The Highlands under the Tourist Gaze

One effect of the pacification of the Highlands was that the area now became accessible for visitors who would previously have regarded it as beyond the ambit of civilisation. One of the ways in which the two Scotlands became one was in the perception of tourist visitors (as opposed to those who visited for business purposes or for reasons of state) to the country from 1746 onwards. For those who complain about the 'inauthenticity' of the tourist event, John Urry points out that: 'Cultures are invented, remade and the elements reorganised. Hence, it is not clear why the apparently inauthentic staging for the tourist is so very different from what happens in all cultures anyway.'

Leaving aside the note of postmodern apologetics in this (if everything is socially constructed, how can we choose between them in terms of value?), Urry is correct to point to the invented aspects of all culture. It is possible to go further, however, and argue that the 'staging for the tourist' in fact contributes to the invention of national cultures, or more precisely, the formation of national consciousness. Tourism is not simply a question of *identity* – in the sense of how Scotland was represented to non-Scots – rather than one of the *consciousness* of its inhabitants, but the process of constructing an image of Scotland for external consumption also contributed to the construction of an internal sense of what it meant to be Scottish. In the process of directing 'the tourist gaze':

> ...each centre of attraction involves complex processes of production in order that regular, meaningful and profitable tourist gazes can be generated and sustained. Such gazes cannot be left to chance. People have to learn how, when and where to 'gaze'. Clear markers have to be provided and in some cases the object of the gaze is merely the marker that indicates some event or experience which previously happened on that spot.[17]

The Scottish Highlands were the first European region to see the transition from what Urry calls 'a scholastic emphasis on touring as an opportunity for discourse, to travel as eyewitness observation':

> The character of the tour itself shifted, from the earlier 'classic Grand Tour' based on the emotionally neutral observation and recording of galleries, museums and high cultural artefacts, to the nineteenth-century 'romantic Grand Tour' which saw the emergence of 'scenic tourism' and a much more private and passionate experience of beauty and the sublime.[18]

Christopher Smout has argued that the domestication of the Highlands as a tourist destination took place in four stages, each with a wider appeal than its predecessor. Only two of these fall into the decisive phase in the construction of Scottishness. In the first, which followed on immediately from 1746, '[the Highlands] appeared to contain anthropological or natural curiosities that a man might go far to see, if he was brave and hardy enough to undertake the journey.' In the second, which opened in the last quarter of the eighteenth century:

> ...with the evolution in taste and the rise of ideas of the sublime and the picturesque [they were] for the first time seen as a wilderness which, though still frightening, contained, partly because of that, a rewarding quality which the trained eye might learn to perceive, and also sites associated with events in history or literature that a scholar might appreciate.[19]

The site of many of the events recounted in the best-selling Scottish poems and novels, imaginary or otherwise, was now within the reach of their readers. Paul Baines refers to the development of 'Ossianic touring' during the period between 1760 and 1830:

> The process of dissemination was enhanced not only by the huge popularity of the poems, which took them across Europe and America, by the burgeoning Scottish tourist industry, for which Ossian acted as both stimulus and telos, a reason for going and the summation of what you would find.[20]

What seems likely is that much of the apparatus created to support the Ossianic myth was suitably adapted to meet the expectations of tourists. One loch to the east of Fort William appeared as 'Loch Oochan' in maps produced in 1789 and 1807, the latter also showing a 'Glen Ouchan' alongside. By the time of the Ordnance Survey of 1876, it is being shown as 'Loch Ossian', alongside 'Strath-Ossian', 'Amhainn-Ossian' and 'Amar-Strath-Ossian' – not because the names had formally been changed, but because it was assumed that this was what they had really been all along, in the local tradition.[21]

The desire to see the reality of the backdrop behind history and literature, 'the events or experiences which previously happened on that spot' did not diminish once the authenticity of the Ossianic canon was opened to question. The willingly deceived simply shifted their affections onto Scott himself. A German doctor, Eduard Meissner, who visited the Highlands in 1817, noted the presence of boats ready to transport tourists to Ellen's Island on Loch Katrine, the real life setting for *The Lady In The Lake*: 'That which was only reality in the poets imagination has now become historical fact to these people.'[22] A later example from the same site – 'which the Scots, in thankful homage to the poet who has made here every inch of earth glorious, have called "the country of the Lady of the Lake"' – can be found in an account by the German writer, Theodore Fontane in 1858:

> As a picture the whole thing is quite perfect, and Walter Scott knew quite well what he was doing when he made Ellen Douglas put her boat ashore and made the King step forth from the underground by the lakeside just at this particular point. The place seems positively to compel the poet to speak in a romantic vein, and no maiden could step ashore from the lake without being immediately taken for the Lady of the Lake herself.[23]

Nor was this restricted to the Highlands. During a visit to Scotland in 1825 an Englishman called John Bowman observed of the crypt at Glasgow Cathedral that:

The readers of *Rob Roy* will recollect that it was in these vaults that Francis Osbaldistone sought for MacVittie on his arrival in Glasgow; and where he was seen by Rob Roy, who appointed to meet him at midnight on the bridge and accompanied him to the tollbooth to search out Owen.[24]

By 1811, three years before the publication of his first novel, *Waverley*, Scott was already the most popular poet in the United States, although this did not amount in terms of sales to more than 5,000 copies of the *Lay Of The Last Minstrel*. It was the Waverley novels themselves that reached deep into the consciousness of an American reading public who would otherwise not have considered themselves interested in 'literature': one estimate from 1823 claimed that 200,000 copies, or 500,000 individual volumes, had appeared since 1814.[25] In 1834, two years after Scott died, the *American Monthly Magazine* carried an article by an American visitor to Scotland whose view of the country is entirely refracted through the prism of Scott's writing:

How completely with the name of Scott is every river, hill, and ruin, in the land of his birth associated – he has given them names – he has made them immortal. ... In a word, From Thule to the Tweed, travel where you may, at every step there is something to remind you of Scott.[26]

Scotland had become what Andrew Hook calls 'Walter Scottland'. As Calvin Colton, the European correspondent of the New York Observer between 1831 and 1835 wrote:

The genius of a single man has consecrated those wide regions, as modern classic ground, and the history of that country a classic legend. Italy and Greece have at this moment, if possible, less interest in the eyes of travellers for their classic associations, than the land which gave birth to Walter Scott.[27]

Tartanry

The second development was associated not with the past, but with the current role played by the male population of the Highlands, after their integration into the operation of the British armed forces. The uniform of these soldiers and the representations made of it now began to evoke the Scottish nation – for Scots as well as the English – in a way that would have been inconceivable before 1746.

Until the early eighteenth century male Highlanders tended to wear a belted plaid adorned in tartan, but not 'clan' tartans – colouration would be determined by the availability of dyes and the position of the wearer within the clan hierarchy. It was this form of clothing that the British government considered, but eventually rejected, banning after the '15. By the time Highland costume *was* banned after the '45 it had been subtly altered.

During the 1730s the plaid was adapted by a Lancashire Quaker called Thomas Rawlinson into the garment which, in all essentials, we know today as the kilt. Acting as the manager of an iron ore smelting works in Invergarry, Rawlinson wanted a garment that would allow his workers to fell trees and tend the furnaces more easily. The resulting kilt began to be adopted in place of the traditional plaid, far beyond his works, not least because it was easier to manufacture and more convenient to wear. The modern kilt is therefore literally a creation of industrial capitalism, designed for the Highlanders, in the immortal words of Trevor-Roper, 'to bring them out of the heather and into the factory.'[28] After the '45 both the traditional plaid and the modern kilt were banned under the Disarming Act, except, of course, for the Hanoverian Highland regiments and individual members of the ruling class, who now began to dress the part in private, as several portraits from these years testify. More importantly, a *popular* fashion for things Scottish, including the plaid worn by the rebels, now manifested itself. This cult of tartanry had four precedents.[29]

The first was at the Scottish court of James VI at the time of his marriage to Anne of Denmark. The second was during the final years of the Restoration regime, when James VII and II made a display of cultivating some of the Highland chiefs, particularly Cameron of Locheil. 'He seems to have been fascinated and amused by the behaviour of this bizarre tribesman from the Gaelic north', writes David Stevenson, 'and to have patronised him unmercifully.'[30] The third, and by far the most popular use of the plaid outwith the Highlands was in England, immediately before the '45. The English Jacobites were naturally at the forefront of this sartorial display of loyalty, Sir John Hynde Cotton having a tartan suit made for him in Edinburgh during 1744. The unifying factor in all three of these examples is the symbolism of the Stuart dynasty and its supporters – Hynde Cotton could scarcely have worn his suit as an expression of *Scottish* national identity. The fourth precedent can be found after the '45: 'In the past the English Tories had been as suspicious of the Scots as the rest of England, but now they adopted the plaid as their emblem, a thing inconceivable a few years before.' One of the last serious displays of popular Jacobitism in England took place in the eastern Midlands during the county elections of 1747, when Tory supporters were seen wearing plaid waistcoats, plaid ribbon and even white cockades in their hat bands.[31] Nor was the wearing of such apparel restricted to political events or public occasions. In Manchester the plaid was popular with both apprentices and the sons of the local gentry; tartan dresses, supposedly modelled on the one worn by Charles while hiding after Culloden, were manufactured in Scotland in 1748 and bought by one member of the Anglican clergy for the female members of his family in York.[32] In short, as Paul Monod has argued: 'Highland dress became a stigma in the iconography of the 1760s, but it had a more positive connotation for some in the decade after 1745.'[33] There is however, a difference between adopting the symbolism of a movement that is engaged in a struggle for power, and one that has become a historical memory. The seriousness of Jacobite support indicated by these gestures may therefore be doubted, but given the identification of the plaid with the Scottish invaders of little over a year before, it does suggest that not everyone felt that identification to be discreditable.

The combination of the Lancashire kilt and the tartan in the dress of the Highland regiments ensured not merely their survival but their absorption into an emergent Scottish mass culture. It would appear that differentiated 'clan' tartans, far from originating in antiquity, first became widely introduced to distinguish between different regiments and were only subsequently adopted generally by the clans that spawned them. Trevor-Roper's summary of these events should be savoured in all its dark irony: '[The kilt] having been invented by an English Quaker Industrialist, was saved from extinction by an English imperialist statesman [i.e., Pitt the Elder].'[34] In due course the (re-)invention of Highland dress spread to areas outwith Britain or its Empire, to wherever Scots or their descendants had settled. By the time the process of nation-building was nearing completion in the United States of America, during the Civil War, Scots or their descendants from both sides of the Highland line were willing to adorn themselves in what was now considered to be Scottish national dress. Companies and regiments of Scottish immigrants raised to fight for the Union, such as the Highland Scots of the 79th New York adorned themselves in the full regalia of kilted dress uniforms.[35] Although the regiment was consciously modelled on the 79th Cameron Highlanders in the British army, here the kilts were at least being worn in pursuit of a cause more worthwhile than any a British army had supported for over a hundred years.[36]

It was Walter Scott who first suggested that the modern kilt had been traditional Highland dress, ironically enough, in the same article of 1805 for the *Edinburgh Review*, which disputed the authenticity of the Ossianic poems. More importantly, Scott was also responsible for stagemanaging the ceremony surrounding George IV's state visit to Edinburgh in August 1822 where the king, himself dressed in a tartan kilt, was greeted by the assembled Highland landowners ('chiefs' as Scott insisted on calling them) and the Edinbourgeoisie in similar apparel – at a time when he was quite aware of the historical falsity of the enterprise. As Macaulay noted with disgust at the contemplation of this spectacle:

> The last British King who held a court at Holyrood thought that he could not give a more striking proof of his respect for the usages which

had prevailed in Scotland before the Union, than by disguising himself in what, before the Union, was considered by nine Scotchmen out of ten as the dress of a thief.[37]

Yet this was precisely the point: they no longer did so. Paul Scott has claimed that the credit for this should go to Sir Walter: 'He created an image of the Scottish past which welded the Highlands and the Lowlands together in heightened national consciousness, and made the rest of the world aware of it for the first time.'[38] Scott did not create this fusion, since events were pressing the two regions of Scotland together in any case, but certainly gave it literary form. Nor was he alone. Several institutions, most notably the London Highland Society, carried out comparable ideological work. From 1806 in particular, when the Duke of Sussex accepted the presidency, the Society was involved in a number of activities which were listed in a report of 1808 as: promoting the teaching of the Gaelic language, history and culture (including the Ossianic poems); establishing a college of pipe music; setting up branches in the colonies and Scotland; building and running a Caledonian Asylum to educate the children of 'deserving' Scottish soldiers and sailors; and helping economic development in the Highlands, in association with the British Fisheries Society. Given the geographical location of the Society, it is interesting that the manager of the Edinburgh Highland Society at this time was moved to comment in 1827 that: 'The London Society did more to preserve the Highland Spirit than any other institution that I know'.[39]

The significance of the 'Celtification' of Scotland is better understood by John Prebble than Paul Scott:

It gave [the Scots] a picturesque national identity where none had been wholly satisfying since the Union, and reminded them, as Scott had hoped, of 'all those peculiarities' which had distinguished them as Scots. It also, and pre-eminently, united Lowlander and Borderer as one nation with a diminishing Gaelic minority whose existence had once aroused uneasy guilt or derisive contempt, but whose costume and history might now be honourably assumed by all.[40]

Some modern Scottish nationalists, anxious to defend their own appropriation of tartan imagery, have claimed that examining the origins of tartanry is tantamount to colluding in 'Unionist' attacks on Gaelic culture, or even Scottish culture as such.[41] Such claims are grotesque. In fact, tartanry attained its dominance at precisely the moment in which the existing Gaelic culture was being destroyed. As Kidd notes: 'The kitsch Gaeldom of the nineteenth century would conveniently obscure the sacrifice of the Highland peasantry on the altars of political economy.'[42] It is to this moment that we now turn.

The Reality of the Highlands: Social Assimilation and the Onslaught on Gaelic Culture

We have followed the inhabitants of the Highlands in their role as conquerors and settlers of the British Empire, and have seen how both this contemporary role and their past reputation was incorporated into a mythical version of Scottish history. How did the changing pattern of social life in the Highlands itself affect the construction of the dual Scottish-British identity? It perhaps goes without saying that the new-found admiration for Gaelic culture among the ruling class did not extend to recognising the wishes of any actual Gaelic speakers. As Christopher Smout records:

> A group of tenants on Sir John Sinclair's estate in the 1790s nicely, if unwittingly, exposed the dilemma when they petitioned him for a Gaelic-speaking minister, complaining that their needs could not be more neglected than if they had been American Indians, but reminding him that theirs was an ancient Scottish language and hoping that his expressed enthusiasm for Ossian would incline him to listen to them. He ignored the petition, of course.[1]

Many tenants of Highland estates would have considered themselves lucky to be merely ignored. One observer, John Ramsay of Ochtertyre, noted: 'The whole weight of Government, for a number of years, was employed to dissolve every tie between the chief and the clan, and to abolish all distinctions between the Highland and Lowland Scots'.[2] What form did the attempt to abolish these distinctions take?

There was still a vital Gaelic culture in existence during the eighteenth century, the most important elements of which were the Gaelic language and the Episcopalian religion. Both language and religion had been targeted since 1723 by the Society in Scotland for the Propagation of Christian Knowledge (SSPCK), which had the chance after 1746 to operate in the areas which had previously been denied to them. Armed with an English language dictionary in one hand and the King James Bible in the other, they set about the unsuspecting natives, intending to purge them of their linguistic and devotional deviations. Sir John Sinclair's tenants had been correct, of course, to compare their treatment to that of American Indians, for this is precisely how the SSPCK saw them. As early as 1729 the Society had spread its activities to North America, assisting missionaries who were seeking to convert the Native Americans as an extension of their evangelical work with the non-English-speaking peoples of Scotland.[3] The SSPCK clearly regarded the Native Americans as similar to the Highlanders in respect of their savagery, or perhaps their barbarism. Tragically, Highland colonists in North America behaved, in the main, no better to the Native Americans than their Lowland equivalents.

In 1766 the Society, while retaining its prohibition on the use of Gaelic as a means of instruction within the classroom and a vehicle for conversation between students, introduced reading in Gaelic as an aid to the understanding of English, and indeed published the New Testament in Gaelic the following year – steps which would never been contemplated before the region had been pacified. These innovations were permitted, however, to strengthen the hold of English, not as a concession to the students. How effective were these measures in reducing the incidence of Gaelic speaking?

A comparison of the Scottish population figures calculated by Alexander Webster in 1755 with those drawn up by James Walker for the Gaelic-speaking parishes ten years later suggests that, out of a total population of 1,265,380, 22.9 per cent or 289,798 spoke Gaelic. By 1806, out of a population of 1,608,420, 18.5 per cent or 297,823 did. This decline does not at first look precipitate, but concealed behind the totals are two important trends.

First, the overall territory encompassed by the *Gaidhealtachd* was decreasing. In the county of Perth, the classic border region, the percentage of Gaelic speakers fell from 38 per cent in 1765 to 27 in 1806. In other internal border areas where the language had previously been spoken, English was now completely dominant. These included the counties of Aberdeen (8.3 per cent Gaelic-speaking in 1765) and Stirling (12.1 per cent Gaelic-speaking in 1765).

Second, the number of Gaelic speakers included those who also spoke English and, increasingly, spoke it as their first language.[4] A comparison by Charles Withers of the original *Statistical Account Of Scotland* with the *New Statistical Account* (1831–1845) illustrates the shift that subsequently took place. In the parish of Comrie, the report of 1794 noted:

The common language of the people is Gaelic. All the natives understand it; but many, especially the old, do not understand the English well. All the young people can speak English; but in order to acquire it, they must go into service in the Low Country. The Gaelic is not spoken in its purity, neither here nor in the bordering parishes.

The indications here are both of a decline in Gaelic but a lack of opportunity for the English alternative to be absorbed. By 1843 the situation in the same parish is quite different:

The English language is generally spoken, and has gained ground greatly within the last forty years. At present, scarcely a fourth part of the congregation attended afternoon Gaelic service, whereas forty years ago, the attendance in English was very limited.[5]

The attack on Highland culture had been a two-sided affair, aimed at religion as much as language. Episcopalianism, unlike the Gaelic language, had been the target of direct state repression after the '45, but despite this advantage, the efforts of the SSPCK and the construction of new churches on the orders of the government, the hold of Presbyterianism on the population, other than at the level of purely formal adherence, was not secure until the first decades of the nineteenth century.[6] It was, however, an unusual triumph, for the faction which was both most responsible for carrying the word, and the chief beneficiary in organisational terms, was the Evangelical wing of the Church of Scotland, not the ruling Moderate faction. The result was that while the inhabitants of the Highlands, particularly in the Western Isles, became followers of the most extreme form of Presbyterianism with mass following in Great Britain, the Church of Scotland did not ultimately benefit. When the kirk split in the Disruption of 1843, entire congregations left to join the Free (i.e., free from patronage) Church of Scotland. In Sutherland perhaps as many as 99.8 per cent abandoned the Established Church.[7] The remaining 0.2 per cent were presumably the landowners themselves. Whether the Free Church subsequently helped or hindered the movement for land reform that exploded in the 1880s is still a matter of dispute among historians.[8] What cannot be disputed, however, is the impact its formation had on the Established Church. In the words of the most recent historian of religion in Scotland: 'Rarely can such a cataclysm have befallen a major Christian church.'[9] From the perspective of an inclusive national identity, however, the significant outcome was the abandonment of Episcopalianism for Presbyterianism, not the subsequent divisions within that camp.

Not every factor eroding Highland distinctiveness was consciously planned. At least one contributor to the Statistical Account Of Scotland saw movement of population, mainly of tenant farmers, from the Lowlands to the Highlands, and the increasing intercourse with Lowlanders which resulted, as a significant element in the 'civilising' process:

The military roads, which were made after the year 1745, opened a free communication with other parts of the kingdom, and an intercourse with strangers. ... The settlement of some graziers here, from the low country, contributed likewise to produce these happy effects.[10]

Another considered the impact of inward migration to the Highlands of equal importance to the activities of the SSPCK:

The language of the parish [i.e., Dunoon] is changed much, from the coming in of low-country tenants, from the constant intercourse our people have with their neighbours, but above all, from our schools, particularly those established by the Society for propagating Christian Knowledge. Hence the English or Scottish language is universally spoke by almost all ages, and sexes. But the Gaelic is still the natural tongue with them, their fireside language, and the language of their devotions.[11]

The process of familiarisation also operated in reverse. For the assault on Gaelic culture did at least have one – not entirely unintended – beneficial side effect: it enabled Highlanders to seek employment in English-speaking areas that would have previously been more difficult to obtain. This was a more positive development, ironically made possible by the spread of the English language. The search for work by Highlanders had always brought them into the Lowlands, usually as seasonal labourers on estates near to the Highland line. Now many of them, particularly from the north and northeastern Highlands, came permanently to become part of the settled workforce in the new manufactories. One study of Greenock estimates that in 1700 a mere 80 out of 1,300 inhabitants, or 6 per cent, were of Highland origin. Numbers increased during the eighteenth century, particularly after 1745, until by 1801 5,000 inhabitants, or 29 per cent, were of Highland origin.[12] Even then, integration did not take place overnight, for many of the Highlanders continued – as migrants from further afield still do to this day – to maintain their own language and to be confined to the same industries, sometimes the same factories. In Greenock, Highlanders formed the majority of workers in sugar refining and glass making; at the Dunchatten works in Glasgow the entire labour force was from the Highlands, a roll-call being taken in Gaelic each morning.[13] Seasonal workers would return to the Highlands with money and stories of relatively greater prosperity, or at least of greater opportunity, existing in the Lowlands, encouraging others to take the same road. Their very presence as workers, rather than thieves or combatants gradually wore down the separateness that had previously been their fate. Nor were the occupations which the Highlanders filled always the most unskilled. Of the 30 individuals with Highland surnames listed in the *Dundee Register* for 1782, four were schoolmasters of various sorts, three were merchants, two were officers of the Excise (one being Chief Collector) and one was a Customs Officer.[14]

Walter Scott rightly remarked of the Highlanders in 1816: 'The more intelligent [of the English], when they thought of them, by chance, considered them as complete barbarians; and the mass of the people cared no more about them than the merchants of New York about the Indians who dwelt beyond the Allegheny mountains.'[15] This was said retrospectively, in recognition of the changes in attitude that had occurred by that date. Only in one area did earlier attitudes still prevail. Perhaps the most notorious figure involved in the Clearances, Patrick Sellar, the factor on the Sutherland estate, continued to view the Highlanders 'as complete barbarians'. In a memorandum written in the same year as Scott penned the words quoted above, he refers to: 'Their obstinate adherence to the barbarous jargon of the times when Europe *was possessed by savages*'. As we have seen, these prejudices have a long pedigree, but Sellar has a theoretical justification for maintaining them:

> Their seclusion, I say, from this grand fund of knowledge, places them, with relation to the enlightened nations of Europe in a position not very different from that betwixt the American colonists and the Aborigines of that Country. The one are the Aborigines of Britain shut out from the general stream of knowledge and cultivation flowing in upon the Commonwealth of Europe from the remotest fountain of antiquity. The other are [sic] the Aborigines of America, equally shut out from this stream...[16]

Yet the significant fact here is that Sellar was a Scot, born in English-speaking Morayshire on the northeastern border of the Lowlands and trained in Scots Law at Edinburgh. Nowhere else in Britain could such remarks have been committed to paper at that time – with the Scots Greys newly triumphant at Waterloo – than as part of an attempt to justify the clearing of the estate at Strathnevar. Their exceptional nature can be seen by considering comments made in 1837 by the Reverend John Dunmore Lang, the prolific advocate of emigration to Australasia, on the need to dilute the Irish component in Australian colonial society with 'virtuous and industrious families and individuals'. And where were such people to be found?

> [A] free [i.e., as opposed to convict] emigrant population of such a character, as the Highlanders and Islanders of Scotland is, both

morally and politically speaking, the kind of population which is peculiarly required in the present circumstances and condition of the colony of New South Wales.[17]

Donald McLeod made part of his attack on the government and the landowners precisely the fact that they had failed to treat the Highlanders as Britons, as was their due:

To enumerate the many victories and laurels the Celtic race gained for ungrateful Britain would be an easy task, had history done them justice; but when put to the test their enemies will find it a difficult task to point out where they have failed to gain victory where bravery would obtain it.

One strand of his argument was therefore that the Clearances should be opposed for this very reason: 'I conclude by calling upon every British subject, every lover of justice, every sympathiser with suffering humanity, to disapprove of such unconstitutional and ungodly doings, and to remonstrate with the Queen and Government, so as to put an end to such systems.'[18] The biggest test of how far the Highlanders were now considered to be both Scottish and British came, however, during the 1840s and showed conclusively that the Highlanders were no longer regarded in the same way as the native Irish by the British ruling class.

The Potato Famine and the Test of Nationhood

In his work on the origins of racism, Theodore Allan defines racial oppression as the reduction of 'all members of an oppressed group to an undifferentiated social status, a status beneath that of any member of any social class within the colonising population'. Allan argues that racism originated, not from innate propensities on the part of different groups to distinguish themselves from and discriminate against other groups (the 'psycho-cultural' argument) but as a conscious ruling class strategy to justify slavery as an economic system in the epoch where formal equality (for males) was increasingly the norm (the 'socioeconomic' argument). Although his argument is mainly concerned with the racial oppression in the Americas, Allen sees a precursor of white colonial attitudes to the Native Americans and African slaves in the British (i.e., Lowland Scot and English) treatment of the Irish from the Anglo-Norman period onwards. With the Reformation, however, the religious difference between the Protestantism of the British settlers and the Catholicism of the Irish natives provided an additional element to the racism of the former: 'What had fed primarily on simple xenophobia now, as religio-racism, drank at eternal springs of private feelings about "man and God".'

There were also more material reasons. As Allan strongly argues, the construction of 'religio-racism' against the entire Irish population was a conscious choice on the part of the English ruling class and their Scottish allies. Ireland was a crucial strategic territory in the struggle between Catholic and Protestant Europe, hence the impossibility of co-opting sections of the Catholic Irish ruling class for the purposes of social control: they could not be trusted to take the British side in the conflicts with Catholic Spain and France. The alternative was of course, to attempt to convert the Catholic population to Protestantism, but this was unthinkable for most of the eighteenth century for two reasons. First, the Ascendancy comprised a relatively small minority of the population whose wealth and power would have been threatened if a majority had been allowed to share its legal privileges. Second, the majority of Protestants below the ruling class proper were Dissenters, most of them Presbyterians, and consequently excluded from the privileges available to communicants with the Anglican Church of Ireland. Mass conversion of the Catholic population was likely to lead to the converts joining the Dissenting branch of Protestantism, rather than that of the great landowners, raising the prospect of the majority of the population uniting against the Ascendancy. After this came near to happening anyway, in 1798, the British ruling class and their Irish extension responded by incorporating the Dissenting element through the Orange Order, but more importantly by shifting the nature of Catholic oppression from a racial to a national basis '*by the incorporation of the Irish bourgeoisie into the intermediate buffer social control system*'. In short, once Catholics were allowed to participate in ruling Ireland, the system of 'religio-racial' oppression had to be abandoned.[19]

Phytopthora infestans affected potato crops across western Europe during the 1840s and early 1850s, but Ireland and the Scottish Highlands suffered to a greater extent than elsewhere in two respects. First, the blight persisted for longer due to favourable climatic conditions: 1846 saw the maximum incidence of crop failure at the European level; in Ireland it continued until 1850 and in the western Highlands until 1855. Second, the extent of crop loss was greater: the average fall in potato yields on the continental mainland was around 33 per cent; during 1846 the fall in Ireland was 75 per cent and in 87 per cent of Highland areas sampled the failure was 100 per cent, or as near as made no difference.[20] Therefore, in terms of both duration of the blight and the extent of crop failure, the Highlands were actually in a worse situation than Ireland, yet the outcome in Ireland in terms of mortality was of a qualitatively different kind.

The population of Ireland in 1841 has been calculated at 8.1 million. Even if we exclude 'averted births', the overall excess mortality between 1841 and 1851 amounted to perhaps 1,082,000 people. In addition, between 1845 and 1855, 2.1 million people emigrated. James Donnelly has calculated that, taking into account both excess deaths and emigration, the total impact of the famine can be summarised as follows:

> Only six of the thirty-two counties lost less than 15 per cent of the population between 1841 and 1851. In another six counties the population in 1851 was from 15 to 20 per cent lower than it had been a decade earlier. Of the remaining twenty counties, nine lost from 20 to 25 per cent of their population, while eleven lost over 25 per cent between 1841 and 1851.[21]

In the Highlands, although a crisis of mortality was feared during 1847 and, to a lesser extent, 1848, it never transpired. During this time higher than normal numbers of deaths were reported in seven parishes, but only seven people were reported to have died directly from starvation and, after judicial investigation, the number was reduced to two. Nor does it appear that death from starvation was 'displaced' from the Highlands themselves by migration abroad or to the Lowlands. Between 1849 and 1850 there were three incidents where large numbers of emigrants died *en route* to North America, but these were exceptional. In 1847 the mortality rate on board ships sailing direct from Ireland to Canada was 8 per cent, and on board ships transporting Irish emigrants via Liverpool, 15 per cent; the mortality rate on board ships sailing to the same destination from Scottish ports was 3 per cent. There was an increase in mortality rates across Scotland as a whole between 1847 and 1851, but this was concentrated in the urban Lowlands, where epidemics, first of typhus, then of cholera, found breeding grounds in the towns thrown up by the industrialisation process. Ironically, the predominantly rural Highlands largely escaped this particular disaster. The figures for emigration do bear a greater resemblance to those of Ireland, but even here some caution must be exercised. Out-migration (i.e., migration to both the Lowlands and overseas) had been proceeding for decades before the 1840s and the areas in which it was now concentrated were those in the predominantly crofting regions of the western Highlands, where the population had fewer resources than that of the inland farming districts. Between 1841 and 1851 estimated average net migration from this area was 16.08 per cent. Between 1851 and 1861 it was 15.87 per cent.[22] The real difference with Ireland is this: in the Highlands the scale of out-migration may have *prevented* a noticeable rise in the rate of mortality; in Ireland emigration was *in addition to* just such a rise.

Why was there such a difference between outcomes in two areas, both supposedly integral to the United Kingdom? The native Irish and the Scottish Highlanders were both heavily dependent on the potato as a staple crop. Both were ruled by a class which had almost in its entirety embraced the principles of the Reverend Thomas Malthus, according to which populations unable to provide for themselves – even through no fault of their own – were literally redundant and could not be helped without violating the laws of political economy. Most crucially of all, both populations had been regarded as cultural and social inferiors by the Anglo-Scottish ruling class. A number of conjunctural answers have been offered by Devine: the Highlanders were not so dependent on the potato as the native Irish; Scotland was in an earlier and more buoyant stage of the economic cycle than Ireland and could therefore still offer employment to temporary migrants from the Highlands in agriculture, fishing and railway construction; communications networks had been developed in Scotland to a degree unknown in Ireland; the Highland population was smaller, partly as a result of previous emigration, and so relief could be more easily provided; the landlords were sufficiently solvent to be able to provide relief in a way that their Irish counterparts were not; local church organisation took the initiative in providing relief on a non-denominational basis, rather than the state in Ireland, which insisted on the performance of work for pay, to the detriment of those already most weakened by hunger; and so on.[23] Some of these have greater relevance than others. Clearly, having access to other sources of nourishment (through fishing, for example), or the ability to buy food as a result of continuing paid employment are important factors, but the others cited by Devine were efficacious only to the extent that relief was *already* being provided. No matter how accessible the transport networks, how small the population requiring assistance, how affluent the landowners – unless aid had been forthcoming in the first place these would not have come into play as factors of importance.

Sir Charles Trevelyan, Under Secretary at the Treasury and the man most responsible for implementing government policy in both regions, wrote of the Highlands in 1846: 'The people *cannot, under any circumstances*, be allowed to starve.'[24] Yet the same man, in his 1848 apologia for British policy in Ireland, could treat the fact that hundreds of thousands were being allowed to starve as an act of Providence:

Unless we are much deceived, posterity will trace up to that famine the commencement of a salutary revolution in the habits of a nation long singularly unfortunate, and will acknowledge that on this, as on many other occasions, Supreme Wisdom has educed permanent good out of transient evil.

Here there is no doubt that political economy must be allowed to function unimpeded:

Ireland has awakened from this dream [i.e., of the necessity of state intervention] by the occurrence of the most frightful calamities, and it has at last begun to be understood that the proper business of a

Government is to enable private individuals of every rank and profession to carry on their several occupations with freedom and safety, and not itself undertake the role of the land-owner, merchant, money-lender, or any other function of social life. ... God grant that the generation to which this great opportunity has been offered may rightly perform its part, and that we may not relax our efforts until Ireland fully participates in the social health and physical prosperity of Great Britain, which will be the true consummation of their union.[25]

But, as Terry Eagleton writes of the Famine in Ireland: 'As far as this particular catastrophe goes, it was not the union which contributed to Ireland's ills, but Britain's self-interested decision to set it aside.'[26] This verdict can be put more strongly: Ireland was not part of the British nation, the Union simply masked the prevailing colonial relationship; the Highlands of Scotland were part of the nation, and the treatment it received in this period of crisis reflected that fact. It is difficult to say exactly when this change in attitude occurred. It is worth noticing however, the comments of Robert Southey – who had long abandoned his youthful radicalism – during a tour of Scotland in 1819. Remarking on the appalling nature of peasant housing in the Highlands (on the Sutherland estate, in fact) he ventures some comparisons with equivalent accommodation in Ireland:

The Irish cabin, I suppose, must be such a heap of peat with or without stones, according to the facility of collecting them, or the humour of the maker. But these men-sties are not inhabited, as in Ireland, by a race of ignorant and ferocious barbarians, who can never be civilised till they are regenerated – till their very nature is changed. Here you have a quiet, thoughtful, contented, religious people, susceptible of improvement, and willing to be improved.

In so far as Southey feels there are any similarities between the Highlanders and the Catholic Irish, it is not between the majority of the population but between the minority who ruled them, and this is not to the advantage of the former:

The Highland Laird partakes much more of the Irish character than I had ever been taught to suppose. He has the same profusion, the same recklessness, the same rapacity; but he has more power and uses it worse; and his sin is greater, because he has to deal with a sober, moral, well-disposed people, who if they were treated with common kindness, or even common justice, would be ready to lay down their lives in his service.[27]

Even past Highland behaviour disruptive of the fledgling bourgeois order was retrospectively rehabilitated as Macaulay – himself of Highland descent – demonstrated in his *History Of England* (publication of which began in 1848, as the famine was still raging in Ireland). He compares the respective historical significance of two battles held during the same week in 1689: Killiecrankie in Scotland and Newton Butler in Ireland. At Killiecrankie an irregular Jacobite minority won an overwhelming, if short-lived, victory over the regular Williamite majority. At Newton Butler an irregular Williamite minority won an equally overwhelming, but longer-lasting, triumph over the regular Jacobite majority. Why has the former become part of the Scottish martial tradition but the latter almost unknown outside the ranks of Ulster Loyalism? 'The Anglosaxon and the Celt have been reconciled in Scotland, and have never been reconciled in Ireland', he writes. If we leave to one side the imaginary racial distinctions with which Macaulay labels his subjects, it is possible to appreciate the honesty of a bourgeoisie which had not yet learned to wax hypocritical on the subject of John Bull's Other Island:

In Scotland all the great actions of both races are thrown into a common stock, and are considered as making up the glory which belongs to the whole country. So completely has the old antipathy been extinguished that nothing is more usual than to hear a Lowlander talk with complacency and even with pride of the most humiliating defeat that his ancestors ever underwent. ... We cannot wonder that the victory of the Highlanders should be more celebrated than the victory of the Enniskilleners, when we consider that the victory of the Highlanders is a matter of boast to all Scotland, and that the victory of the Enniskilleners is a matter of shame to four fifths of Ireland.[28]

If the British ruling class had been intent on perpetuating racism against the Highlanders in the same way as they were against the Irish, it is unlikely that the 'common stock' of which Macaulay speaks would ever have come into existence. The native Irish remained an ever-present threat to the integrity of the British state, while the Highlanders no longer did. Indeed, many Highlanders themselves expressed this racist opposition to the Irish. Hugh Miller, the writer and geologist from the Black Isle in Cromarty, noted in his autobiography what he called the degradation of the new working class 'which is scarcely less marked than that exhibited by the negro' and partly blamed the Irish:

The immigrant Irish form also a very appreciable element in the degradation of our large towns...and are chiefly formidable from the squalid wretchedness of a physical character which they have transferred from their mud cabins into our streets and lanes, and from the course of ruinous competition into which they have entered with the unskilled labourers of the country, and which has had the effect of reducing our lowlier countrymen to a humbler level than they perhaps ever occupied before.[29]

Two qualifications need to be made to this picture of acceptance. First, although Highlanders were included in the British nation, their ancestors continued to be subjected to literary abuse that now clearly echoed the racist doctrines used to justify British rule over non-European peoples. 'It is clear,' wrote John Pinkerton in 1794, 'that the manners of the Celts perfectly resembled those of the present Hottentots.'[30] Second, although the Highlanders were not allowed to starve, this should not obscure the fact that they, and the majority of the Scottish population, continued to be exploited more straightforwardly in class terms. Walter Scott wrote to the Duchess of Sutherland at the beginning of her experiment in terms that capture the contempt felt by the ruling class towards those upon whose labour they relied:

I have very little doubt that your ladyship's patriotic attempts to combine industry with such relics of ancient manners as still dignify the highlanders who have the good fortune to be under your protection, will succeed, though perhaps not with the rapidity that your philanthropy may anticipate. It has taken a generation to convert a race of feudal warriors (for such were the highlanders previously to 1745) into a quiet and peaceable peasantry, and perhaps it will take as long to introduce the spirit of action and exertion necessary to animate them in their new profession. Man in general is a vile prejudiced animal... In the mean time a new race is gradually arising who will be trained in those sentiments and habits which the present state of society requires, and which it is your ladyship's wish to introduce, and who will in the course of twenty years, look back in wonder at the prejudices of their fathers, and with gratitude to their mistress who pursued their welfare in spite of themselves.[31]

But as Rosalind Mitchison writes: 'While the consciousness of common nationality was being extended to the highlander, it was being withdrawn from the bottom of the social scale.'[32] Increasingly, however, those at 'the bottom of the social scale' were not the peasants and artisans of old Scotland, but a new class of workers, most importantly industrial workers. They would assert their own claims to belong to the nation, or rather, the nations, since they too displayed a dual national consciousness, but one now as charged with class consciousness as that of their masters. These different class perspectives on nationhood were captured in the writings of the two greatest Scottish literary figures of the Age of Revolution: Burns and Scott.

Burns and Scott: Radical and Conservative Nations

Robert Burns (1759–1796) and Walter Scott (1771–1832) were so different in their class position and political attitudes that fruitful comparisons between their views of nationhood may seem impossible.

Take their class positions first. Burns was the son of an Aberdeenshire farmer who had migrated to Ayrshire. Unlike many of his peers, his education went beyond that of the parish school since his father, together with some neighbours, paid for a private schoolmaster to educate their children. In addition to his writing, which would not have been lucrative enough to sustain himself or his family, Burns first combined tenant farming and work for the Excise, before failure in the first role made him turn to the latter full-time, where he eventually rose to the position of acting supervisor at Dumfries. Scott's grandfather had been a farmer, but his father was a lawyer and Writer to the Signet and he was trained to follow in the same profession, in which he gained entry to the Faculty of Advocates and rose to the position of principal clerk of the Court of Session. Between 1805 and his financial collapse in 1826 Scott was also a partner in the printing firm of James Ballantyne and Co.. Unlike Burns, Scott latterly gained most of his income from his writings and, indeed, after his near-bankruptcy in 1826 was eventually able to pay off his creditors in this way. In short, Burns was born into the lower petty-bourgeoisie and remained at that level for most of his life, climbing eventually (while remaining within the same class) into one of the few forms of state employment available at the time outside of the armed forces. Scott belonged to the classic pre-industrial bourgeois profession, the law, and became one of the first members of the new profession of 'novelist'.

The political differences are no less marked and can best be illustrated by their respective verses to the tune of 'For a' That'. In words probably written in 1794 Burns concludes by foretelling of an age of universal solidarity in which class distinctions have been overturned:

> Then let us pray that come it may,
> (As come it will for a' that,)
> That Sense and Worth, o'er a' the earth,
> Shall bear the gree, an' a that.
> For a' that, an' a that,
> It's coming yet for a' that,
> That man to man, the world o'er,
> Shall brithers be for a' that.[1]

No nations are mentioned here, but rather the world. As Thomas Crawford writes, this is 'the anthem for the whole human race', 'the "Internationale" of those days and of many Scottish generations since'.[2] Now contrast these sentiments with those of Scott in a verse first sung at the inaugural meeting of the Pitt Club of Scotland in 1814, after the defeat of Napoleon. The entire song is a sigh of relief at the suppression of the French Revolution ('guns, guillotines, and a' that'). The nations of Britain had played their part in restoring the French fleur-de-lis to her rightful place:

> We'll twine her in a friendly knot
> With England's rose, and a' that;
> The Shamrock shall not be forgot,
> For Wellingtons made bra' that.
> The Thistle, though her leaf be rude,
> Yet faith we'll no misca that,
> She sheltered in her solitude
> The Fleur-de-lis, for a' that.

The solidarity of the European reaction which had contained the virus is celebrated, with each absolutist regime named and its virtues acclaimed:

> The Austrian Vine, the Prussian Pine
> (For Blucher's sake, hurra that,)
> The Spanish Olive, too, shall join,
> And bloom in peace for a' that.
> Stout Russia's hemp, so surely twined
> Around our wreath we'll draw that,
> And he that would the cord unbind,
> Shall have it for his gra-vat!

In the last verse Scott rounds on the Americans who had been so bold as to declare war on the British in 1812 (in response to a Loyalist invasion from Canada supported by Britain, although this seems to have eluded Scott.):

> There's ae bit spot I had forgot
> America they ca' that!
> A coward plot her rats had got
> Their fathers flag to gnaw that:
> Now see it fly top-gallant high,
> Atlantic winds shall blaw that,
> And Yankee loon, beware your croun,
> There's kames in hand to claw that!

Finally, Scott sets forth his confidence in British imperialism:

> For on the land, or on the sea,
> Where'er the breezes blaw that,
> The British Flag shall bear the grie,
> And win the day for a' that![3]

At a literary level this is an unfair comparison: Burns' 'A Man's a Man' is great verse; Scott's 'For a' That' is wretched doggerel. Insofar as it illuminates some aspects of their politics, however, the opportunity is too good to pass up. Burns appears as an internationalist and a radical; Scott as a British nationalist and counter-revolutionary. But their attitudes are more complex than at first appears.

Burns and Radicalism

Take the song which is most often taken to embody the Scottish nationalism associated with Burns:

> Fareweel to a' our Scottish fame,
> Fareweel our ancient glory;
> Fareweel ev'n to the Scottish name,
> Sae fam'd in martial story;
> Now Sark rins over Solway sands,
> An' Tweed rins to the ocean,
> To mark where England's province stands –
> Such a parcel of rogues in an nation![4]

'Such a Parcel of Rogues in a Nation' may suggests that Burns was uncomplicatedly nationalist in his politics, and this interpretation is strengthened by another poem written in 1793, 'Robert Bruce's March To Bannockburn', or, as it is better known, 'Scots Wha Ha'e':

> Scots, wha hae wi' Wallace bled,
> Scots, wham Bruce has often led,
> Welcome to your gory bed,
> Or to victory![5]

The melody of this song is based on 'Hey Tuttie Tattie', the march Burns believed Bruce played at Bannockburn. Burns himself described the composition of this song in a letter, saying that 'I had no idea of giving myself any trouble on the subject, till the accidental recollection of that glorious struggle for Freedom, associated with the glowing ideas of the same nature, *not quite so ancient*, aroused my rhyming mania.'[6] What were these more modern ideas to which Burns refers?

For his most recent editor this is: 'A reference to the trial of Muir and Palmer for sedition, then taking place at Edinburgh.'[7] For other writers the ideas in question are more directly those of the French Revolution, whose armies were then driving back the combined might of the British state and European absolutism. As Marilyn Burns writes: 'If the Scottish reader were to apply these verses topically, he or she would have difficulty fitting serfdom and usurpation to the French republic, but might feel the words fitted the Government in London.'[8] Read in this way Burns can be seen as linking two separate events to the Scottish political scene: the historical struggle to maintain the independent feudal state and the contemporary struggle to defend the French Republic. Such interpretations have been challenged by William Donaldson, who writes of Burns that 'Jacobitism was the only political principle consistently present throughout his creative life' and argues that 'Scots Wha Ha'e', 'the nearest thing we have to a national anthem, was inspired by the Jacobite rebellions.' Donaldson therefore interprets Burn's own reference to 'struggles...*not quite so ancient*' in the context of Jacobitism, not that of the French Revolution: 'How a song which celebrates the traditional theme of heroic independence under a line of native kings could be construed as an essay in republicanism is less than clear.':

> The word 'Usurper' also featured prominently in the song. To an eighteenth century Scot, this had only one connotation, and it directly links the Wars of Independence with the Jacobite risings as heroic national struggles. It is not revolutionary libertarianism, but Scottish independence that is celebrated here.[9]

There are, however, some major difficulties with this interpretation.

First, no one in Scotland regarded the Jacobite rebellions as examples of a 'heroic national struggle', either during the Jacobite era or 40 years later: if Burns did take this view then he was introducing it into the literature, not reflecting an existing attitude.

Second, there is considerable doubt as to whether he took this view anyway. On the previous page to the one on which Donaldson commends Burn's Jacobitism, he conducts an excellent analysis of one of Burn's greatest songs, 'Ye Jacobites By Name', in which the singer identifies the 'meddlers, adventurers and foolish partisans blinded by their own propaganda' who supported that ideology. Donaldson attempts to overcome this contradiction by saying: 'The torturous complexity of his politics may conceal a very simple fact: maybe he didn't believe much in any of it, and assumed and discarded party labels in order to survive.'[10] But how then is it possible to claim that 'Jacobitism was the only political principle consistently present throughout his creative life'? Nor is this a case of an artist taking one position in his art and another in his life. The first letter Burns wrote for publication was a reply to a sermon by the Reverend Joseph Kirkpatrick on the centenary of the Glorious Revolution, in which Kirkpatrick had launched the by then traditional Whig onslaught on the person of James VII and II and his progeny. Burns reply insists that, as individuals, the Stuarts were no worse than any other monarchs, but this did not amount to a political endorsement of their cause. Burns notes the success of French Absolutism, but: 'With us, luckily, the Monarch failed, and his unwarrantable pretensions fell a sacrifice to our rights and happiness.'[11]

Third, it is not clear why Scottish independence should be seen as incompatible with political republicanism. It was certainly a minority position among the radicals of the 1790s, but was eventually adopted by Thomas Muir, the most famous, albeit during the period of repression and his exile in France.[12] Indeed, most modern nationalists assert that this was also Burns' position. There is some evidence in his work to support such a claim. Take a song of the 1790s called 'The Tree of Liberty', which Thomas Crawford has convincingly argued was written by Burns.[13] In these verses, the Tree of Liberty is unambiguously the fruit of the French Revolution ('It stands where ance the Bastille stood/A prison built by kings, man') and this is contrasted with the British failure to follow the French road:

> Let Britain boast her hardy oak,
> Her poplar and her pine, man,
> Auld Britain ance could crack her joke,
> And o'er her neighbours shine, man,
> But seek the forest round and round,
> and soon 'twill be agreed, man,
> That sic a tree cannot be found,
> 'Twixt London and the Tweed, man.

Can 'sic a tree' be found *north* of the Tweed? The last verse declares: 'Syne let us pray, auld England may/Sure plant this far-famed tree, man'.[14] These references imply that it is England, not Scotland (which goes unmentioned in the song), that most requires the Tree of Liberty. If the words of 'Such a Parcel of Rogues In a Nation', written two years later in 1795 are also taken into account, then the Scottish Nationalist character of his work would seem incontestable. In fact, Burns had a considerably more complex attitude towards Britishness than these remarks would suggest.

As early as 1793 Burns wrote to Robert Graham of Fintry to refute allegations that had been circulating about his allegiances. Two passages are interesting in the context of this discussion. In the first Burns writes that he is unable to judge George III as an individual, but 'in his Public capacity, I always revered, and ever will, with soundest loyalty revere, the Monarch of Great-britain, as to speak in Masonic, the sacred KEYSTONE OF OUR ROYAL ARCH CONSTITUTION.' In the second he distances himself from the development of the French Revolution: 'As for France, I was her enthusiastic votary in the beginning of the business. – When she came to show her old avidity for conquest, in annexing Savoy, etc. to her dominions, and invading the rights of Holland, I altered my sentiments.'[15] Once again, there is no division between art and life. Only weeks after the publication of 'Such a Parcel of Rogues In a Nation' he composed the song now usually known as 'The Dumfries Volunteers'. It begins:

> Does haughty Gaul invasion threat?
> Then let the louns beware, Sir;
> There's wooden walls upon our seas,
> And volunteers on shore, Sir:
> The Nith shall run to Corsincon,
> And Criffel sink in Solway,
> Ere we permit a Foreign Foe
> On British ground to rally!
> We'll ne'er permit a Foreign Foe
> On British ground to rally!

Scotland is now part of 'British ground' rather than as in the earlier song, 'England's province'. It concludes:

> The wretch that would a tyrant own,
> And the wretch, his true sworn brother,
> Who would set the Mob above the Throne,
> May they be damn'd together!
> Who will not sing 'God save the King',
> Shall hang as high's the steeple;

> But while we sing 'God save the King',
> We'll ne'er forget The People!
> But while we sing 'God save the King',
> We'll ne'er forget The People![16]

Burns had, of course, joined the Dumfries Volunteers and various explanations have been advanced for both this and his subsequent celebratory verse, ranging from the plausible (Thomas Crawford delicately suggests 'that there may have been an element of expediency in his volunteering'[17]) to the truly phantasmagoric (Berresford Ellis and Mac a' Ghobhainn believe that 'Burns joined the Yeomanry as part of an overall plan by the republicans being carried out throughout Scotland to infiltrate the ranks of the soldiery.'[18]). The first explanation is certainly plausible given the level of repression in Scotland during these years. Was Burns then simply playing a double game, affecting loyalty in public, while associating with radicals, and providing their publications with poems and songs in private?[19] Both 'Does Haughty Gaul Invasion Threat?' and Burns' membership of the Dumfries Volunteers can however be explained without invoking a public/private split in this way.

On the one hand, Burns' radicalism was perfectly compatible with a reformist attitude to the British state, as the counterposition of 'God Save the King!' and 'We'll ne'er forget The People' in the last verse of the poem indicates. As Angus Calder has pointed out: 'France under Napoleon was again despotic.' Consequently: 'There was no contradiction in setting British libertarianism against French tyranny'.[20]

On the other hand, Burns' Scottishness was also perfectly compatible with his Britishness. William Ferguson has argued that, between Scott and Burns, the latter 'proved the stronger supporter of Scottish National identity':

> Both authors had their North British Moods, but in Burns they did not strike deep. When in the North British or Augustan mood Burns poetry was at its weakest. 'Doth Haughty Gaul Invasion Threat?' is passionless fustian compared to 'Scots Wha Hae', Scotland's true national anthem.[21]

Few would dispute this as a literary judgement, but aesthetic quality is not necessarily the best guide to the consciousness of the artist. 'A Man's a Man' is at least as great a poem as 'Scots Wha' Hae', but presumably Ferguson does not thereby assume that the international-ism of the former overrides the nationalism of the latter – even assuming that it can be judged as solely nationalistic in content. Burns did not suddenly make himself over as British for reasons of political expediency:

the letter replying to Reverend Kirkpatrick quoted above was signed 'a Briton'.

As far as Burns political attitudes were concerned, Jock Morris is surely right to say that: 'He had a mixed, contradictory consciousness.'[22] His national consciousness, however, was not so much contradictory as *combinatory* of both Scottish and British identities, and it is this, as Ferguson suggests, which he shares with Walter Scott, albeit from the other side of the political divide.

Scott and Conservatism

If Scott appears an ambiguous figure in relation to the balance between the Scottish and British aspects of his own identity, it is only through a confusion between national *consciousness* and national*ism*. Some episodes in his life do indeed give a superficial impression that his sympathies lay primarily with the Scottish side. His first biographer, for example, noted his reaction to proposed changes in the Scots law and his passionate contribution to a debate on this subject in the Faculty of Advocates during 1806, in which he was set against his friend, the Whig Francis Jeffrey:

> When the meeting broke up, he walked across The Mound, on his way to Castle Street, between Mr Jeffrey and another of his reforming friends, who complimented him on the rhetorical powers he had been displaying, and would willingly have treated the subject-matter of their discussion playfully. But his feelings had been moved to an extent far beyond their apprehension: he exclaimed, 'No, no – 'tis no laughing matter; little by little, whatever your wishes may be, you will destroy and undermine, until nothing of what makes Scotland shall remain.' And so saying, he turned round to conceal his agitation – but not until Mr Jeffrey saw tears gushing down his cheek – resting his head until he recovered himself on the wall of the Mound. Seldom, if ever, in his more advanced age, did any feelings obtain such mastery.[23]

Scott expressed similar views, if rather more restrainedly, in 1826 when the government responded to a collapse in value of the pound by attempting to force the Scottish (and English) banks to curtail the issue of banknotes under the value of £5. His response was to compose three letters pseudo-anonymously (as Malachi Malagrowther) for publication in the *Edinburgh Weekly Journal*: 'What I *do* complain of is the general spirit of slight and dislike manifested to our national establishments, by those of the sister country who are so very zealous in defending their own'. What he does *not* complain of is the Union itself. Scott absolutely resists any suggestion that the Scots might rise up against English rule in the same way that the Irish did against British rule in 1798: 'We had better remain in union with England, even at the risk of becoming a subordinate species of Northumberland, as far as national consequences is concerned, than remedy ourselves by even hinting the possibility of a rupture.'[24]

Some very forced interpretations have been imposed on these letters. In the most audacious, Paul Scott argues that the last quoted passage merely indicates his opposition to violence, not to separation as such. This scarcely accords with the violence Scott was quite prepared to see exercised against the Scottish working class or rebellious colonial subjects of the British crown. According to Paul Scott, however, 'the Malachi Letters amount to a coherent statement of the philosophy of Scottish nationalism...it would be no exaggeration to describe them as the first manifesto of modern Scottish Nationalism.'[25] In fact, in the same letter Scott makes quite clear where his sympathies lie:

> ...our blood has flowed as freely as that of England or of Ireland – our lives and fortunes have been as unhesitatingly devoted to the defence of empire... We have in every respect conducted ourselves as good and faithful subjects of the general Empire.

And was Sir Walter now prepared to abandon this devotion and subjection?

> We do not boast of these things as actual merits; but they are at least duties discharged and in an appeal to men of honour and of judgement, must entitle us to be heard with patience, and even deference, on the management of our own affairs, if we speak unanimously, lay aside party feeling, and use the voice of one leaf of the holy Trefoil, – one distinct and component part of the United Kingdoms.[26]

Scott's novel, *Guy Mannering* (1815) is set in the 1760s and 1770s, roughly between the conquest of Canada and the loss of the American colonies. At one point the hero, Brown, writes to a Swiss friend about the role which the Scots have played in India:

> The English are a wise people. While they praise themselves, and affect to undervalue all other nations, they leave us, luckily, trap doors and back doors open, by which we strangers, less favoured by nature, may arrive at a share of their advantages.

As Andrew Lincoln writes: 'The phrase "trap-doors and back-doors" captures the ambiguity of the English position – ostensibly secure in its exclusive identity, but in practice forced to let others find a way into its cultural space.'[27] Lincoln cites the example of the East India Company as one of these openings for the Scots, and while this is true, I think that the passage also tells us something else about the ambiguity with which Scott regarded the relationship with England, an attitude quite different from the Scottish nationalism asserted by Paul Scott. What is revealed rather is an *uncertainty* about the relationship, a determination not to jeopardise Scottish access to the 'advantages' which the 'wise' English (wise because they recognise the abilities and capacities of the Scots) have made available.

These apparently contradictory attitudes were not personal to Scott, but typical of his class. His protégé, James Hogg, despite an evident sympathy for Jacobitism which he displayed both in presenting the Jacobite songs and in reconstructing their aesthetic values in compositions like 'Donald MacGillivary', had a political attitude to the British state which was, in practical terms, identical. In letters to his friend written in the Highlands during 1803, he describes travelling along the banks of Loch Arkaig, where the Hanoverian troops ('malevolent brutes') searched for Charles Stuart after Culloden:

> While traversing the scenes where the patient sufferings of the one party, and the cruelties of the other, were so affectingly displayed, I could not help being a bit of a Jacobite in my heart, and blessing myself that, in those days, I did not exist, or I would certainly have been hanged.

This emotional identification with the Cause Forlorn had, however, no bearing on his actual attitude to the place of contemporary Scotland in the British state. Another letter expresses his depression after listening to a fellow traveller expound on the Scottish victories at Falkirk and Bannockburn: 'I wish from my heart that the distinctions of Englishmen and Scot were entirely disannulled and sunk in that of Britons.'[28]

As Nicholas Phillipson has famously written, what Sir Walter did was to give the Scottish element of this dualism a mode of expression:

> ...the Malachi letters were not a call to action but a substitute for it. ... Scott showed Scotsmen how to express their nationalism, by focusing their confused national emotions upon inessentials... By validating the making of a fuss about nothing, Scott gave to middle class Scotsmen and to Scottish nationalism an ideology – an ideology of noisy inaction.[29]

On the one hand Paul Scott argues that the *Letters* are 'a passionate protest against English interference in Scottish affairs and a demand for Scottish cultural distinctiveness' and sees these sentiments as also informing his other work: 'I think that the emotional force behind the best of Scott's poetry and novels was precisely a deep regret at Scotland's loss of independence and a fierce desire to defend and enhance the Scottish identity in spite of it.' On the other hand, he quotes Hugh MacDiarmid's view that Scott's position 'led naturally to the separatist position' and describes the *Letters* as 'the first manifesto of Scottish nationalism'.[30] Which is it then? Culture and identity or separatism and nationalism? In fact, at one level Paul Scott is right about Sir Walter. He did indeed display a form of Scottish national consciousness, but as I have argued throughout, this is not the same as nation*alism* and does not necessarily lead to any political conclusions. It is perfectly possible to possess a Scottish identity without it making one iota of difference to seeing politics as taking place in an essentially British context.

Those who possess a dual national identity in which – inevitably – one half of that identity is stateless, do not inevitably demand that it be embodied in a nation state unless they have good material reasons for doing so. Scott had no such reason. Mitchison gives as an example the attitude to the poor rates. 'By the end of the century the Scottish upper classes were being able to claim it as a sign of superior national virtue that they carried only about a fifth of the burden of poor relief of their English counterparts.'[31] Among those claiming to defend their superior national virtue was one Malachi Malagrowther, Esquire. Referring to 'the fatal progress of her *poor-rates*', Scott was adamant that 'some system or other must be proposed in its place':

> Suppose the English, for uniformity's sake, insist that Scotland, which is at present free from this foul and shameful disorder, should nevertheless be included in the severe treatment which the disease demands, how would the landholders of Scotland like to undergo the scalpel and cautery, merely because England requires to be scarified.[32]

What exercised Scott and the rest of his class was not simply the necessity of keeping the victims of the Poor Law in their place, but the possibility that they might take matters into their own hands.

Leaving the Eighteenth Century

Both Burns and Scott can therefore be seen as embodying transitional forms of consciousness, pointing back to the type of dual national consciousness and class consciousness typical of an agrarian society undergoing rapid change in the class structure, but from which a permanent, industrial working class has still to emerge. If the sentiments Burns expresses in a 'A Man's a Man' still resonate for socialists today, it is because the democratic and egalitarian vision will only be accomplished in a socialist future, not because Burns envisaged or *could have* envisaged that future. Burns is the last great figure of the old, rural Scotland in transition, touched by the political influence of the French Revolution, but not yet industrialised. Scott on the other hand lived to see the new world that was being created in the West of Scotland, and if the ambiguity of his response to that world still speaks to us today, it because it is recognisably still *our* world, where that of Burns is not. Therefore, although my political sympathies, like those of most socialists, lie with Burns, it is with Scott that I want to close this chapter.

Scott is often seen as the last great figure of the Scottish Enlightenment, and in one sense this is fitting, since he had internalised its theory of historical change, and given it concrete artistic expression in his novels. In another sense, however, he can be more usefully seen as the literary representative of the class of improving landowners, who were being replaced in the Scottish class structure by the manufacturers, who brought both factories and workers in their wake. He admires both Union and Empire, but is unwilling to pay the price in the transformation of the Scottish social structure. His disquiet is revealed clearly in his corre-spondence during the great demonstrations of 1819, where he constantly frets over the possibility of armed insurrections. Towards the end of 1819, when some sort of social explosion was clearly preparing itself, Scott wrote to his son in tones of dark foreboding:

> I am concerned I cannot give a very pleasant account of things here. Glasgow is in a terrible state. The Radicals had a plan to seize on 1,000 stand of arms, as well as a depot of ammunition... The fearful thing is the secret and steady silence observed by the Radicals in all they do. Yet, without anything like effective arms or useful discipline, without money and without a commissariat, what can they do, but, according to their favourite toast, have blood and plunder?[33]

As Christopher Harvie points out, the 'mental substructure' of his novels is not 'the idea of an accelerating social progress' discerned by Lukacs:

> ...but an image of stability achieved by a fruitful combination of enterprise, authority, good sense and paternalist responsibility. ... Such stability and consistency were innovations in eighteenth-century Scotland and rejoicing in them didn't imply allegiance to a dogma of continuous social change.[34]

Again, these were not simply his personal sentiments. His son-in-law and biographer, James Lockhart also took up his pen to defend the Scotland which had emerged from the Union and was preserved by the defeat of the last Jacobite rebellion. The issue here was not the Scottish currency, but the far more significant issue of the unreformed legal system. Yet the form of his argument is that it is Scotland which is being undermined by the reformers: 'It is not to be denied, that the Scottish lawyers have done more than any other class of their fellow-citizens, to keep alive the sorely threatened spirit of national independence in the thoughts and feelings of their countrymen.'[35] But these sentiments, like those of Scott in relation to the currency, are expressive of a battle already lost. The advent of industrialisation in Scotland, to which we now turn, would transform the eighteenth-century consciousness of being Scottish and British, as new classes entered the historical stage quite removed from the agrarian radicalism and conservatism which had previously characterised the extremes of both national identities.

Class Consciousness and National Consciousness In the Age of Revolution

I now turn to the last stage in the formation of dual national consciousness in Scotland, the period of *social diffusion* among the majority of the population. By the end of our period that majority consisted, like England, but unlike anywhere else on earth, of wage-labourers, and increasingly of urban, industrial wage-labourers. Was the balance of Scottishness and Britishness in their consciousness the same as for the dominant class, or indeed for the subordinate classes which had come before them in Scottish history? And what was the relationship between this national consciousness and the class consciousness that was to be displayed so dramatically in and around 1820? In this chapter I will argue against the answers which are most frequently given to these two questions.

The first concerns the extent to which a British identity had been adopted below the level of the Scottish ruling class. One group of historians argues that, even as late as 1815, 'Britishness' was a 'primary and permanent identity' only for those at the top of society, a small minority in relation to the population as a whole, who 'operated in an all-British context':

Socially, this was a group confined to the aristocracy and the upper reaches of the gentry, who met together, if not annually, then at least periodically, in their London houses, intermarried and sent their sons increasingly to the top English public schools. Occupationally, the group was limited to the officer corps of the army and navy, the expatriate officials of the East India Company and the retinues of the embassies abroad – careers that brought people together, often in a confined space at an early age and for a long time, people from all over the United Kingdom whose sense of personal identity was reinforced by their frequent and often perilous contacts with the 'other'.[1]

Richard Finlay has gone further, suggesting that British identity was not even a national identity for the ruling class but merely an 'elite identity'. And for the social classes below elite level, 'there was a marked ambiguity...when it comes to British identity'. Indeed, Finlay implies that the continuation of a Scottish identity after 1707 was largely the work of the subordinate social classes.[2]

The second answer assumes the first is valid, but goes on to identify Scottish identity with a joint opposition to both the British state and the capitalist society which developed in Scotland after the Treaty of Union. Peter Berresford Ellis and Seumas Mac a' Ghobhainn have claimed that:

> The Scottish Radical tradition has always gone hand in hand with Scottish nationalism, a belief that the Union with England, the removal of Scottish government from Scottish soil, and Scotland's future placed subject to the majority of English representatives in the House of Commons, was the major source of Scottish ills.[3]

And James Young, referring more specifically to the period between 1770 and 1820, has argued that:

> While a class-conscious working class began to emerge in a new context of industrialisation, the colonial relationship between the two countries was a decisive factor in shaping the social and cultural formation of the Scottish working class.

In the struggles which followed, 'the nationalism of the lower orders was increasingly seen by the English [sic] Government as evidence of a threat to the stability of Empire'.[4] The climax of this period in April 1820 took the form of what was probably the first general strike – and furthermore a *political* general strike – in the history of capitalism. The fact that this level of industrial action took place in Central Scotland, rather than say, the northwest of England, is implied by these authors to result from the fact that Scottish workers displayed a greater level of militancy than the English, which is in turn said to be a reaction to colonial domination by England. Both of these positions sit uneasily with the evidence.

As I have tried to demonstrate in previous chapters, no Scottish national consciousness had been consolidated by the time of the Union and, insofar as one had begun to form in the Lowlands, it was mainly the preserve of the emergent bourgeoisie, rather than the classes below it in society. Furthermore, this protonational consciousness was in any case substantially recast by the acceptance of the Highlands as part of the

Scottish nation in the second half of the eighteenth century. It is true that by the end of the eighteenth century the majority of people in Scotland had developed a consciousness of Scottish nationhood, but many of them – many more than there were members of the ruling class – had also developed a consciousness of British nationhood. That should be clear even from the brief discussion of Burns in the previous chapter – unless it is argued that he was considerably more removed from the experience of the common people than is usually thought to be the case.

Can we prove this one way or the other? 'We can say...how many Scots lived in one-roomed houses in Glasgow', writes Finlay, 'but we cannot tell how many of them felt more Scottish than British.'[5] Not by the same kinds of evidence, certainly, but we can infer some conclusions on the latter subject from the forms of cultural life through which the Scots expressed their feelings and beliefs, and, more importantly, from their political actions. For, although the Scottish element of that consciousness was part of the daily fabric of lived experience, in politics the British element was dominant; and this was as true for Paisley weavers as it was for Edinburgh lawyers. This may seem obvious: since there was no Scottish state, political activity would naturally have to take place at the British level. If, however, working-class radicalism was aligned to a militant Scottish nationalism, as Berresford Ellis, Mac a' Ghobhainn and Young believe, then we should expect to find as its goal, not participation in the reform or even revolutionary overthrow of the British state, but the separation of Scotland from Britain – particularly if, as Young insists, membership of the British state involved a colonial relationship with England. As we saw in Chapter 5, however, there is little evidence for such a relationship. And since the subsequent history of the labour movement in Britain does not suggest that Scottish workers are intrinsically more militant than their English or Welsh brothers and sisters, the answer to their particular militancy in 1820 must lie in combination of specific material conditions under which Scotland entered the process of capitalist industrialisation, and the responses which it generated. In what follows I will examine these conditions and the influence they exerted over the class consciousness and national consciousness of the working class.

The Consequences of Combined and Uneven Development 1: Economic

The transformation which took place in Scotland between 1746 and 1820 was unprecedented in European history and would not be seen again on such a scale until the industrialisation of Russia after 1929. Indeed, the experience of Scotland was far closer to that of Russia than England in terms of the speed and intensity with which it occurred. The middle of the eighteenth century is clearly a turning point. Before, according to Devine: 'There had been real advances within the *existing* structure of economy and society, but precious little indication yet the *overall* social fabric of Scotland was being altered.'[6] After, as Rosalind Mitchison writes: 'Scotland packed into about thirty years of crowded development from 1750 to 1780 the economic growth that in England had spread itself over two centuries.'[7] As a result of what Immanuel Wallerstein calls 'The Scottish Great Leap Forward', the Scottish economy rose in a relatively short time to equal and temporarily even surpass that of England.[8] The social consequences of 'catching up and overtaking' England have tended to be overlooked because the very act of doing so created a single British national economy whose existence has then been read back into the preceding historical period. Yet because Scotland was a society different from and less developed than England at the beginning of industrialisation and urbanisation, there were different social responses to the same experiences.

The theory that all countries must undergo the same stages of development in the same order can be traced back to the beginnings of the capitalist system.[9] In this perspective, development is characterised by an unevenness which is overcome as the backward gradually attain the same level as the more advanced. When Marx wrote in the preface to *Capital* that: 'The country that is more developed industrially only shows, to the less developed, the image of its own future', he was not suggesting that all countries would reach the future by the same route, or that arriving there would have the same implications for late developers.[10] Crucially, the prior development of some states cannot but affect the conditions under which later developers enter the world system, not least through imperialist domination which prevented the latter from becoming independent centres of capital accumulation.[11] Scotland was affected by uneven development in both senses. In the case of the Glasgow merchants during the seventeenth century, for example, their English equivalents were both in advance of them (thus showing 'the image of their own future') and used that position to prevent their achieving parity (thus affecting the conditions under which the late developing Scottish merchants entered the world system). A theory of uneven development alone, however, even in a modified form, is inadequate to explain the pattern of development in Scotland, or indeed anywhere else. We also require a theory of *combined* and uneven development.

Such a theory was developed by Leon Trotsky in an attempt to explain what he called 'the peculiarities of Russian development' in the early twentieth century, but it is capable of application in other historical periods. Trotsky argued that in relation to the advanced countries, the backward are neither condemned to *repeat* their experience, nor to find their progress towards development *blocked* by them, but under certain conditions they could *adopt* their technological, organisational and intellectual achievements. 'The privilege of historic backwardness – and such a privilege exists – permits, or rather compels, the adoption of whatever is ready in advance of any specified date, skipping a whole series of intermediate stages.' Often this process of assimilation takes place within an overall socioeconomic structure still characterised by archaism: 'Savages throw away their bows and arrows for rifles all at once, without travelling the road which lay between those two weapons in the past.' [12] The reference is to the Native American response to the European colonisation of their continent, and this is the most extreme example possible. Nevertheless, we can see the same principle at work in Scotland, which, prior to 1746, was at a far greater distance from England in socioeconomic terms than absolutist France, the greatest rival of the British state.

This is not an interpretation into which the historical record has to be forced after the event. In 1814, Walter Scott published his first novel, *Waverley*, which recounts the adventures of the eponymous hero during the '45. Near the end, the omnipresent narrator looks back from his vantage point in 1805 at the changes which had taken place in Scotland over the preceding 60 years:

> There is no European nation, which, within the course of half a century, or little more, has undergone so complete a change as the kingdom of Scotland. The effects of the insurrection of 1745, – the destruction of the patriarchal power of the Highland chiefs, the abolition of the heritable jurisdictions of the Lowland nobility and barons, – the total eradication of the Jacobite party, which, averse to intermingle with the English, or adopt their customs, long continued to pride themselves upon maintaining ancient Scottish manners and customs, – commenced this innovation. *The gradual influx of wealth, and extension of commerce, have since united to render the present people of Scotland a class of beings as different from their grandfathers, as the existing English are from those of Queen Elizabeth's time.*[13]

Near the beginning of the process, in 1755, the first issue of the *Edinburgh Review* contained an editorial in which the extent of Scottish development was considered in biological terms: 'If countries have their ages with respect to improvement, North Britain may be considered as in a state of early youth, guided and supported by the more mature strength of her kindred country.'[14] But early youth has advantages lost to the more mature. As Robert Wallace observed in 1758:

> In a smaller nation, where good agriculture and manufactures have been lately introduced, improvements will be more sensible, than in a kingdom of greater extent, more populous, and where good

agriculture and extensive commerce have been of longer standing. For this reason, though England is much richer than Scotland, and the improvements of the English much greater, the improvements in Scotland may be more striking and sensible.[15]

After outlining the 'advantages' possessed by the English in their skill at agriculture, manufacturing and trade, Wallace gives the first hint of what Alex Callinicos calls 'the disadvantages of priority' – the obverse of the 'privilege of historical backwardness' – from which British capitalism as a whole has suffered in the twentieth century.[16] The English 'have less curiosity than the Scots' and 'confine themselves to fewer branches of trade or manufactures', which, although allowing them to master these specialisms, led to new difficulties:

All these are so great advantages, that it is scarce to be thought, the English have not made proportionally greater advances than the Scots; unless it is supposed, that their more early application to trade, and their having carried it to greater a height before the Revolution, hath rendered it impossible, or very difficult, for them to multiply their trade in the same proportion, as may easily be done by the French or Scots, who may have more lately applied themselves to trade.[17]

This was not a view many shared at the time. Even as late as 1776 – the year in which *The Wealth Of Nations* was published – Lord Kames implied that economic maturity was some way off: '...may we not hope, that our progress may be rapid; and that agriculture will soon be familiar among us, and as skilfully conducted as in England?'.[18] It is instructive, therefore, to compare this very tentative optimism with the following verdict from an anonymous supplement to the sixth edition of the same book in 1815:

...it may suffice to observe in general, that there never were greater agricultural improvements carried on in any country than there have been in Scotland during the last thirty years; that the progress of the most correct systems of husbandry has been rapid and extensive beyond what the most sanguine could have anticipated; and that, in short, when we contrast the present state of agriculture in the south-eastern counties with what must have been its state about the middle of the last century...*the efforts of several centuries would seem to have been concentrated in the intermediate period.*[19]

Anonymous was right. Take, for example, the increase in levels of rent, using 1660 as our base year. Between 1660 and 1740 the national average of real rent doubled, between 1660 and 1770 it increased threefold, between 1660 and 1793 it increased 7.6 times and between

1660 and 1811 it increased 15 times. When the rate of increase finally began to stabilise at the end of the Napoleonic Wars in 1815, the total increase in real terms from 1660 may have been in the order of 15.6 times. These increases reflected prior increases in productivity. The yield of oats increased between 200 and 300 per cent between 1750 and 1800, and meat output may have increased by 600 per cent between the 1750s and the 1820s.[20] As Christopher Whatley notes: 'Such productivity and output gains have to be accounted for, as without them the industrialisation and urbanisation of Scotland could not have taken place on the scale and at the speed which they did.'[21] Let us now assess the extent of these twin processes.

Industrialisation

Industrialisation is not simply the dominance of the capitalist mode of production within an economy, since most countries have been through a stage where capitalist relations of production prevailed, but in which the agricultural sector was still the largest in the economy. Scotland was still in this position when Adam Smith published *The Wealth Of Nations* in 1776, which is one reason why, contrary to popular belief, the contents of that book are mainly devoted to agriculture.[22] Nor does industrialisation necessarily involve the dominance of large-scale or heavy industry, although in later, more consciously planned industrialisation such as that of the USSR, it has done so. During his visit in 1802 and 1803 the Swedish industrial spy, Eric Svedenstierna, passed up the opportunity to visit the Carron Iron Works – then the largest and most famous of Scottish heavy industrial plants – partly because it had apparently been hidden from prying eyes by a wall, but mainly because by English standards it was not particularly exceptional:

> The reserve of the present manager of Carron, even towards his own countrymen, is said by those who have seen the works to be a mere caprice, for this works is now neither the largest, nor is anything made there which could not be made in most of the foundries of Great Britain. It consists merely of five blast furnaces in operation, and produces little bar iron, and this, so it is said, merely for is own purposes.[23]

In fact, heavy industry – pig iron production, and consequently steamship building, railway construction and the increased demand for coal – became central to the Scottish economy only in the two decades following 1830.[24] Nevertheless, industrialisation had taken place even by the time Svedenstierna was passing up to chance to visit Carron.

Before the mid-nineteenth century, industrialisation generally fell between the advent of a capitalist economy *per se* and the shift to heavy industry, and provided the link between these processes. It involved two key stages. The first was the transition from artisanal manufacture – which had existed under all previous modes of production – to what Marx calls 'the manufacturing period proper' where 'manufacture is the predominant form taken by capitalist production'. As Marx points out, this can happen in two ways: either the capitalist assembles craftsmen together under one roof to perform their different handicrafts in the production of a commodity (i.e., cloth manufacture), or the capitalist assembles craftsmen under one roof, all of whom are skilled in the same handicraft. 'On the one hand...manufacture either introduces division of labour into a process of production, or further develops that division; on the other hand it combines together handicrafts that were formerly separate.' The end result in either case is 'a productive mechanism whose organs are human beings'. The second stage was the replacement of labour power by the instruments of labour themselves:

> In manufacture the transformation of the mode of production takes labour-power as its starting point. In large scale industry, on the other hand, the instruments of labour are the starting point. ... In manufacture the organisation of the social labour process is purely subjective: it is a combination of specialised workers. Large-scale industry, on the other hand, possesses in the machine system an entirely objective organisation of production, which confronts the worker as a pre-existing material condition of production.[25]

As Harry Braverman summarises the process, the transition from manufacture to machinofacture involves a shift from a process where the *organisation* of labour has changed to one where the *instruments* of labour have changed.[26]

The first industry to see these changes was textiles and, more specifically, cotton. We saw in Chapter 5 how the growth of the Scottish linen industry and the commanding position which it held in the British market made claims that Scotland was an English colony highly implausible. It was in this industry in particular that, that between 1730 and 1780, capitalist industrialisation was first established in the form of factories of skilled spinners and weavers, with the latter beginning to base their loom shops in proximity to the merchant warehouses and to be employed as wage-labourers, reliant on the merchants for access to the means of production, the loom. Yet within the ten years from 1780 to 1790 the technology and the skills of the employees was redirected towards cotton. Between 1770, when James Hargreaves took out the patent on his jenny which transformed cotton spinning operations, and 1822, when the Stampmaster of linen cloth made his last records, the amount produced in the west of Scotland fell from 40 per cent of the Scottish total output to less than 0.5 per cent. In 1780 there were precisely two cotton spinning mills in Scotland, but by 1787 there were 17 and by 1834 134, the majority of which were within a 25 mile radius of Glasgow. The way in which the Scottish cotton industry borrowed from the English is a classic example of combined and uneven development at work:

> In Scotland the transition was even simpler than in England, for Lanarkshire followed Lancashire into the cotton industry with a lag of some twenty years, just sufficient time for the Lancashire producers to have proved the feasibility of the new techniques, to have discovered the insatiable market for the products and to have demonstrated that substantial profits came the way of the innovator in the cotton industry.

What did the Scottish cotton masters borrow?

> The borrowing of new machines, jennys for the home and waterframes and mules for the factories, was an obvious move for the Scottish producers, and gave them the immediate advantages of late starters, since the costs of pioneering had been borne by their Lancashire rivals. It was also logical to borrow and imitate the organisational structure which had been evolved by the local linen industry, and to carry this forward to factory production as had Arkwright and others in England. The English experience was again imitated in the search for water-power sites and the building of large spinning mills and factory villages. The Scottish cotton masters did not have to bear the costs of the pioneer in any of these areas; this helps to explain the speed with which cotton grew to prominence.

Even the areas into which the Scottish industry did not follow the English, such as the production of cheaper cotton goods, were influenced by the need to find markets outside those already captured by the Lancashire pioneers, in this case fine cotton yarn.[27]

Norman Murray has estimated that the number of handloom weavers in Scotland increased from 25,000 in 1780 to 58,00 in 1800 to 78,000 in 1820, and the figure continued to grow, although at a slower rate, until decline began around 1840.[28] Approximately two thirds of these operatives worked for houses in the Glasgow and Paisley area.[29] The people who became weavers came from three different sources (in ascending order of numerical importance): the Highlands, Ireland and the rural Lowlands, migration from which, unlike similar areas in England, was not blocked by the operation of the Poor Law.[30] In Paisley during 1821, for example, only seven per cent of the inhabitants were originally from the Highlands, and these do not appear to have been primarily involved in weaving. By 1816, however, we find around 600

Highlanders employed as farm servants or labourers, and 800 in the printfields and bleachfields. One report claimed that, with their backgrounds in agriculture and fishing, Highlanders were 'not suited' for employment in such an alien activity as factory work. The role of the Irish was more significant, with perhaps as many as 25 per cent of weavers in Scotland being native Irish by 1820, of which the number employed in Glasgow and its environs was greater, reaching perhaps a third of those employed in the occupation.[31]

Urbanisation

Industrialisation was at the centre of a wider process of transformation. In 1755 the Scottish population was calculated by Alexander Webster as being 1,265,380.[32] This was only 2.5 per cent of an increase from the 1691 figure of 1,234,575.[33] By the first reliable census of 1801 it had risen to 1,608,420 and by 1831 to 2,364,368.[34] Between 1755 and 1801, the population of the west of Scotland grew by 82.7 per cent, or three times that for Scotland as a whole, while Lanarkshire grew by 80.7 per cent and Renfrewshire by 194.6 per cent.[35]

Most of the new population lived in towns. As Devine observes of Scotland in the 1750s: 'The proportion of town dwellers was increasing but the overall distribution of population was still more akin to that of Ireland, the Scandinavian countries and Poland than to the more advanced economies of England and Holland.'[36] This changed as Scotland itself became the leading 'industrial economy'. In 1700 Scotland was only the tenth most urbanised country in Western Europe, but by 1750 it was seventh, by 1800 fourth and by 1850 second only to England and Wales. By the latter date fully 35.9 per cent of the population lived in towns of over 5,000 and the *rate* of urban expansion was the highest anywhere.[37]

Take, for example, cities with more than 100,000 inhabitants. In 1800, 959,300 people, or 10.5 per cent of the total population of England and Wales lived in cities of that size; no one in Scotland did. By 1850, the figures for England and Wales were 3,992,100 people or 21.7 per cent of the total population, but for Scotland they have leapt to 490,700 people or 16.8 per cent of the total population.[38] As Iain Whyte notes: 'Urban expansion began later in Scotland and occurred at a much more rapid rate than south of the Border.' Across the eighteenth century the percentage of the English population living in towns of over 1,000 rose from 13.3 per cent to 20.3 per cent; the percentage of the Scottish population rose from 5.3 per cent to 17.3 per cent – more than a threefold increase.[39]

Given the way in which population and industry had shifted to the southwest, the experience of Glasgow is central. It grew more rapidly than any other town, expanding by 270 per cent between 1755 and

1801. As many as 50 new streets and squares may have been built in the city in the three years between 1788 and 1791.[40] And who lived in these streets and squares? On the eve of 1820 nearly one out of every ten inhabitants of Glasgow was Irish born.[41] More generally, as a parliamentary report of 1836 noted: 'There are few persons you meet with in Glasgow who can say that their fathers were born in that town.'[42] Nor was Glasgow unique in the west in this respect. Between 1755 and 1801 the population of Paisley grew from 2,509 to 31,179 and it has been estimated that between 15,000 and 20,000 of these were immigrants, the majority from either the surrounding Ayrshire countryside or from the Highlands and the Western Isles. 'Thus Paisley acquired a work-force the majority of whom were experiencing for the first time the conditions of employment in industrial production.'[43]

The conditions in which these migrants were expected to live and work were inhuman. Again, the experience of Glasgow is central. 'The city which boasted it was the second in Empire', writes Devine, 'was apparently also the first in human degradation'. The population rose from 7,385 in 1801 to 274,533 in 1841, the biggest increase of 45.9 per cent taking place between 1811 and 1821, the very decade when average real wages began a 20 year fall, or rather, collapse, across the range of occupations. Of the other major British cities only Manchester, with an increase of 40.4 per cent, experienced comparable growth. The infrastructure of the city was unable to cope with increases of this magnitude, especially in the provision of basic amenities like housing and sanitation. One outcome was that mortality per 1,000 of the population, which had fallen from 32.2 to 17.1 between 1791 and 1801 now began to rise again, reaching 21.2 in 1811 and averaging 24.8 between 1821 and 1824. From 1818, and contributing to these figures, there were recurrent epidemics of infectious diseases, of which typhus proved the biggest killer. Yet the growing urban crisis coincided with the dominance of the very ideology which was least prepared to countenance public intervention to deal with it. The funds available through the Scottish Poor Law were inadequate and fell throughout the period: totalling £14,487 in 1813, they temporarily rose in 1815 at the beginning of the post-war slump, but declined thereafter reaching a low of £11,413 in 1822.[44] As social need increased, the funding necessary to meet it decreased, as the bourgeoisie abandoned the paternalist attitudes which had softened inequalities in the old, fundamentally rural Scotland where social power had also carried personal obligation.

The mere statistics of social transformation can only hint at the change in life experience undergone by the people they represent. What were the new forms of consciousness, ideology and solidarity which arose from the impact of combined and uneven development in Scotland?

The Consequences of Combined and Uneven Development 2: Social and Political

Combined and uneven development is indeterminate in its results. In the period of the transition from feudalism to capitalism as a world system societies where the transition was at an early stage often assimilated the achievements of those which had completed it – not to speed up the process, but the better to preserve the existing form of society. Consequently, as Trotsky noted: 'The [backward] nation...not infrequently debases the achievements borrowed from outside in the process of adapting them to its own more primitive culture.' In the case of Russia itself, a feudal absolutist state initiated the process of capitalist industrialisation during the 1860s, principally in order to compete militarily in a European state system where mass-produced armaments were indispensable. As a result the most backward society in Europe also contained the largest factories with the most up-to-date technologies.[45]

Naturally this had implications for the class consciousness of the working class produced by the process of industrialisation. That class was not originally drawn, as it had been in England, from members of the existing urban craft guilds, but mainly from the peasantry, who were plunged into urban life and the discipline of factory labour and denied political expression for their grievances by the same autocratic regime which had called them into being for its own ends:

> Strikes forbidden by law, underground circles, illegal proclamations, street demonstrations, encounters with the police and with troops – such was the school created by the combination of a swiftly developing capitalism with an absolutism slowly surrendering its positions. The concentration of workers in colossal enterprises, the intensive character of government persecution, and finally the impulsiveness of a young and fresh proletariat, brought it about that the political strike, so rare in western Europe, became in Russia the fundamental method of struggle. [46]

These developments were central to the way in which the Russian revolutions of 1905 and 1917 developed in the cities. As we shall see, no direct parallels with Scotland are possible, but the two key elements identified by Trotsky – a rural, undisciplined working class and a state apparatus inherited from the transitional period – were both present and exercised a profound influence over the initial formation of the working class movement. We will examine these in turn.

The Condition of the Working Class

The development of the British *industrial* working class has been infinitely more unified than that of the peasantry or of pre-industrial artisans. But just because it came into existence on both sides of the Border at the same time, and underwent the same experiences, we should not assume that the response to these experiences was the same. As Edward Thompson recognised in the 'Preface' to *The Making Of The English Working Class*:

..the Scottish story is significantly different. Calvinism was not the same thing as Methodism, although it is difficult to say which, in the early nineteenth century, was worse. We [i.e., the English] had no peasantry in England comparable to the Highland migrants. And the popular culture was very different. It is possible, at least until the 1820s, to regard the English and Scottish experiences as distinct, since trade union and political links were impermanent and immature.[47]

I think that Thompson is right, both about the difference in national experience and the point at which these differences were overcome. Although industrialisation took place more or less simultaneously in both nations, Scotland largely 'skipped the intervening stages' between peasant self-sufficiency and wage labour which England had experienced. 'Scotland entered on the capitalist path later than England' wrote Trotsky in 1925, 'a sharper turn in the life of the masses of the people gave rise to a sharper political reaction.'[48]

Of course 'the masses' did not consist solely of migrants from the rural Lowlands plus the Highlands and Ireland. Some were members of the urban guilds, or their descendants, but they too experienced the 'sharpness' to which Trotsky refers. Unlike their equivalents elsewhere in western Europe, or the merchants in their own country, Scottish craftsmen did not begin to organise themselves into artisan guilds until the fifteenth and sixteenth centuries. Once they had taken this step, however, the 'incorporations' provided them with effective economic control over the various crafts, most importantly by controlling the number of entrants into the profession and the nature of the training which apprentices had to undergo in order to become time-served. In England, where the organisation of the artisan guilds was in any case more fluid, reflecting an economy where capitalist relations of production had already made far more inroads than across the Border, guild privileges came under increasing legal attack from the end of the seventeenth century in particular. It was not until the latter half of the eighteenth century that equivalent moves were made in Scotland. This was partly a result of the expansion of the market. On the one hand, skilled journeymen chose to set up on their own account, either within the burgh (thus risking a fine) or outside, where the incorporation had no authority. On the other hand, because of the increase in legitimate numbers, the master might began to treat apprentices as workers, to be trained by the journeymen, not as someone who was effectively part of the household for the five or seven years of his training. In some cases, masters hired skilled labour from the country who had no formal training at all. The result, in the case of the first, was to weaken the guilds externally, by placing masters outside their powers of regulation, and in the case of the second, to begin the process of class differentiation within the craft. Increasingly, as the eighteenth century drew to a revolutionary close, those working in the various trades – most importantly the handloom weavers – began to be, and to perceive themselves to be, wage-earners who would never rise to become masters themselves.[49]

The situation of these workers was still relatively privileged, however, compared to the conditions which the majority of the new working class found in the slums of Glasgow and its satellite towns. The social explosion which this combustible human material threatened was widely recognised by the ruling class and its ideologues. Walter Scott was one of the first to do so. Underneath the surface optimism of the famous passages from *Waverley* quoted earlier in this chapter lay a deeper pessimism over the changes which capitalism was bringing to Scottish society. At the beginning of 1820 he was consoling himself in a letter with this thought: 'The poor ARE to be trusted in almost every situation where they have not been disunited by circumstances from their natural superiors.' But as he goes on to say in the same letter, these circumstances of disunity were becoming the norm, as the very nature of industrial capitalism was undermining the sense of obligation which had supposedly regulated the attitude of feudal superiors to their tenants or even the relationship between master and man that had been a feature of manufacture before the coming of the factory.[50] He was not alone in making these observations. As one anonymous contributor to *Blackwood's Edinburgh Magazine* noted, again in 1820:

> The immense extent of the manufacturing establishments in many parts of England and Scotland, has rendered it...a matter of extreme difficulty for those at the head of them to keep up anything like those habits of minute acquaintance and tangible sympathy with their people, which prevailed among the masters and apprentices of the comparatively limited and trifling establishments of former days.[51]

Scott, however, went further. In the spring of 1820, as the crisis broke, he extended his analysis: 'The unhappy dislocation which has taken place betwixt the Employer and those under his employment has been attended with very fatal consequences. Much of this is owing to the steam engine.'

In the days when manufacture was dependent on the water-mill the employer had no choice in his location, but had to recruit workmen from the nearest village and consequently spent time trying to influence their behaviour. 'This is now quite changed':

The manufactures are transferred to great towns where a man may assemble 500 workmen one week and dismiss the next without having any further connection with them than to receive a week's work for a week's wages nor any further solicitude about their future fate than if they were so many old shuttles. A superintendence of the workers considered as so many moral and rational beings is thus a matter totally unconnected with the Employer's usual thoughts and cares. They have now seen the danger of suffering a great population to be thus separated from the influence of their employers and given over to the management of their own societies in which the cleverest and most impudent fellows always get the management of the others and become bell-weathers in every sort of mischief.[52]

And this mischief was not generated only by the workplace where they laboured, but by the environment in which they lived. As Hugh Miller noted, at the distance of the mid-century:

When the dangerous classes of a country are located in its remote districts, as they were in Scotland in the early half of the last century [i.e., the eighteenth century], it is comparatively easy to deal with them: but the sans culottes of Paris in its First Revolution, placed side by side with its executive Government, proved very formidable indeed: nor is it, alas! very improbable that the ever-growing masses of our large towns, broken loose from the sanction of religion and morals, may yet terribly avenge on the upper classes and the Churches of the country the indifferency with which they have been suffered to sink.[53]

It would be wrong to imagine, as many commentators like Miller did, that working class organisation was simply propelled by inchoate rage; in many cases it embodied a political response which drew on the previous experience of migrants to the industrial towns. This was particularly the case for those who came from the Highlands and Ireland. As William Knox notes of the popular reaction to the Peterloo massacre:

The actions of the landowner's government...alienated large numbers of people migrating to urban centres from the Scottish Highlands and Ireland. Their historical experiences of dealing with the landowning classes and the bitterness which that had induced in them were intensified by these displays of aristocratic arrogance.[54]

We know far more about the attitudes of the Irish than the Highlanders. James Paterson of Kilmarnock, who later owned a newspaper in the town, recalled in his memoirs how during his apprenticeship as a printer he came into contact with one of the local radical groups, whose members were virtually all handloom weavers. Among these was an Irishman, an ex-soldier, whose political demands exceeded those normally associated with the radical movement, including those for 'no king, no lords, no gentry, no taxes!'.[55] For the Catholics in particular, there were additional reasons for political radicalism which were not solely connected with the situation in Ireland itself, but also with their position within Scottish society: 'They are very numerous', wrote Bishop Andrew Scott to Lord Sidmouth in August 1819, 'very poor, have nothing to lose in a revolution, and are flattered by the reformists with the hopes of ameliorating their circumstances by a revolution'.[56] As the Bishop was no doubt all too painfully aware, the Catholic Irish were also under less direct ideological control than they would have been in Ireland: there were no Catholic schools in the west of Scotland until 1816 and as late as 1836 'there was only one priest in Glasgow for every 9,000–11,000 Catholics'.[57]

What was the level of Irish involvement in the events between 1815 and 1820? The point to note is that the Irish presence in Scotland was simply much greater than in England: 'Only 2.9 per cent of the population of England and Wales were Irish in 1851, compared to 7.2 per cent in Scotland.'[58] Martin Mitchell has presented evidence that suggests that the Irish presence among the radicals was at least proportionate to their presence in the workforce, if not to the population as a whole. Around 30 leaders of the underground radical organisation were arrested in February 1817. Of the 13 whose nationality or occupation have been established, five were Irish and four were weavers. The events of 1820 reveal a similar picture. Two of the 16 men sentenced to transportation for their part in the Battle of Bonnymuir were originally from County Down: one was a stocking-maker, the other (and this will come as no surprise) a weaver. Two of the seven men arrested for their part in the riot in Greenock were Irish, both labourers.[59]

What were the religious backgrounds of the Irish who were involved in the movement? Here we encounter two disabling assumptions. The first is that the Protestant Irish in Scotland were invariably Loyalist defenders of British imperialism and the Ascendancy in Ireland, and were able to fuse with the native Scottish working class through a shared Protestantism:

Among the immigrants the Protestant Irish were in a clear minority but they felt far more at home in Scotland than the more numerous Catholic Irish, since they were familiar with Scottish institutions, shared the same Protestant faith and were, in many cases, returning to the land of their forefathers.[60]

According to this assumption these religious and social solidarities invariably led, not only to differentiation from the Catholic Irish immigrants, but also to opposition to them in a way that prevented solidarity as workers. The second is that the Catholic Irish in Scotland were mainly 'preoccupied with the unfolding of nationalist politics at home' and that 'their lack of engagement with Scottish affairs helped restrict opportunities for concerted action for decades to come'.[61] In some versions of this thesis (although not that of Elaine McFarland quoted here) the obverse of Catholic withdrawal from Scottish or British working class political life was that they allowed employers to use them as blacklegs or cheap labour, thus legitimising the opposition of Protestant workers. Neither of these assumptions stands up to an examination of what happened between 1815 and 1820.

First, although the careful discussion by Mitchell suggests that Irish participation in the secret societies was limited to Protestants, they did not aim to exclude Catholics from their organisations and indeed consciously sought to involve them in activity. Mitchell notes that these Protestants must be distinguished from those who were involved in the anti-Catholic Orange Lodges being established in Scotland at this time: 'The Protestant Irish reformers in Scotland in these years should be regarded as being part of the radical Presbyterian United Irish tradition, which was non-sectarian and which desired the same political, social and religious rights for all.'[62]

Second, even if Irish Catholics played only a limited role in the secret societies, there is strong evidence to suggest that they, alongside the Protestant Irish, were heavily involved in the general strike of April 1820. Aside from evidence concerning particular individuals (which Mitchell presents) the unanimity of the response to the strike call among weavers and spinners – given the extent to which the Irish had filled the latter occupation in particular – makes the following conclusion difficult to avoid:

> As the overwhelming majority of spinners in this period appear to have been Irish and most spinners stopped work in April 1820, it is not unreasonable to argue that Irish spinners, like Irish weavers, went on strike in support of the radicals.[63]

Finally, we must ask whether involvement on the part of both the Protestant and Catholic Irish principally intended to aid the movement for a republic in Ireland, rather than in Britain. There is evidence that Irish membership of the United Scotsmen or participation in their activities during the 1790s was conducted on this basis.[64] By the second wave of radicalism, immigration had taken on a permanent character and motivations correspondingly shifted:

> During 1816–20 most of the Irish workers who were involved in the political agitations in the west of Scotland almost certainly participated not for the sake of Ireland, but for the same reasons as Scottish workers: they were suffering as a result of the economic distress of the

time and became convinced that only drastic political change would end their agony.[65]

The Unreformed State

It is possible that the pressures building up on the side of the working class might have been less had the British state in Scotland been more responsive to its demands. But, as I argued in Chapter 3, this quasi-independent apparatus retained all the most reactionary attributes of the Scottish state which merged with England in 1707. Feudalism was destroyed in Scotland after 1746 more thoroughly and consciously than it had been in England, but the superstructure which had grown up during the feudal epoch remained in place and provides the second parallel with the Russian situation of 100 years later. As Devine notes:

> After the Union there were 45 parliamentary seats in the Scottish counties and 15 in the burghs, each with 2,600 and 1,500 voters respectively. This amounted to approximately 0.2 per cent of Scotland's population in the later eighteenth century. This tiny electorate was unique even by the pre-democratic standards of eighteenth-century Britain, as both Ireland and England had a signif-icantly larger franchise. For instance, the Dublin electorate of 3,000–4,000 was greater than the total number of those with the vote in all the counties of Scotland and nearly as much as the entire electorate combined.[66]

In fact, as even such an apologist for the Dundas regime as Michael Fry is forced to admit:

> For the Commons, Scotland had the most narrow and oligarchical franchise of any of the three kingdoms under the Crown. ... The electoral system seemed designed for corruption. In the thirty county seats eccentric rules for the suffrage, based on a motley collection of antique laws, restricted it to large landowners, keeping out the lesser gentry and small farmers who often enjoyed it in England.[67]

To be precise, the county franchise in 1790 was 2,655. 'This meant that the entire Scottish [county] electorate equalled that of Preston in England (2,800), was less than half as large as that of Bristol (6,000), one fifth that of the City of London (12,000) and one-seventh that of Westminster.' In individual counties the number of voters could be as few as three, as was the case in Bute.[68] The burghal electorate was even smaller:

> ...the electoral manipulation was less complex but worse. So far from there being any popular franchise, not even richest and most respected

citizens were necessarily represented. The MP was chosen by the corporations on which, as variously defined in the sett (or constitution), membership was confined to certain interests, usually the old merchant's or craftsmen's guilds. Moreover, each council elected its successor, and was naturally inclined to elect itself. Only a minute fraction of the urban population thus enjoyed the franchise.[69]

Only 33 people were enfranchised in the Scottish capital of Edinburgh. In 1790 only nine county and burgh elections were even contested.[70]

One pamphlet of 1782 attacked not the Union, but the fact that the Scots had 'been excluded that proportion of liberty which had been enjoyed by England', as a result of which: 'The members of the aristocracy have monopolised the blessings of government, and carefully retained in their pay a chosen band of inferiors, who have celebrated the praises of a government, the benefits of which were confined to themselves and their employers.'[71] It was not merely the franchise that was restricted: before 1832 Scotland was virtually a one-party state in a way that England had ceased to be. And that party was the Tory party. As Henry Cockburn recounts in his memoirs:

This party engrossed almost the whole wealth, and rank, and public office, of the country, and at least three-fourths of the population. ... With the people put down and the Whigs powerless, Government was the master of nearly every individual in Scotland, but especially in Edinburgh, which was the chief seat of its influence. The infidelities of the French gave it all the pious; their atrocities all the timid; rapidly-increasing taxation and establishments all the venal; the higher and middle ranks were at its command, and the people at its feet. The pulpit, the bench, the bar, the colleges, the parliamentary electors, the press, the magistracies, the local institutions, were so completely at the service of the party in power, that the idea of independence, besides being monstrous and absurd, was suppressed by a feeling of conscious ingratitude. ... [p]ersons were sent to the criminal courts as jurymen very nearly according to the discretion of the Sheriff of their county; and after they got there, those who were to try the prosecution were picked for that duty by the presiding judge, unchecked by any peremptory challenge. In other words, we had no free political institutions whatever.

The consequences of this were exactly what might have been expected, and all resolved into universal prostration. ... There was no free and, consequently, no discussing press. ... Nor was the absence of a free public press compensated by any freedom of public speech. Public *political* meetings could not arise, for the elements did not exist. I doubt if there was one during the twenty-five years that succeeded the year 1795. Nothing was viewed with such horror as any political congregation not friendly to existing power. No one could have taken a part in the business without making up his mind to be a doomed man. No prudence could protect against the falsehood and inaccuracy of spies; and a first conviction of sedition by a judge-picked jury was followed by fourteen years transportation. *As a body to be deferred to, no public existed.* Opinion was only recognised when expressed through what we acknowledged to be its legitimate organs; which meant its formal or official outlets. Public bodies therefore might speak each for itself, but the general community, as such, had no admitted claim to be consulted or cared for. The result, in a nation devoid of popular political rights, was, that people were dumb, or if they spoke out, were deemed audacious. The wishes of the people were openly despised, but it was thought and openly announced, as a necessary precaution against revolution, that they should be thwarted.

Cockburn cites as an example the case of a congregation who applied, in 1800, to the government, as patron of their church, for an admired deputy clergyman to be given the place of minister on the death of the incumbent: 'The answer, written by a member of the cabinet, was, that the single fact of the people having interfered so far as to express a wish was conclusive against what they desired; and another appointment was made.'[72]

Several Scottish reformers wrote to their English counterparts on the theme of the greater level of repression which they faced. Lord Daer, the eldest son of the Earl of Selkirk, but a radical nevertheless, wrote to Charles (future Earl) Grey at the beginning of 1793 responding to the suggestion that the reformers in Scotland should take the lead because they were proportionally more numerous than those in England. Daer agreed with this assessment, but added that their numbers would not be enough to protect them:

If we are more numerous I believe also we are much more oppressed. By every act implying favour to Reform the people here expose themselves either to the heavy hand of government or to the unceasing weight of little aristocratic oppression. If set forward alone, the arbitrary attacks will be more pointed than if countenanced by their friends in England: at least they may think so, which is the same, and they will feel all the bitterness of desertion in distress.[73]

Thomas Fyshe Palmer wrote to the same correspondent later that year from the Tolbooth in Perth, while awaiting trial:

If the servants of the crown can pack the jury which is to sit on the accused, if they have the dreadful power of any punishment short of death which servility or interest may dictate, and if from their proceedings, no appeal lies, it is evident that a despotism equal to that under the Stewarts prevails in Scotland, insulting in proportion as a semblance for the forms of freedom is presumed.[74]

At the beginning of 1793 Charles Grey moved a motion in Parliament to appoint a committee of enquiry into parliamentary representation. Reformers in both Scotland and England began a petitioning movement in support of Grey which produced 21 petitions presented to the House of Commons from Scotland, as opposed to 14 from England. Neither of these results is very creditable but, considering that the Scots were subjected to a level of repression as yet unknown in England, 'in comparison with the outcome of the English campaign, the achievement of Scots radicals could be viewed as a triumph'.[75]

Thompson has summed up the difference between England and Scotland. In the former:

> ...the Government was faced with a series of obstacles: an indefinite law, the jury system (which humiliated authority by twice acquitting Daniel Eaton and by acquitting Thomas Walker in 1794), a small but brilliant Foxite opposition among whose number was the great advocate Thomas Erskine (who led the defence in several trials), a public opinion saturated with constitutionalist rhetoric and willing to spring to the defence of any invasion of individual liberties.

In the latter, 'the judges were docile or partisan, the juries could be picked with impunity.' The protections enjoyed by the English provided real limits to the activities of the state. 'If any – faced by the records of Tyburn and of repression – are inclined to question the value of these limits, they should contrast the trial of Hardy and his colleagues with the treatment of Muir, Gerrald, Skirving and Palmer in 1793–4 in the Scottish courts.'[76] The greater presence of the middle class in the reform movement in Scotland than in England is therefore explicable, not as the result of some intrinsic backwardness on the part of Scottish workers, but because the middle class in Scotland had far more to protest about than their English equivalents.

The situation for artisans and workers was, however, in some respects even worse than Thompson suggests. For the only aspect of the state in Scotland which met the needs of workers with anything approaching regularity – the juridical apparatus through which the wages and conditions of workers in the guilds were regulated – was also the only aspect which was under threat from the bourgeoisie.

The new employers opposed the use which the guilds could make of the courts to increase their wages. For the former it offended against the doctrines of market supremacy that increasingly characterised bourgeois ideology. (And which, as we have seen, was also leading them to oppose municipal taxation as a means of solving the urban crisis.) The ferocity with which members of the Scottish legal establishment responded to the Radical movement of the 1790s, was not inconsistent with a degree of paternalism towards the guilds, as long as they kept their place. The same attitude which informed Braxfield and his colleagues in sentencing Muir and his comrades for stirring up the lower orders against the system itself, also lay behind his support for the arrangement by which workers could find some redress, and which consequently gave at least partial legitimacy to society in their eyes. If industry had remained in the traditional forms long established in the burghs along the Scottish east coast, the use of the courts might have been tolerated, but in the hands of an industrialised and volatile workforce it no longer played the same stabilising role. For the new employers and their ideologues, education in a version of Adam Smith's ideas which emphasised the free market at the expense of his mistrust of employer organisation, the system of regulated order typical of the feudal and transitional economy was an obstacle to accumulation and had to be destroyed. The judges, magistrates and justices who had operated the existing system rapidly adapted to that which was replacing it. Hamish Fraser argues that the transformation from a 'social' economy (perhaps based on a deeper 'moral' economy) to a 'market' economy within the law occurred between 1808 and 1813, when trade union organisation in itself became a criminal offence after the defeat of the Handloom Weavers' Association and the trial of its leading members. Even as late as 1808 Lord Meadowbank was in a minority when he rhetorically asked 'what it is that fixes the rate of reasonable wages, except a free market'. Only six years later, after the statutes on wage regulation, which had existed since the sixteenth century, had been abolished in both England and Scotland, Sir John Sinclair could pretend that the answer had never been in doubt: 'It does not appear...that [the authority of magistrates to regulate wages] was often exercised; these magistrates, with much wisdom have commonly left the price of labour like any other commodity in a well-regulated market, to find its own level.'[77] So fell the last remaining defence offered by pre-industrial Scottish society to the new capitalist order.

Scottish Radicalism and British National Consciousness

Harold Perkin has written that: 'It was between 1815 and 1820 that the working class was born.'[78] If he means by this that the development of separate working-class *consciousness* was completed during these years then the claim can be sustained for both Scotland and England. The Battle of Waterloo in 1815 saw the end to nearly 20 years of war against France. The collapse in demand for armaments and munitions more generally brought widespread unemployment, which was then exacerbated by the return of demobilised soldiers and renewed emigration from the north of Ireland. Adding further to working class distress was the abolition of income tax and the consequent shifting of taxation onto essential consumer goods like salt and soap. Hardest hit of all occupational groups were the handloom weavers.[79]

Norman Murray has demonstrated the involvement of weavers in the reform movement, for which there seem to be three reasons specific to them. First, the defeat of their attempts to unionise in 1812 and the consequent blocking of any road to improved conditions through workplace organisation. Second, the decline in living standards (evidence suggests their wages may have halved between 1815 and 1818), partly as a result of the wage-cuts imposed after the defeat of 1812, partly as a result of a cyclical downturn in demand. Third, the political doctrines associated with the movement after 1815 and articulated by, for example, William Cobbett, were compatible in their demands for male suffrage and the secret ballot with those traditionally supported by the weavers since the 1790s. The question of why they tended to belong to the physical force wing of the movement is less clear, although Murray suggests that the peculiar intensity of economic hardship in the 1810s, combined with the realisation, at least among a minority of weavers, that their difficulties stemmed from the beginnings of long-term decline of the industry, rather than short-term cyclical fluctuations.[80]

A radical tradition had existed in Scotland since the formation of the Friends of the People in 1792. However it was the post-war crisis which brought for the first time the mass of artisans and workers into the movement for political reform, which had previously been dominated by the petty bourgeoisie and dissident members of the bourgeoisie themselves. Their core demands for the right to vote for working men and annual parliaments met, however, with the same contempt that they had when voiced by their social superiors. On 1 April 1820 a group calling itself the Committee of Organisation for Forming a Provisional Government issued a proclamation across the western central belt calling for a general strike and rising in pursuit of these demands. The response was dramatic. The Lord Provost of Glasgow, Monteith, claimed in a letter to the Home Office that: 'Almost the whole population of the working classes have obeyed the orders contained in the treasonable proclamation by striking work.'[81] Around 60,000 struck along the Clyde valley, which, given the centrality of this region to the industrial revolution, must have been a large proportion of the world working class at that date. The human material for the industrial revolution in Scotland had, in most cases, not experienced artisanal labour or even urban life before employment in the mills and factories. Inevitably the speed and completeness with which Scottish society changed had an impact on the emergent working class movement and its politics. It seems possible, therefore, that even though the leadership of the movement between 1815 and 1820 came from an established occupation in decline – the handloom weavers – the greater level of industrial militancy in Scotland at this time was the reaction of an unprepared population to the speed and intensity of the industrialisation process.

The general strike of 1820 clearly demonstrated a qualitative shift in the emergence of working-class consciousness, although the separation between reformist and revolutionary consciousness was not – and could not – be clear at this date, if only because of the nature of the state meant that reforms themselves required insurrectionary activity. The shift was, however, also evident in much smaller ways. Knox draws attention to the changed rules of the Edinburgh Society of Bookbinders which had originally allowed both masters and journeymen to be members, but in 1822 were amended to allow only the latter to do so.[82] To what extent had national consciousness also emerged by this time? And, if so, *which* national consciousness?

The risings which accompanied the strike itself were abortive, largely because they were intended to occur simultaneously with insurrections in the north of England which the Scottish insurgents believed – mistakenly, as it happened – had been called off.[83] This should not be seen as a dependence on English workers. Clarke and Dickson (in an article with which I am otherwise in broad agreement) write that: 'Even in the insurrectionary phase of 1819–20, the assault on the British state was to be led by the English working class.'[84] The problem with this formulation, changing what needs to be changed, is the same as with those which identify the Scottish bourgeoisie as the 'junior partner' in the British Empire. Although Scottish workers were aware that different conditions pertained on either side of the border (since their demands were intended to remove these differences), they do not appear to have considered themselves as being 'led' by their English brothers and sisters, but to have realised that the British state was susceptible to overthrow on one side of the border. I will return to this point, but it is important to realise that these attitudes go back to the very beginning of Scottish radicalism.

I have already quoted a letter from Lord Daer to Charles Grey highlighting the greater levels of oppression suffered by the Scots. Daer believed that Scotland was also oppressed by England: 'Scotland has long groaned under the chains of England and knows that its connection there has been the cause of its greatest misfortunes.' Or again: 'We have existed a conquered province for two centuries.' It is significant therefore that he did not advocate separation, but rather a closer Union based on the unity of the people, rather than the state: 'We have suffered a misery which is perhaps inevitable to a lesser and remote country in a junction where the Governing powers are united but the Nations are not.' Even though, according to Daer, many of the Friends of the People were opposed to the Union he was not:

> I for one should still be of that opinion did I not look upon it that a thorough Parliamentary Reform would necessarily place us in a much better situation whilst at the same time relieve you from that vermin from this country who infect your court, your parliament and every establishment. I, therefore, wish a closer Union of the Nations...

Daer stresses the need for a Convention in England similar to that already being planned in Scotland, and for the two to unite in one British body ('I look upon it as of the highest consequence...to get Scotland to unite in the same Assembly without sending its Delegates thro' any intermediate Assembly for Scotland alone.') The individual Scottish societies should be able to correspond directly with the English. Not only would this strengthen the movement but it would effectively disarm those in the Scottish movement who wanted to follow a separate path:

> One of the greatest bonds of union betwixt the two nations at present is that the Reformers here feel that they have need to lean on you [i.e., the English reformers]. If it is possible once to teach them that they can take the lead many may be for bidding you farewell. The very grievance of our present persecution may therefore be turned to account. Were you to neglect us, it might excite the worst spirit of indignation and despair and even if contrary to our information, you are as much persecuted as us, but still show that you think of us and that you exert yourselves for us; tho' it should be in vain, it will help to rivet us to you.[85]

At no time in the history of the radical movement between 1792 and 1820 was Scottish nationalism the predominant political ideology. As John Brims has written:

> ...it is surely significant that the United Scotsmen's oath called upon prospective members to swear that they would persevere in endeavouring 'to form a brotherhood of affection amongst Britons of every description' and 'to obtain an equal, full and adequate Representation of all the People of Great Britain'.[86]

Virtually the same form of words reappears in the oath which one of the secret societies which emerged in 1815 required its members to swear:

> In the awful presence of God, I, A.B., do voluntarily swear that I will persevere in my endeavours to form a brotherhood of affection

amongst Britons of every description who are considered worthy of confidence; and that I will persevere in my endeavours to obtain for all the people of Great Britain and Ireland not disqualified by crimes or insanity the elective franchise at the age of 21 with free and equal representation and annual parliaments.[87]

It is true that Scottish radicals continued to look to their own national history for inspiration. William Aiton, the Sheriff-Substitute at Hamilton, describes how, on 13 June 1815, a crowd of perhaps 10,000 marched from Strathaven to Drumclog:

They went first to the place where the Covenanters defeated Claverhouse, and from thence to a cairn of stones or tumulus, on the farm of Allanton, Ayrshire, about two miles from the field of Drumclog, where they imagined Sir William Wallace had fought his first battle with the English.

Yet as the Sheriff plainly saw, the search for revolutionary ancestors was not primarily inspired by nationalist motives:

Ever since the lower orders in Scotland gave up the study of religious opinion, and wrangling about abstruse points in divinity, and the purity of religious sects, and began to study politics, *too many of them have shown an inclination to notice and bring to view every occurrence, whether recent or ancient, wherein successive resistance has been opposed to any regular and established authority.* It can only be from such motives that the skirmish at Drumclog was pompously celebrated on the 13th June, 1815, by an assemblage of people, who marched to the field of action with military ensigns and music, for the purpose, as they said, of 'Commemorating the Victory obtained by their ancestors, the Covenanters, over the Kings Troops, commanded by Captain Graham.'[88]

At demonstrations in Paisley during 1819 the banners not only bore the names of William Wallace and Robert the Bruce but also invoked the Magna Carta and the rights of Britons. One resolution passed by a meeting of reformers at Rutherglen on 23 October 1819 stated their opposition to government 'subversion of the British constitution' while another called for 'Universal Suffrage and Annual Parliaments: without which, and election by Ballot, it is impossible to save this country (Britain) from Military despotism.'[89] Those attending the Rutherglen meeting sang 'God Save the King' and 'Rule, Britannia' – expressions of a reformist attitude to the British state similar to that expressed by Burns in 'The Dumfries Volunteers'.[90] (Even those radicals whose work is tinged more explicitly with Scottish nationalism did not lose all sense of

historical perspective. James Callender, in a polemic against Samuel
Johnson, was perfectly capable of registering the greater radicalism of
the Independents compared with the Covenanters during the War of the
Three Kingdoms, noting in particular the absence of religious bigotry
among the former compared with the latter.[91]) Nor is it the case that
Scottish radicals were unconcerned with contemporary events in
England. On 11 September 1819 the second meeting in that year to
demand reform was held on Meikleriggs Muir near Paisley:

> They marched to Meikleriggs in military style, each body of men
> carrying banners with political slogans, and headed with a brass band.
> The most popular marching song was 'Scots Wha Ha'e'. The flags
> were edged with black crepe, black cloth draped over the platform,
> and most of the speakers were dressed in the cloths they reserved for
> funerals, all in token of mourning for those who had been killed in the
> 'Battle of Peterloo'...

After the speeches were over a collection was held for the widows and
orphans of those who had died on St. Peter's Fields.[92] The clearest
example of the predominance of Britishness is, however, given by the
general strike of April 1820 itself.

The proclamation which detonated the strike was addressed to 'the
Inhabitants of Great Britain and Ireland', whom it calls 'Britons', evoking
'those rights consecrated to them, by MAGNA CHARTA and the BILL of
RIGHTS'.[93] For some modern Scottish nationalists such an assumption
of the primacy of British identity combined with a reliance on the
symbols of English Radicalism can only mean one thing – the
proclamation must be the product of English *agents provocateurs*![94] In
fact, as Peter Holt has demonstrated, the text was most probably a collaborative effort between four Glaswegian weavers and an English
Radical called Joseph Brayshaw, who might have introduced the
references to Magna Carta.[95] This is of twofold significance: first, because
none of his Scottish colleagues felt it necessary to remove this or other
references to the English historical tradition; and second, because
saturated with the imagery of English radicalism as the proclamation is,
the workers who read it took it as their cue to begin strike action in
support of the Radical demands.

The same attitudes prevailed down to the final dissolution of the *ancien
regime* in Scotland. According to Henry Cockburn at the Jubilee to
celebrate the passing of the 1832 Reform Bill on 10 August, between
30,000 and 40,000 people assembled on Bruntsfield Links in Edinburgh
where: 'They passed an address to his Majesty, the House of Commons,
and Earl Grey, and sang "God Save the King", "Rule, Britannia" and
"Scots Wha Hae Wi' Wallace Bled"'.[96] The report in *The Scotsman* gives
the figure as double that stated by Cockburn and indicates that the

procession also included models of William Wallace and a thistle nearly ten foot high.[97]

The adoption of English radical imagery in Scotland was reciprocated by the adoption of Scottish radical imagery in England. Indeed, the appropriation of one song – Burn's 'Scots Wha Ha'e' – by English Radicals is a perfect illustration of this process. Edward Thompson reports on one English demonstration of 1819: 'At Sheffield a monster procession marched to the Brocco behind bands playing the '"Dead March in Saul" and "Scots Wha Ha'e Wi' Wallace Bled".' (Indeed, the matter is more complex still for, at a similar event in Newcastle, the demonstration assembled to the tune of the Jacobite song 'Johnnie Cope', although presumably this is more to do with the excellence of the tune than an indication of latent support for the Stuarts.)[98] 'Scots Wha Ha'e' was still being sung in the Lancashire cotton mills in the 1830s 'as a rallying song for liberty'.[99] In his history of the Chartist movement R.G. Gammage records a meeting of 'several thousand persons' at Sunderland in 1838: 'Before the business of the meeting commenced the united bands struck up with the fine old martial and patriotic air of "Scots Wha Ha'e Wi' Wallace Bled".'[100] As Eric Evans writes of the English radicals of this period: '"British" is the dominant descriptor of patriotic identification; and at any level more local than that of "Britain", the English were more likely to identify with their own regions and localities than with the whole country of England *per se*.'[101] It is clear that, for the workers referred to above, 'British' now included 'Scottish'.

Finally, we should note the following song:

> What land has not seen Britain's crimson flag flying,
> The *meteor of murder, but justice the plea*,
> Has the blood of her sons, in her ruthless wars dying,
> Been the warm showers! to nourish fair liberty's tree.
> Yes! if placemen and paupers in myriads unceasing,
> If nations degraded, white slave trade increasing,
> if scorn with oppression be reckon'd a blessing,
> Then Britain has nourish'd fair liberty's tree.

Here Britain features both as the leadership of the alliance that crushed the revolutionary hopes of 1789 ('For kings have resolved that in Europe for ever/The tocsin of freedom shall sound never again'), and as one of the sources of power which will eventually overthrow them:

> May the time soon arrive when the tyrant and minion
> Shall be heard of no more save in tales of the evening,
> When freemen from labour in circle conveying,
> Tell them o'er, in the shade of liberty's tree.

The site of action for the singer is Britain, but the subject is the international upheaval between 1789 and 1820. What nationality was the author? In fact, this is an anonymous Scottish piece, first performed in Paisley at the Saracen's Head Inn to celebrate the release from prison of the English radical Henry 'Orator' Hunt on 22 October 1822.[102] Yet without this knowledge, there is no way of saying whether the author is Scottish or English.

The Britishness of Scottish Radicalism

A hundred years of capitalist development lay between the general strike of April 1820 across the central belt and the general strike of February 1917 in Petrograd. The first announced that the Scottish workers had joined their English counterparts on the historical stage, but that they were virtually alone; the second announced that Russian workers were in the vanguard of an international class based in Glasgow, Belfast, Sheffield, Turin, Berlin, Chigago and the rest, and which was shortly to join them in the upheavals that characterised the end of the First World War. In other words, the development of the productive forces meant that by 1917 socialism had become – perhaps had only just become – a historical possibility on a world scale; by 1820 the development of the productive forces meant that industrial capitalism had only just become a reality in England and Lowland Scotland, and nowhere else. The result of industrialisation and urbanisation in Scotland was therefore to remove the unevenness between Lowland Scotland and, with it, the special conditions which had produced the militancy of the Scottish response. As we have seen, however, the dominance of the British over Scottish consciousness among Scottish workers remained. Why, given the difference in life experience down to 1832, was the reverse not the case?

Taylor has summarised the view of many writers in identifying the emergence of British nationalism between 1789 and 1848 as inherently reactionary, built as it was around the institution of the monarchy rather than the identity of the people.[103] I have already rejected the view that the monarchy was decisive in forming the British nation, but there is a greater mistake here, which is the assumption that any national consciousness can be solely composed of reactionary elements. National consciousness can and, indeed, *must* contain all possible social impulses (revolutionary socialist internationalism apart), even where these embody contradictions. What led to the dominance of 'British' over 'Scottish' consciousness in politics? From some point between 1746 and 1820, *all* classes in Scotland began, for different reasons, to treat the British aspect of their national identity as *politically* decisive. In the case of the working class there appear to be four reasons for this.

First, there were no material obstacles in the way of this merging of classes. The apparent contrast here is with the Irish working class. As Marx wrote of Irish workers in Britain during the nineteenth century: 'In relation to the Irish worker [the English worker] feels himself a member of the *ruling* nation and so turns himself into a tool of the aristocrats and capitalists of his country *against Ireland*, thus strengthening their domination *over himself.*' The English worker 'cherishes religious, social and national prejudices against the Irish worker' and, in return, the Irish worker 'sees in the English worker the accomplice and stupid tool of the *English rule in Ireland.*'[104] These comments provide a useful general insight into the way in which racism can divide the working class, nevertheless there is some evidence to suggest that they are not entirely accurate with regard to the Catholic Irish. As Hobsbawm writes of their presence in Britain:

> Most of them were workers and, very consciously, Catholic and Irish. Until the twenty-six counties separated from the United Kingdom, most of them found a formula which combined national and class identification by supporting, or allying with, parties and movements which claimed to be in favour of both, or at any rate hostile to both. ... After Irish separation had been achieved, the bulk of the Catholic Irish in Britain, insofar as they organised and voted at all, undoubtedly gravitated to the parties of their class. ... Nevertheless [despite Protestant anti-Irish racism], for the majority group among the Irish, perhaps just because they were so evidently a majority, the double identification as Irish and (when in Britain) British workers, seems to have been relatively unproblematic.[105]

Certainly as far as Scotland is concerned Mitchell has demonstrated in detail that even during the first half of the nineteenth century the Catholic Irish 'were not as isolated and despised as some historians have claimed' and that some at least 'participated in strikes, trade unions and political movements with native workers' and were embraced in turn by native Scottish political reformers.[106]

In fact the real contrast is the relationship between Scottish and English workers *in Britain* and that between Protestant and Catholic workers *in pre-Partition Ireland* itself. As James Connolly noted immediately before the outbreak of the First World War:

> Here [i.e., in Ulster], the Orange working class are slaves in spirit because they have been reared up among a people whose conditions of servitude were more slavish than their own. In Catholic Ireland the working class are rebels in spirit and democratic in feeling because for hundreds of years they have found no class as lowly paid or as hardly treated as themselves.[107]

If Scottish workers had suffered racial or national oppression at the hands of the English similar to that which Catholic Irish workers suffered at the hands of the British, then joint British industrial and political organisation would have been impossible. They did not. As John Pocock has emphasised, the Scottish national identity stands in stark contrast to that of the Catholic Irish:

> Irish history presents the case of an agony, a classic identity crisis capable of solution only by the death of the divided self and its rebirth in a new, exclusive and revolutionary form. By comparison, Scottish history has been, and may remain, a mere matter of choice, in which the acceptance of Anglicisation, the insistence on the concept of Britain, Lowlands localism and Gaelic romanticism, remain equally viable options and the problem is to reconcile one's sense of identity with one's awareness of so open-ended a structure of choice.[108]

The second reason was that earlier notions of what it meant to be Scottish, including those which defined Scottishness in relation to not being from the Highlands, Ireland or England, were being completely restructured. When the centre of population gravity switched from rural to urban, all the existing towns increased in size to some extent and this changed perceptions of Scottishness. Hugh Miller wrote of these years in his autobiography that:

> Of the wilder Edinburgh mechanics with whom I formed at this time any acquaintance, less than one-fourth were natives of the place. The others were mere settlers in it, who had removed mostly from country districts and small towns in which they had been known, each by his own small circle of neighbourhood, and had lived, in consequence under the wholesome influence of public opinion. In Edinburgh – grown too large at the time to permit men to know aught of their neighbours – they were set free from this wholesome influence, and, unless under the guidance of higher principle, found themselves at liberty to do very much as they pleased.[109]

But none of these towns, not even Edinburgh, expanded to the same degree as Glasgow. As we have seen, the social effects of industrialisation were immense. Not only had the economic centre of the nation moved to the west, but the very conception of what it meant to be Scottish was moved with it. In part these changes were geographic and occupational. The industrial west increasingly became identified with Scotland, and for many of the people who lived and worked there, it was the only Scotland they had ever known. Many of these people were Irish. Tom Gallagher, who generally accepts that there was anti-Irish feeling in Lowland Scotland, nevertheless argues that it was 'pressed into a number of deep but narrow channels which only rarely burst their banks to swamp

society as a whole'. One of the reasons for this was that the period of industrialisation, to which the Irish immigration contributed so much,
involved the most intensive social change Scotland had yet experienced,
'[s]o at a time of maximum transition and great economic upheaval, the
influx of the Irish was far less traumatic and dislocating than it would
have been at other moments'.[110] But a Scottishness which included not
only Highland immigrants but also Catholic Irish would have been
unrecognisable to, for example, Lord Kames. As Henry Hanham writes:
'Many of the new industrial areas were virtually indistinguishable from
their English counterparts and were largely populated by immigrant Irish
Catholics to whom the Scottish Presbyterian tradition was alien.'[111]

The third reason was the fact (to which I have already alluded) that
the state against which both Scottish and English workers were ranged
was a British state. The significance of this is often overlooked in effusions
concerning the wonders of Scotland's supposed civic nationalism.
Graham Morton has suggested that eighteenth century Scotland was 'a
very modern form of nationalism': 'One that was sustained primarily
within civil society and was therefore highly undirected because it was
not state created.'[112] Leaving aside the fact that Morton is conflating
what I call national consciousness with nationalism as such, the claim
that Scottish nationhood was the creation of civil society, rather than
the state, implies that in most (all?) other nation states the opposite was
the case. No nation – at least among the 'historic' nations of Europe with
whom Morton is presumably comparing Scotland – has ever been just
the creation of a state apparatus, but neither was Scotland just the
creation of civil society. The exceptional nature of Scottish civil society
has been stressed (to the point of exaggeration) by Tom Nairn: 'What it
reflected was a one-off conjuncture: institutional endowment from a
previous state; a new, remote and wildly corrupt state authority; and
then, after 1745–46, further military defeat and suppression, followed
by heady colonial and mercantile expansion.' As Nairn implies, the
nature of Scottish civil society was hardly 'undirected' by the state. Later
he makes the point explicit:

> In fact, 'self-management' owed its being to the state, albeit indirectly:
> the political violence and counter-violence of the civil wars, the
> Cromwellian occupation and the Restoration all lay behind the
> moment of the Scottish Enlightenment, as well as the Boyne and
> Culloden.[113]

In short, nationhood in Scotland, both at the stage of Scottish protonational consciousness before 1707 and dual Scottish-British national
consciousness after, was always conditioned by the state. What has
confused the issue, of course, is that after 1707 it was a *British* state
which undertook the conditioning, *including that relating to the Scottish
aspects of British identity*. As I have tried to demonstrate, representations

of Scottish participation in the British Empire were central to this. Morton has recently argued that a nation does not require a state in order to become a nation state. In defence of this somewhat startling thesis, he claims that in Scotland civil society acted as a substitute for this absent state, notably in the period between 1830 and 1860. The period discussed by Morton begins more or less at the point where mine ends, nevertheless his argument raises a point which is of more general interest for Scotland after 1707. Morton claims that 'the very concept of the British "nation-state" is untenable because of the disparity between a number of civil-societies and the one unitary British state', and argues that what he calls 'Unionist Nationalism' arose as 'a product of the "gap" between Scottish civil society and the British state – a gap which precluded the setting up of a Scottish state to rival that of Westminster.'[114]

It might be useful to begin from the British state, rather than the civil society for which Scottish historians show such an inordinate and misplaced fondness. Charles Tilly has stressed how the nature of what he calls 'contention' in Britain in the late eighteenth and early nineteenth centuries increasingly took on a parliamentary and national (rather than local) character:

> With increasing frequency people, including ordinary people acting collectively, made claims on Parliament, individual members of Parliament, and national officials. Local powerholders and the crown became less salient objects of claims. The timing of claim-making came to depend more closely on the rhythms of parliamentary discussion and governmental action. While authorised local assemblies such as wardmotes and vestry meetings continued to provide the setting for many claims on national authorities, workers organisations, special-interest associations and public meetings open to all inhabitants (or at least to 'respectable' inhabitants) took on increasing importance as vehicles for claim-making.

According to Tilly, this was the result of four processes:

> First, war-driven expansion, strengthening, and centralisation of the British state gave increasing political advantage to groups that could convey their demands directly to Parliament, whose fiscal and regulative powers augmented from decade to decade. ... Second, capitalisation, commercialisation and proletarianisation of economic life undermined old networks of patronage, weakened local craft organisation as a basis of collective interaction, sharpened the division between wage-earners and employers, gave workers increasing incentives and opportunities to band together on a regional or national scale, and promoted an alliance (however contingent and temporary)

among workers and capitalists in favour of democratic openings in national politics. ... Third, population growth, migration, urbanisation, and the creation of larger producing organisations transformed local social ties, giving political advantages to actors that could create, manipulate, alter, or infiltrate efficient assemblies and associations. Assemblies, associations, and political entrepreneurs provided the means of connecting and coordinating the actions of many dispersed clusters of people simultaneously. Not only the idea but also the feasibility and effectiveness of a union federation or a national network of political clubs generalised. ... Fourth, within the limits set by these first three processes and in constant interaction with authorities, contention accumulated its own history of shared beliefs, memories, models, precedents, and social ties, which underlay the use for claim-making of public delegations, and special-purpose associations. The recurrent effort to organise general unions and stage general strikes in the 1830s rested in part on the venerable program of the mass platform and on shared memories of the simultaneous meetings and insurrections between 1815 and 1820.

Their importance lay in the fact that they focussed attention on the state – the British state – as the object of amendment or overthrow. As Tilly concludes:

...Great Britain had created citizenship, a greatly expanded set of mutual rights and obligations linking the state to a whole category of people defined chiefly by long-term legal residence within the state's territory. New rights and obligations concerned military service, taxation, voting, assembly, association, religious practice, access to the judicial system, legal penalties, economic welfare, working conditions, and other significant zones of human activity.[115]

The fourth and final reason was the absence of a 'useable' Scottish history embodying the values which the organised section of the class wished to assert. Wallace, Bruce and the later Covenanters were not enough from which to construct an entire radical tradition. And so although the early Labour movement in Scotland incorporated radical symbolism from earlier periods of Scottish history into its traditions and iconography, it was equally open to English influences. In a sense, this is the proletarian equivalent of the way in which Robertson and the other Enlightenment historians 'plugged in' to English history after 1746, and for similar reasons: Smout argues that the radicals positively embraced:

...a reading of English history as a whole series of events in which true-born Englishmen had asserted themselves against royal and aristocratic tyranny... All this was very appealing to the Scottish

Friends of the People in the 1790s and their successors in the nineteenth century, and they adopted the simple device of arguing that in 1707 the new Britain inherited all the English and all the Scottish past, so the Scots plugged in to English history.[116]

In short, they treated Scottish history in the same way as their Whig predecessors and contemporaries. As Colin Kidd has argued: 'Neither in the responses of Scottish radicals to the French Revolution, nor in the 'tory' mythology of Sir Walter Scott...was there a major reversal of the sociological whig denigration of the political value of the Scottish past.'[117]

In one sense, however, Kidd goes too far. As we have seen, Scott was under no illusions as to the class nature of the conflicts which arose after 1815. But his remarks have a deeper significance in the context of a discussion of national consciousness, for it was not merely the middle classes that Scott hoped to imbue with an 'ideology of noisy inaction'. He also saw Scottish national identity as a narcotic to be applied to an increasingly restless working class. Rosalind Mitchison has written that 'increasingly, class divisions...came to obstruct national consciousness and solidarity rather than political, religious or geographic.'[118] Scott was concerned to mobilise his version of Scottish national identity precisely to stop this happening and the spectacle of the royal visit in 1822, which Scott did so much to organise and direct, was at least a partially successful attempt to do so.[119]

There irony here, surely, is that the major contribution made by Scottishness to the events of the radical years was a component, not, as is so often claimed, of working class militancy, but of the ideology of counter-revolution. In a letter written during the Malachi Malagrowther episode of 1826, Scott suggested that only the retention of the Scottish identity prevented Scottish people, or at least their lower orders, from becoming 'damned mischievous Englishmen':

The restless and yet laborious and constantly watchful character of the people, their desire for speculation in politics or anything else, only restrained by some proud feelings about their own country, now become antiquated and which late measures will tend to destroy, will make them under a wrong direction the most formidable revolutionists who ever took the field of innovation.[120]

We may be grateful that Scottish workers ignored his advice and overcame 'proud feelings about their own country' to become 'formidable revolutionists' in 1820.

Conclusion

The basis for Scottish nationhood was laid between 1746 and 1820. Identifiable components pre-existed the former date, but they were no more constitutive of nationhood in themselves than eggs, flour and butter separately constitute a cake: certain processes have to be undergone first. Scottish nationhood, as it endures to this day, involves three sets of relationships, two of which have been attended to at different times in this book.

The one which has not is the first, the distinction between Scottish national *consciousness* and Scottish national*ism*, for the simple reason that until the 1920s, and more seriously the 1960s, the latter did not exist in measurable terms. James Kellas has distinguished between 'the electoral history of the SNP, and the demand for political devolution' and 'the continuing development of Scottish national consciousness in all its forms'. These have different histories and, although linked, are not interchangeable with each other:

> The former is a chronicle of 'waves' of support, followed by troughs of decline; the latter is a steady growth to the position today in which national consciousness is to be found throughout Scottish society. The fortunes of the SNP have of course affected the intensity of national consciousness, but such consciousness is greater than the number of votes won by that party at elections. It is not necessarily concerned, as is the SNP, with 'national self-determination', or with political devolution. It is rather an assertion of Scottishness on the part of an amorphous group of interests and individuals, whose identity is caught up with that of Scotland.[1]

One survey conducted in Glasgow during the mid-1970s showed that the number of Scots who considered themselves British rather than Scottish increased from 29 per cent in 1973 to 33 per cent in 1976, at the same time as the SNP vote was rising. The implication is that the rise of Scottish nationalism had 'politicised' the question of Scottish nationality: 'It may be that to identify oneself as a Scot implies that one is a Scottish Nationalist.'[2] Today this is no longer the case. There is a growing tendency for Scots to claim that they feel more Scottish than British: 33 per cent in June 1998 compared to 29 per cent in September 1991 – although this is less than the figure of 40 per cent recorded in the immediate aftermath of the general election of 1992.[3] And this increase has occurred at the same time as the Labour vote has risen and the SNP vote has remained steady or fallen. The authors of one survey conducted at that time conclude that:

> Although Scottish identity is negatively related to Conservative identity, the SNP is not the sole beneficiary. Labour attracts a high level of support from Scottish identifiers. Nor do Scottish identifiers demand separation from Britain. A Scottish parliament is the most favoured constitutional option.

Interestingly, this option was one which they shared with Scots who felt themselves to be primarily British: '53 per cent of Scottish identifiers and 49 per cent of British identifiers favoured the creation of a Scottish parliament within Britain'.[4] These findings were borne out by the referendum of September 1997 and the Scottish elections of May 1999. An ICM poll taken in April 1990 found that 25 per cent of respondents considered themselves Scottish not British, 32 per cent more Scottish than British and 26 per cent equally Scottish and British. Yet this was only one month before Scottish parliamentary elections where 28.7 per voted for the SNP in the constituencies and 27.3 per cent in the regional lists.[5] In short, there is no necessary connection between Scottish national consciousness and Scottish nationalism.

This is partly because of the second distinction, between *Scottish* national consciousness and *British* national consciousness. Christopher Smout has written of the Scots that they exhibit 'a kind of dual ethnic consciousness, composed partly of loyalty to the actuality and opportunity of modern Britain; and partly of loyalty to the memory and tradition of Scotland.' Smout notes that this dualism cuts across class lines (although I would wish to add that each class understands its significance in a different way) and 'represents a real emotional tension, a contradiction within the citizen which is never resolved.'[6] It has often been observed that, while the English often conflate Englishness with Britishness, the Scots can opt for Scottishness or Britishness according to circumstance. What is rarely recognised is that, for the Scots, their British and Scottish identities do not merely exist in parallel, but inter-penetrate each other at every point. In other words, Scottishness as we know it today not only emerged at the same *time* as Britishness, but is *part* of Britishness, and could not exist (at least in the same form) without it. Crick suggests that it is wrong to equate the emotional power of 'Britishness' with that of 'Scottishness':

> The question then arises, is 'British' a concept of nationalism with at all the same function as Scottish? If a nationalism at all, it is not a comprehensive ideology, like most nationalisms, but a very specific one, I contend, limited to a particular function: that of holding the United Kingdom together. ...the forging of Britishness was not about an imagined national community so much as about holding the kingdoms together with the minimum of force, indeed, reasonably peacefully.[7]

In fact many of the most demonstrative exhibitions of Scottishness are simply because, as Joyce McMillan once noted: 'Scottish identity requires constant assertion, whereas British identity is something taken for granted by every institution with which [the Scots] have to deal, and inclined to assert itself in the half conscious assumption that politics is something that happens at Westminster.'[8]

The third distinction is between British national *consciousness* (of which Scottish national consciousness is a part) and British national*ism*. It is remotely possible, I suppose, that the arguments contained here might be presented as an apologia for 'Britishness' or even the British Empire itself. It is neither of these things. Indeed, one of the objects of my writing was to make it more difficult for celebrations of 'Scottishness' to continue avoiding, or continue treating as a joke, the way in which the Scottish nation was itself partly formed through our participation in British imperialism. And not only formed, but continually reformed. Claims that Scots have remained tied to the British state since 1945 because of the Welfare State contain a partial truth – the provision of welfare is a major underpinning of reformist consciousness – but in other respects are complacent in the extreme.[9] And this has other implications. If 'Scottishness' itself is at least partly the product of imperialism and ethnic cleansing, then it is futile to imagine that merely setting up a Scottish nation state will *by itself* remove the attendant poisons of racism and hostility towards cultures which are perceived to be 'different'.

The point here is not that there is anything inherently desirable about feeling British rather than Scottish (or any other nationality), but rather that, precisely because the central economic, social and political issues have tended to be resolved at a British level, it is at a British level that working class unity has also tended to be expressed. It is in this context that the opposition between 'state' and 'civil society' has some significance. The acceptance by Scottish workers of British nationhood has by no means been unconditionally positive. Where it has encouraged working class identification with the British state – where it has been channelled into nationalism – then it has acted as a barrier to socialism, but where it has involved recognition of the collective interests of workers on both sides of the Border – interests formed as the level of civil society – then it has offered the possibility of achieving socialism, and of escaping from the prison of nationhood altogether. The latter attitude is well expressed in a song by the Paisley Radical John MacGregor (1790–1870). Given the way in which the events of 1820 have been portrayed as embodying Scottish nationalist aspirations, there is some irony that these words were first read at the 1867 ceremony where the monument to Hardie and Baird, two of the martyrs of the rising, was unveiled. It is based on a poem written by MacGregor in 1820:

> O may fair liberty expand
> And spread her pleasure's round;
> And sweet contentment bless our land,
> And righteousness abound.
> May Britain claim a precious fame
> For all that's great and grand;
> And nation's found in intercourse,
> Obey her just command.[10]

Afterword

All nations have myths. Terry Eagleton argues that it is in the nature of myth to remove events from their real historical context and represent them merely as moments in an 'infinitely repetitive' pattern which typically takes the form of a narrative.[1] As Cairns Craig writes:

> The fundamental role of narrative in the formation of national identity has come increasingly to be recognised in 'nation theory': indeed, it is now often argued that nations are nothing more than narratives and that it is through the narrative arts that national identities are established, maintained and elaborated.[2]

It is sometimes said that Scotland has more of these than the other 'historic' or 'continuous' European nations whose territorial boundaries were largely set in the late medieval period. According to one group of sociologists: 'In a society in which national consciousness has had few outlets for nearly three centuries, the creation of myths is perhaps an inevitable corollary.'[3] In fact, Scottish myths are no more numerous than those of other nations, including England. Nor, contrary to what David McCrone and his colleagues suggest, do the existing myths stem from a frustrated national consciousness, for, as we have seen, statelessness has not prevented the Scots from developing national consciousness to an extremely high level.

I began this book by stating my intention to undermine what I see as the central myth of Scottish history. The project of demystification has, however, come under attack from both Scottish nationalists and academics by no means committed to that political perspective. In this Afterword I want to defend, not so much the specifics of my own case (which will no doubt have to be undertaken in due course), but the project itself.

Often these attacks are launched over what are apparently trivial issues. Take, for example, the historical origins of the kilt and tartan. It is usually claimed that the actual historical origins are irrelevant, because their importance lies in the fact that they are regarded as representations of Scottish identity in the minds of the Scots themselves. Recently, these arguments have begun to be couched in terms derived from postmodernism, the notion that history is a narrative (and consequently a myth) like any other, that it can be put to work for a number of different purposes, and that arguments concerning the 'truth' in this context are merely attempts by Whig or Marxist historians to use their ('grand') narratives of progress to attack Scottish identity. Two assertions are usually made in this context.

First, that the onslaught on 'Scotch Myths' conceals an ulterior 'Unionist' motivation. According to Murray Pittock, 'such demythologisation is effectively only the creation of a new myth':

> This exposure of myths is held to be of service, I cannot find it so...the destruction of myths is itself a manifestation of the values of a centring 'British' history. The attack on tartanry is only another attack on self...

Second, that the problem is not the existence of myths but, as Pittock says, 'what is done with them'.[4] The argument has been extended by Craig Beveridge and Ronald Turnbull:

> What is known is that tartan is now used as a symbol of Scottishness by people whose commitment to genuine forms of political and cultural nationalism is not in question. If it is undoubtedly true that establishment groups and commercial forces have attempted to appropriate this powerful semiotic system and shape its meaning to their own ends, it is equally indisputable that tartan has been invested with many other meanings, and that it can and does function as an iconography of opposition to Scotland's current political status.[5]

One correspondent to *Scotland On Sunday* during 1998 argued that to attack the use of tartan as a symbol was to misunderstand its 'creative potential':

> Surely the main thrust of post modernism as derived from the work of Levi Strauss and Barthes is that once we are aware and conscious of 'the dominant narrative of Scotland' we are free to construct our own narratives. ...the most effective way to resist 'the subconscious narrative of tartanry' is to bring it into opposition with the conscious narrative of Scottish independence.[6]

Why this hostility on the part of people who might be expected to approve of demythologising Scottish history? Three reasons suggest themselves.

First, although there is a perfectly rational case to be made for Scottish nationalism as a political movement, no nationalist cause has ever sustained support without mobilising the myths of which, to a large extent, every national identity consists. This is true even of national movements like Irish Republicanism whose goals, if not whose methods, socialists have been inclined to support. Tom Nairn has argued that some set of symbols was inevitable in the communication of national identity both to fellow Scots and to others, since the real identity would involve a 'long story...incomprehensible in normal conversation' and the alternative of silence 'would imply oblivion':

Shorthand is as inescapable as nationalism: the culture requires it. It must therefore be faked, with whatever materials come to hand. It is in this sense that the fakelore of Gaelicism and assumed Highland identity is by no means accidental, or simply the consequence of bad faith and culpable romantic escapism. Phoniness is its unavoidable accompaniment, of course, as is the kind of uneasy half-belief which most Scottish Lowlanders have half-indulged in about it since Victorian times.

Nairn counsels intellectuals against 'sanctimoniousness' when confronted with the 'follies of tartanry': 'A cure will be found for in politics, not in aesthetic disdain or a stand-off intellectualism.'[7] Ultimately, therefore, the task of deconstruction *cannot* be endorsed by nationalists, for the process, if pursued systematically, would leave the national movement in question bereft of all its mythical underpinning.

Second, despite the indeterminacy of semiotic systems invoked by Beveridge and Turnbull, it is extremely difficult to separate out the signs of Scottish identity from those of the Empire that the Scots did so much to build and sustain. Subjects like the kilt and the tartan, which at first seem peripheral to the main contours of Scottish history, nevertheless have – for nationalists – the inconvenient effect of emphasising that their current usage is intimately bound up with the process of imperialist expansion. If tartanry is, at least in part, a cultural embellishment of British imperialism, then it is difficult to see how an attack on it can be, as Pittock argues, an attack on self, unless they are prepared to acknowledge that imperialism is part of that self – in which case, surely, it is right that it should be attacked.[8]

Third, focus on the construction of an all-Scottish identity after 1746 draws attention to the divisions between Highland and Lowland which helped prevent the formation of an inclusive national identity before that date. This is intolerable to contemporary Scottish nationalists. For, if the Scottish nation is a historical construction of relatively recent date and not one traceable back to the dawn of time, then the possibility exists that it might not continue until the last syllable is recorded either.

The project undertaken by Beveridge and Turnbull in particular is perhaps the most significant attempt to view Scottish history through the theoretical apparatus of postmodernism. Like many theoretical innovations, postmodernism came late to Scottish academic life. In this case, however, it would have been better never than late for it is utterly useless as a vehicle for conducting serious historical work.[9] The warning issued by Eric Hobsbawm against the slide into relativist irrationalism in Western thought is relevant here:

> If there is no clear distinction between what is true and what I feel to be true, then my own construction of reality is as good as yours or anybody else's...then no narrative among the many possible ones can be regarded as privileged.

As Hobsbawm points out, the audience for postmodernism lies in a particular type of social group:

> It is not fortuitous that these views have appealed particularly to those who see themselves as representing collectivities or milieux marginalised by the hegemonic culture of some group (say, middle-class white heterosexual males of Western Education) whose claim to superiority they contest.[10]

Consequently, postmodernism is eminently suitable as a vehicle for nationalist ideology. But as Hobsbawm notes: 'A history which is designed *only* for Jews (or African-Americans, or Greeks, or women, or proletarians, or homosexuals) cannot be good history, though it may be comforting history for those who practise it.'[11] And one might add: neither can good history be designed only for Scots.

The problem, however, is deeper than simply the confluence of nationalism and postmodernism. At the root is the assumption that nations are – or at least, have become – the normal and inescapable forms within which human societies exist. As Cairns Craig writes:

> The nation 'imagines' because it is the nation through which the agency of human groups is primarily exerted in the modern world: the nation acts upon the individual – by the educational opportunities it provides and the economic potentialities it makes available, by the wars in which it engages and the laws that define the limits of individual action – and individuals act through the nation, by extending the effectiveness of their own willpower into the will of the institutions which shape national life.

This certainly describes what currently happens, but whether it is *necessarily* true or *exclusively* true that 'the nation shapes our individual futures' is surely a more complex question.[12]

Nevertheless, I believe that acceptance of the assumption Craig presents here is the reason why many historians regard any attempt to deconstruct national mythologies as futile. Richard Finlay has criticised what he sees as the failure of historians to 'engage' with myths in a positive way: 'The factual invalidation of myths in weighty academic tomes does not and never has invalidated them as complex icons of cultural, social and political belief.' Given the persistence of myths among the Scottish people (Finlay uses the examples of Burns, Wallace and the Jacobites) it is more important for historians to understand them than to attempt their destruction.[13] It is true that it is only possible to dispel myths if their power over people is first understood, and the attempt will fail in any case if it remains confined to academy, but it must nevertheless be made. For to collude in the perpetuation of national myths is not merely patronising in the extreme, implying that mythology is all that the majority of people can understand, or *need* to understand of their history, it actively invites the Scots not to concern themselves with historical truth, but to subscribe instead to whatever mythological version is most pleasing to them. The dangers in this are immense. Christopher Small once wrote, in the context of a discussion of the '45:

> A parallel may be assumed between the growth of identity in a nation and in a maturing individual; common experience as well as psychological theory suggests that in both cases the truth and completeness of what is acknowledged is crucial to the kind of identity achieved.

Small notes that where individuals assume a 'false identity', psychoanalytic theory argues that they must face up to the traumas in their personal history, from childhood on, if this is to be overcome. There can be, he writes, an 'analogous process' in the development of groups or nations where they too assume a 'false identity' and collective history is 'overlaid and distorted by forgetfulness and self-deception':

> It is possible to think of the historian's commitment to 'truth' and to finding out 'what really happened' as the same, even if the aim is not directly therapeutic, as is the psychoanalyst's. A people which forgets or ignores its past will have as much difficulty as has a single mortal, deprived of memory, in retaining any sense of identity. But a people sustained by *false* ideas of the past, by illusions of glory or projections of blame, is not in a healthy state either.[14]

This is very well said, although for those, like the present author, who work within the classical Marxist tradition, it is not the psychic health of 'the people' in general which is a matter for concern ('the Scottish people' being an ideological notion concealing the class-divided nature of Scottish society), but that of the group which makes up the majority of the population: the Scottish working class.

With that in mind, let us turn to a passage from one Scottish writer who is presumably immune from attack on grounds of 'Unionism'. In an essay written in the 1930s, Lewis Grassic Gibbon reflects first on the scale of human misery endured by the working class of the Glasgow slums, then indulges himself in some versions of what an independent Scottish state might be like before pulling himself back to reality with this declaration:

> But I cannot play with these fantasies when I think of the hundred and fifty thousand in Glasgow. They are a something that stills the parlour chatter. I find I am by way of being an intellectual myself. I meet and talk with many people whose interests are art and letters and music. Enthusiasm for this or that aspect of craft and architecture, men and women who have very warm and sincere beliefs regarding the ancient culture of Scotland, people to whom Glasgow is the Hunterian Museum with its fine array of Roman coins, or the Galleries with their equally fine array of pictures. 'Culture' is the motif-word of the conversation: ancient Scots culture, future Scots culture, culture ad lib and ad nauseam. ... The patter is as intimate on my tongue as on theirs. And relevant to the fate and being of those hundred and fifty thousand it is no more than the chatter and scratch of a band of apes, seated in a pit on a midden of corpses.

If the word 'culture' is changed in this passage to 'identity', then Grassic Gibbon seems curiously contemporary, for the 'hundred and fifty thousand' and more are still with us, festering not in the Gorbals of his day but the peripheral estates of Drumchapel and Wester Hailes. For that reason, the polemic with which he continues his argument also maintains its relevance:

> There is nothing in culture and art that is worth the life and elementary happiness of one of those thousands who rot in the Glasgow slums. There is nothing in science or religion. If it came (as it may come) to some fantastic choice between a free and independent Scotland, a centre of culture, a bright flame of artistic and scientific achievement, and providing elementary decencies of food and shelter to the submerged proletariat of Glasgow and Scotland, I at least would have no doubt as to which side of the battle I would range myself. For the cleansing of that horror, if cleanse it they could, I would welcome the English in sovereignty over Scotland till the end of time. I would welcome the end of Braid Scots and Gaelic, our culture, our history, our

nationhood under the heels of a Chinese army of occupation if it could cleanse the Glasgow slums [and] give a surety of food and play – the elementary right of every human being – to those people of the abyss.[15]

This is to make the case in the most extreme terms possible. The author of *Sunset Song* was not, I think, opposed to culture, nor do these passages adequately reflect the complexity of his own engagement with nationalism. Grassic Gibbon did not believe that Scotland lay under English sovereignty, nor did he call on the English (or Chinese) to impose it. Nevertheless the spirit of this passage is one which the left should endorse, for it reminds us that the task of socialists is to seek the abolition of capitalism, not its endless reproduction under new national flags. And for the Scottish left in particular, it reminds us that we are not, or should not be, Scots who happen to be socialists, but socialists who happen to be Scots.

Notes

Preface, Acknowledgements, Dedication

1. My findings are summarised in 'Scotland's Bourgeois Revolution', C. Bambery (ed.), *Scotland, Class And Nation* (London, Chicago and Sydney, 1999), Chapter 3.
2. M. Bloch, *The Historian's Craft* (Manchester, 1976), pp. 29–35.
3. The article, which is a review of T. Dickson (ed.), *Scottish Capitalism* (London, 1980), appeared in *The Bulletin Of Scottish Politics*, vol. 1, no. 2, Spring 1981. The contents page lists the article as 'The Origins of Scottish Nationhood: Arguments Within Scottish Marxism', but the article itself is headed up by the subtitle, which I have used in the citations that follow.
4. N. Davidson, 'In Perspective: Tom Nairn', *International Socialism* 82, Second Series, Spring 1999 and 'The Trouble With "Ethnicity"', *International Socialism* 84, Second Series, Autumn 1999.
5. L. Grassic Gibbon, *Sunset Song*, Volume 1 of *A Scots Quair*, various editions; I. Carter, *Farm Life In Northeast Scotland, 1840–1914* (Edinburgh, 1979 and 1997).

Introduction

1. T. Nairn, 'Empire and Union', *Faces Of Nationalism* (London and New York, 1997), p. 209. The article was a review of two books, L. Patterson, *The Autonomy Of Modern Scotland* (Edinburgh, 1994) and J. Robertson (ed.), *A Union For Empire* (Cambridge, 1995). For my own review of the latter work see 'Union, Empire and Explanation', *Scottish Affairs* 14, Winter 1996.
2. T.M. Devine, *The Scottish Nation, 1700–2000* (Harmondsworth, 1999), p. ix.
3. I. Bell, 'Crucial Test of Self-Belief', *The Scotsman*, 29 September 1999.
4. One outstanding recent example, from which I have drawn in Chapter 10, is the work by Martin Mitchell on the Irish contribution to the labour movement in the west of Scotland before 1848. See M.J. Mitchell, *The Irish In The West Of Scotland, 1797–1848* (Edinburgh, 1998).

5. The recent collaborative work produced jointly by the Open University in Scotland and the University of Dundee is a good example of this. Only one essay, by John Foster, attempts to set out the differences between Weberian and his own Marxist position. See 'Class', A. Cooke, I. Donnachie, A. MacSween and C.A. Whatley (eds), *Modern Scottish History 1707 To The Present*, vol. 2, *The Modernisation Of Scotland, 1850 To The Present* (5 Volumes, East Linton, 1998), vol. 2, pp. 210–17. See A. Law, 'Review: *Modern Scottish History* Vols 2 and 4', *Scottish Affairs* 26, Winter 1999, pp. 126, 127. Rare examples of work in which historians of Scotland have explicitly set out their theoretical affiliations include, for Weber, G. Marshall, *Presbyters And Profits* (Paperback Edition, Edinburgh 1992), pp. 3–35 and (more critically) for Marx, W.W. Knox, *Industrial Nation* (Edinburgh, 1999), pp. 1–27.

6. The main exception to this rule is to be found in the work of Christopher Smout, who has argued that Scottish identity consists of a set of 'concentric' loyalties rising through family, kin or clan, locality, nation, state, empire to supranational body. See T.C. Smout, 'Problems of Nationalism, Identity and Improvement in Later Eighteenth Century Scotland', T.M. Devine (ed.), *Improvement And Enlightenment* (Edinburgh, 1989), pp. 2–3, and the fuller exposition in 'Perspectives On Scottish Identity', *Scottish Affairs* 6, Winter 1994, p. 107. Both draw on A.D. Smith, *The Ethnic Revival* (London, 1981), pp. 55, 164ff. Richard Finlay has commended this model for its supposed 'sophistication' compared to 'crude' Marxist alternatives. See R.J. Finlay, 'Keeping the Covenant: Scottish National Identity', T.M. Devine and J.R. Young (eds), *Eighteenth Century Scotland: New Perspectives* (East Linton, 1999), p. 122. I find it deeply unsatisfactory, largely because of the way in which the term 'identity' is made to carry more explanatory weight than it can possibly bear. See Chapter 1, pp. 15–18.

7. P.P. Cockcroft in *Scotland On Sunday*, 12 September 1999. The series ran for six weeks between 5 September and 10 October 1999.

8. J.G.A. Pocock, 'British History: a Plea For a New Subject', *Journal Of Modern History*, vol. 47, no. 4, December 1975. See also 'The Limits and Divisions of British History: In Search of the Unknown Subject', *American Historical Review*, vol. 87, no. 2, April 1982.

9. G. Kerevan, 'Milosevic's "Nationalism" is Not Ours', *The Scotsman*, 5 April 1999. Compare Lord Acton in 1862: 'These two views of nationality, corresponding to the French and English systems, are connected in name only, and are in reality the opposite extremes of political thought.' Lord Acton, 'Nationality', G. Balakrishnan (ed.), *Mapping The Nation* (London and New York, 1996), p. 29.

10. See Davidson 'In Perspective: Tom Nairn', op cit, p. 113 and D. Gluckstein, *The Nazis, Capitalism And The Working Class* (London, 1999), Chapter 1.

11. T. Nairn, 'The Modern Janus', *The Break-Up Of Britain* (second, revised edition, London, 1981), p. 329.

12. Indeed, in so far as his earlier work was associated with Marxism, some have concluded that the verdict also applies to Nairn himself. See, for example, J. Breuilly, *Nationalism And The State* (second edition, Manchester, 1993), pp. 407–14 and A.D. Smith, *Nationalism And Modernism* (London, 1998), pp. 47–57. The extent to which Nairn had

already moved away from Marxism by the time he wrote 'The Modern Janus' is discussed in Davidson 'In Perspective: Tom Nairn', pp. 102–9.
13. Finlay, 'Keeping the Covenant: Scottish National Identity', pp. 120–1.
14. Finlay gives two references. The first is to T. Dickson (ed.) *Scottish Capitalism* (London, 1980). There is certainly much to criticise in this collaborative effort, but nowhere in the relevant chapter (i.e., K. Burgess et al, 'The Making of a Class Society: Commercialisation and Working Class Resistance, 1780–1830') is there any reference to national identity, Scottish or British, let alone to either being formed in the period which Finlay identifies. The one chapter which does deal with the subject (i.e., J. Foster et al, 'Scottish Nationality and the Origins of Capitalism') places the origins of Scottish nationality in the *feudal* epoch, indeed, cites the very same 'popular character and mass participation of the Anglo Scottish wars of the fourteenth century' to which Finlay draws our attention as proof of this contention! (See ibid., pp. 37–9, 55–6.) The second reference is to Nairn, *The Break-Up Of Britain*, which Finlay describes as a more 'sophisticated treatment'. Indeed it is, but Nairn does not claim that the bourgeoisie 'invented' Scottish national identity in the eighteenth century either. Indeed, at one point he devotes a detailed discussion to the paradox displayed by the strength of Scottish national identity *at the point of Union in 1707* and the weaknesses of Scottish nationalism thereafter. ('Scotland and Europe', ibid., pp. 105–7.) Has Finlay actually read either of these books? As I argue in Chapter 3 below, there is a tendency among Marxists, particularly those, like Foster, influenced by the Stalinist tradition, to place the origins of Scottish nation much earlier than the historical evidence will bear. Finlay also refers to E.J. Hobsbawm and T. Ranger (eds), *The Invention of Tradition* (Cambridge, 1983). This includes Hugh Trevor-Roper's 'The Invention of Tradition: the Highland Tradition of Scotland', which *does* claim that a Highland tradition – a concept which I suppose could be stretched to include 'identity' – was invented at the beginning of the nineteenth century, but Trevor-Roper did not suggest that Scottish identity as whole was invented then, and in any case he is not, I think, a Marxist. So we wait, with bated breath, to discover the identity of these Unknown Historical Materialists whom Finlay invokes, dismisses, but whose names he cannot reveal.
15. See, for example, M. Mann, *The Sources Of Social Power* (2 Volumes, Cambridge, 1986-), vol. 1, *A History Of Power From The Beginning To A.D. 1760*, p. 1.

Chapter 1: What is National Consciousness?

1. M. Lowy, 'Marxists and the National Question', *New Left Review* 96, March/April 1976, p. 81.
2. J.V. Stalin, 'Marxism and the National Question', *Collected Works* (Moscow, 1953), vol. 2, p. 307.
3. R. Mulholland, 'What is the National Question?', *Socialist Scotland* 1, Autumn 1989, p. 18.
4. E.J. Hobsbawm, *Nations And Nationalism Since 1780* (Cambridge, 1990), p. 6.

5. B. Anderson, *Imagined Communities* (revised edition, London and New York, 1991), pp. 135–9.
6. It is perhaps appropriate that Leon Trotsky, the man who did most to uphold the classical Marxist tradition against Stalin, also offered an alternative to his checklist procedure using precisely the example of Switzerland:

    > ...the Swiss people, through their historical connections, feel themselves to be a nation despite different languages and religions. An abstract criterion is not decisive in this question, far more decisive is the historical consciousness of a group, their feelings, their impulses. But that too is not determined accidentally, but rather by the situation and all the attendant circumstances.

    L.D. Trotsky, 'The Negro Question In America', *Leon Trotsky On Black Nationalism And Self-Determination*, edited by G. Breitman (New York and Toronto, 1978), p. 28.
7. E. Kedurie, *Nationalism* (second edition, London, 1961), p. 82.
8. H. Seton-Watson, *States And Nations* (London, 1977), p. 5.
9. A.D. Smith, *National Identity* (Harmondsworth, 1991), p. 21.
10. N. Davidson, 'The Trouble With "Ethnicity"', *International Socialism* 84, Second Series, Autumn 1999, pp. 5–12.
11. For recent defences of this 'key dichotomy', see M. Lowy, *Fatherland Or Mother Earth?* (London, 1998), pp. 1, 27–9 and A. Callinicos, 'Marxism and the National Question', C. Bambery (ed.), *Scotland, Class And Nation*, (London, 1999), pp. 39, 40–2.
12. Hobsbawm, *Nations And Nationalism Since 1780*, pp. 7–8. Hobsbawm does some dextrous fence-sitting with regard to his own position:

    > Neither objective nor subjective definitions are thus satisfactory, and both are misleading. In any case, agnosticism is the best initial posture of a student in the field, and so this book assumes no a priori definition of what constitutes a nation.

    On the same page, however, he comes down on what is essentially a subjectivist position: 'As an initial working assumption, any sufficiently large body of people whose members regard themselves as members of a "nation" will be treated as such.' Ibid., p. 8.
13. Anderson, *Imagined Communities*, p. 6.
14. V.N. Voloshinov, *Marxism And The Philosophy Of Language*, translated by L. Matejka and I.R. Titunik (London and Cambridge, Massachusetts, 1986), pp. 11, 13.
15. G.E.M de Ste. Croix, *The Class Struggle In The Ancient Greek World* (London, 1981), p. 43. (See also p. 32.)
16. K. Marx, *The Poverty Of Philosophy*, *Collected Works* (50 Volumes, London, 1975-), vol. 6, p. 211.
17. G. Lukacs, 'Class Consciousness', *History And Class Consciousness* (London, 1971), p. 51.

    > By relating consciousness to the whole of society it becomes possible to infer the thoughts and feelings which men would have in a particular

situation if they were able to assess both it and the interests arising from it in their impact on immediate action and on the whole structure of society. That is to say, it would be possible to infer the thoughts and feelings appropriate to their objective situation. The number of such situations is not unlimited in any society.

18. E.P. Thompson, *The Making Of The English Working Class* (Harmondsworth, 1980), pp. 8–9.
19. See, for example, R. Suny, 'The Revenge of the Past: Socialism and Ethnic Conflict in Transcaucasia', *New Left Review* 184, November/December 1990, p. 9. For an explicit appeal to Thompson's authority, see ibid., note 7. In at least one case, that of so-called 'proletarian Zionism', there has been an attempt to argue that national and class consciousness can become fused. See the discussion in N. Weinstock, *Zionism: False Messiah*, edited and translated by A. Adler (London, 1979), Appendix 3, 'Borchov and the National Question', pp. 274–9.
20. Hobsbawm has confused the issue further by arguing that two definitions of class can be found in Marx. One based on objective class position (*à la* de Ste. Croix) and the other on subjective awareness of that position (*à la* Thompson). The latter is not, however, a definition of class, but of class consciousness. 'Class consciousness in the full sense only comes into existence at the historical moment when classes begin to acquire consciousness of themselves as such.' How conscious would a proletarian have to be before she or he could be said to 'exist' as a member of their class? And would they cease to be a member if their level of consciousness changed? See E.J. Hobsbawm, 'Class Consciousness in History', I. Meszaros (ed.), *Aspects Of History And Class Consciousness* (London, 1971), p. 6 and 'Notes on Class Consciousness' [the same essay under a different title], *Worlds Of Labour* (London, 1984), p. 16.
21. I owe this formulation to Alex Callinicos, who made it in his reply to the discussion during a meeting on 'Base and Superstructure' at Marxism '90 in London, 13 July 1990.
22. Kerevan, 'Arguments Within Scottish Marxism', p. 119.
23. Anderson, *Imagined Communities*, p. 7.
24. M. Weber, 'Structures of Power', *From Max Weber*, edited by C. Wright Mills and H.H. Gerth (London, 1948), p. 176.
25. A. Cobban, *The Nation State And National Self-Determination* (Glasgow and London, 1969), p. 108.
26. J. Breuilly, *Nationalism And The State* (second edition, Manchester, 1993), p. 6.
27. Smith, *National Identity*, p. 14.
28. M. Guibernau, *Nationalisms* (Cambridge, 1996), p. 3.
29. T. Nairn, 'Empire and Union', *Faces of Nationalism* (London and New York, 1997), pp. 196–7.
30. A.D. Smith, *Nationalism And Modernism* (London, 1998), pp. 73, 75.
31. M. Biddiss, 'Nationalism and the Moulding of Modern Europe', *History*, vol. 79, no. 257, October 1994, p. 414.
32. A. Brown, D. McCrone and L. Patterson, *Politics And Society In Scotland* (Houndmills, 1996), pp. 191, 192.
33. M. Billig, *Banal Nationalism* (London, 1995), p. 60.

34. Another corollary is that perhaps the supposedly fabulous range of identities available to those of us who live during the current stage of capitalism may be little more than those of the various consumer groups identified as targets for niche advertising. Stuart Hall has given the game away to a certain extent when he writes: 'But the fact that greater and greater numbers of people (men *and* women) – with however little money – play the game of using things to signify who they are.' (S. Hall, 'Brave New World', *Marxism Today*, vol. 32, no. 10, October 1988, p. 28.) As Ambalavaner Sivanandan has written of this passage: 'Who are these people...unless it is those who use cardboard boxes under Waterloo Bridge to signify that they are the homeless?' A. Sivanandan, 'All That Melts into Air is Solid: the Hokum of New Times', *Communities Of Resistance* (London and New York, 1990), p. 47.

35. Billig, *Banal Nationalism*, pp. 138–9. These comments are clearly aimed at Lyotard's fatuous claim that 'Eclecticism is the degree zero of contemporary general culture: one listens to reggae, watches a western, eats MacDonalds food for lunch and local cuisine at dinner, wears Paris perfume in Tokyo and "retro" clothes in Hong Kong; knowledge is a matter for TV games.' (J-F. Lyotard, 'Answering the Question: What is Postmodernism?', *The Postmodern Condition* (Manchester, 1984), p. 76.) The attempt by Anthony Smith to characterise Billig as a theorist 'exploring novel postmodern dimensions' of nationalism is therefore quite incomprehensible, particularly since Smith himself quotes from this passage by Billig! See Smith, *Nationalism And Modernism*, pp. 205, 224.

36. Guibernau, *Nationalisms*, p. 43.

37. M. Billig, 'From Codes to Utterances: Cultural Studies, Discourse and Psychology', M. Ferguson and P. Golding (eds), *Cultural Studies In Question* (London, 1997), p. 208.

38. R. Poole, 'On National Identity: a Response to Jonathan Ree', *Radical Philosophy* 62, Autumn 1992, pp. 14–15.

39. Billig, *Banal Nationalism*, pp. 24, 60.

40. E.P. Thompson, 'Introduction: Custom and Culture', *Customs In Common* (London, 1991), p. 1.

41. Billig, *Banal Nationalism*, p. 8. The metonym is developed further on pp. 39–43 and 49–51.

42. Voloshinov, *Marxism And The Philosophy Of Language*, p. 91. Billig does not refer to Voloshinov directly in *Banal Nationalism*, but acknowledges his debt to him in 'From Codes to Utterances'.

43. Billig, *Banal Nationalism*, pp. 55, 57.

44. H. Cunningham, 'The Language of Patriotism', R. Samuel (ed.), *Patriotism: The Making And Unmaking Of British National Identity* (3 Volumes, London, 1989), vol. 1, *History And Politics*, pp. 58–9.

45. B. Crick, 'Essays on Britishness', *Scottish Affairs* 2, Winter 1993, pp. 73–4.

46. E. Gellner, *Nations And Nationalism* (Oxford, 1983), p. 138.

47. R.R. Palmer, 'The National Idea In France Before the Revolution', *Journal Of The History Of Ideas* 1, 1940, pp. 96, 98–9.

48. 'Address from the Society of United Irishmen in Dublin, 1792', E.W. McFarland, *Ireland And Scotland In The Age Of Revolution* (Edinburgh, 1994), Appendix 2, p. 250.

49. P.J. Taylor, 'The English and Their Englishness: "a Curiously Mysterious, Elusive and Little Understood People"', *Scottish Geographical Magazine*, vol. 107, no. 3, 1991, p. 148.

50. For the United Netherlands see J.I. Israel, *The Dutch Republic* (Oxford, 1995), pp. 1085–7 and Chapter 42; for Britain, see L. Colley, 'The Apotheosis of George III: Loyalty, Royalty and the British Nation, 1760–1830', *Past And Present* 102, February 1983, pp. 115–17.

51. B. Crick, *George Orwell: A Life* (London, 1980), p. 22.

52. G. Orwell, 'Notes on Nationalism', *The Collected Essays, Journalism And Letters Of George Orwell* (4 Volumes, Harmondsworth, 1970), vol. 3, *As I Please 1943–1945*, p. 411.

53. J. Huizinga, 'Patriotism and Nationalism in European History', *Men And Ideas*, translated by J.S. Holmes and H. van Marl (London, 1960), pp. 97–9.

54. Any doubt that Orwell means 'nationalism' where he writes 'patriotism' can be dispelled by consulting J. Newsinger, *Orwell's Politics* (Houndmills, 1999), Chapter 4, a critical but sympathetic Marxist account which supersedes all previous discussion of the subject.

55. See Billig, *Banal Nationalism*, pp. 55–9

56. F.M. Barnard, 'National Culture and Political Legitimacy: Herder and Rousseau', *Journal Of The History Of Ideas* 44, April 1983, p. 231.

57. F. Meinecke, *Weltburgertum Und Nationalstaat* (Munich and Berlin, 1908), p. 7, quoted in M.I. Finley, 'The Ancient Greeks and Their Nation', *The Use And Abuse Of History* (Harmondsworth, 1987), p. 123.

58. J. Plamenatz, 'Two Types of Nationalism', E. Kamenka (ed.), *Nationalism* (London, 1976), pp. 23–4.

59. Smith, *Nationalism And Modernism*, p. 90.

60. Ibid., p. 74. (See also p. 90.)

61. Barnard, 'National Culture and Political Legitimacy: Herder and Rousseau', pp. 250–1

62. Finley, 'The Ancient Greeks and Their Nation', p. 131.

Chapter 2: From National Consciousness To Nation States

1. Q. Skinner, *The Foundations Of Modern Political Thought* (2 Volumes, Cambridge, 1978), vol. 2, *The Age Of Reformation*, pp. 351–2, 353, 354. Ian Birchall has argued that Skinner is wrong, in an attempt to defend his thesis that Gracchus Babeuf, organiser of the Conspiracy of Equals against the Directory during the French Revolution, was engaged in the same struggle for freedom as the modern proletariat. (I.H. Birchall, *The Spectre Of Babeuf* (Houndmills, 1997), p. 3.). Birchall makes a convincing case for Babeuf, but would not, I trust, make the same case for Spartacus or Watt Tyler, other than in the most elementary sense that all three men were resisting exploitation and oppression. If this is not so then why do Marxists bother to distinguish between the slave, feudal and capitalist modes of production? Karl Kautsky, although an elephantine pedant and ultimately a renegade, did nevertheless urge a sensible caution against 'two dangers' which faced historical investigators who were also engaged in contemporary politics: '...in the first place, they may attempt to mould the past entirely after the image of the present, and, in the second place, they

may seek to behold the past in the light of the needs of present-day policy.'
Foundations Of Christianity (London, n.d.), p. 10.

2. V.N. Voloshinov, *Marxism And The Philosophy Of Language*. Translated by
   L. Makeika and I.R. Titunik (London and Cambridge, Massachusetts,
   1986), pp. 19, 23.

3. A. Hastings, *The Construction Of Nationhood* (Cambridge, 1997),
   pp. 15–17.

4. S. Reynolds, *Kingdoms And Communities In Western Europe, 900–1300*
   (second edition, Oxford, 1997), pp. 250, 254, 255–6.

5. S. Reynolds, 'Medieval *Origines Gentium* and the Community of the Realm',
   History, vol. 68, no. 224, October, p. 377. Colin Kidd has argued that the
   Japhetan genealogy was dominant down to the seventeenth century at
   least. See *British Identities Before Nationalism* (Cambridge, 1999), pp. 9–10
   and Chapter 2 more generally.

6. Quoted in R. Bartlett, *The Making Of Europe* (London, 1993), p. 198.

7. A.D. Smith, *Theories Of Nationalism* (London, 1971), p. 167.

8. Bartlett, *The Making Of Europe*, p. 202. As Susan Reynolds writes: 'There
   is no foundation at all for the belief, common among students of modern
   nationalism, that the word *natio* was seldom used in the middle ages
   except to describe the *natiores* into which university students were
   divided.' *Kingdoms And Communities In Western Europe*, p. 256.

9. Ibid., pp. 201–2.

10. J.R. Llobera, *The God Of Modernity* (Oxford and Providence, 1994), p. 153.

11. J.R. Hale, *Renaissance Europe, 1480–1520* (London, 1971), p. 55

12. Reynolds, *Kingdoms And Communities In Western Europe*, pp. 251–4.

13. B. O'Leary, 'Ernest Gellner's Diagnoses of Nationalism: a Critical Overview,
    Or, What is Living and What is Dead in Ernest Gellner's Philosophy of
    Nationalism?' J.A. Hall (ed.), *The State Of The Nation* (Cambridge, 1998),
    p. 55.

14. Gellner, *Nations And Nationalism*, pp. 35, 141.

15. The most recent example, which specifically targets the writings of Eric
    Hobsbawm, can be found in Hastings, *The Construction Of Nationhood*, a
    work which inspires William Ferguson to claim that Hastings had
    'exploded' the view that 'nations, nationhood and nationalism cannot
    pre-date 1780.' See *The Identity Of The Scottish Nation* (Edinburgh, 1998),
    p. 301. See also F. Watson, 'The Enigmatic Lion: Scotland, Kingship and
    National Identity In the Wars of Independence', D. Broun, R.J. Finlay and
    M. Lynch (eds), *Image And Identity* (Edinburgh, 1998), p. 31, note 58, for
    similar remarks.

16. E. Gellner, 'Reply to Critics', J.A. Hall and I.C. Jarvie (eds), *The Social Theory
    Of Ernest Gellner* (Amsterdam, 1996), p. 638.

17. J.R. Hale, *The Civilisation Of Europe In The Renaissance* (London, 1993),
    p. 68.

18. Hale, *Renaissance Europe*, p. 320.

19. J. Derrick McClure, 'The Concept Of Standard Scots', *Chapman* 23/4,
    Spring 1979, p. 90–1.

20. Ibid., p. 91. Compare E.J. Hobsbawm: 'Dialects, as everyone knows, are
    just languages without an army and police force', *The Age Of Empire*
    (London, 1987), p. 156.

21. M. Billig, *Banal Nationalism* (London, 1995), pp. 30, 31.

22. L. Febvre and H.-J. Martin, *The Coming Of The Book* (London, 1976), pp. 258–9.
23. Hale, *The Civilisation Of Europe In The Renaissance*, p. 68.
24. Ibid., pp. 153–4.
25. M. Mann, 'The Emergence of Modern European Nationalism', J. Hall and I.C. Jarvie (eds), *Transitions To Modernity* (Cambridge, 1992), p. 162. See also N. Harris, *National Liberation* (Harmondsworth, 1992), pp. 28–9.
26. J.W. Cairns, 'Institutional Writings In Scotland Reconsidered', A. Kirafy and H.L. MacQueen (eds), *New Perspectives In Scottish Legal History* (London and Totowa, 1984), p. 78.
27. E.J. Hobsbawm, *Nations And Nationalism Since 1780* (Cambridge, 1990), p. 46. It should be obvious from these observations that Hobsbawm does not believe that 'nations, nationhood and nationalism' simply appeared around 1780 without any preceding history of development, contrary to what is claimed in the references cited in note 15 above.
28. P. Furtardo, 'National Pride in Seventeenth-Century England', Samuel (ed.), *Patriotism*, vol. 1, *History And Politics*, p. 44.
29. Llobera, *The God Of Modernity*, pp. 141–2.
30. Quoted in F. Braudel, *Civilisation And Capitalism* (3 Volumes, London, 1981), vol. 2, *The Wheels Of Commerce*, p. 467.
31. It is therefore placing the existence of a full-blown English nationalism too early to argue, as Liah Greenfield does, that it arose during the reign of Henry VIII to legitimise the position of a 'new' Henrican aristocracy based on merit rather than birth. (L. Greenfield, *Nationalism* (Cambridge Massachusetts, 1992), Chapter 1.) Nevertheless, Mann is surely right to argue that the transition from 'nation' in 'the medieval sense of a group united by common blood descent' to 'the general population of the territorial state' had been accomplished in England before the outbreak of the War of the Three Kingdoms in 1638. See M. Mann, *The Sources Of Social Power* (2 Volumes, Cambridge, 1986–), vol. 1, *A History Of Power From The Beginning To A.D. 1760*, pp. 435, 463. For an earlier version of this argument see H. Kohn, 'The Genesis and Character of English Nationalism', *Journal Of The History Of Ideas* 1, 1940.
32. E. Meiksins Wood, *The Origin Of Capitalism* (New York, 1999), pp. 13–14.
33. Such as the work of the 'famous historian' to whom Meiksins Wood presumably refers, the anti-Marxist zealot J.H. Hexter. See his 'The Myth of the Middle Class In Tudor England', *Reappraisals In History* (London, 1961), pp. 71–5.
34. In one interview with Lee Humber and John Rees, conducted during 1992, Hill explained this decision on the grounds that:

> Using the word 'bourgeoisie' is like a red rag to most academics. Even the most intelligent of them, Lawrence Stone for example, believes that the bourgeoisie must have something to do with the towns and that if you can prove that the gentry were the main capitalists in England in the 17th century you've disproved the idea of a bourgeois revolution. But to have to explain this every time you use the word bourgeois is a bore. It's much easier to just leave out the word bourgeois...Initially I thought that I had to drop the jargon in order to get people to treat me seriously.

'The Good Old Cause – an Interview With Christopher Hill', *International Socialism* 56, Second Series, Autumn 1992, pp. 130–1.

35. H. Draper, *Karl Marx's Theory Of Revolution* (4 Volumes, New York, 1978), vol. 2, *The Politics Of Social Classes*, p. 169.

36. J. Breuilly, *Nationalism And The State*, (second edn, Manchester, 1993) pp. 3–4.

37. A Gramsci, 'The Renaissance', *Selections From The Cultural Writings*, edited by D. Forgacs and G. Nowell-Smith (London, 1985), p. 226 and 'The Question of the Language and the Italian Intellectual Classes', ibid., p. 169. See also J. Larner, *Italy In The Age Of Dante And Petrarch, 1216–1380* (London and New York, 1980), pp. 1–9.

38. Billig, *Banal Nationalism*, p. 25.

39. Greenfield, *Nationalism*, p. 47.

40. For a useful synoptic account of the Swiss and Dutch states from their formation to their respective transformation into the Helvetic and Batavian Republics during the French Revolution, see M. Forsyth, *Unions Of States* (New York, 1981), Chapter 2. The comments of Fredy Perlman on the United States which emerged from the War of Independence in 1784 can, changing what needs to be changed, also be applied to its Swiss and Dutch predecessors:

> The North American colonizers broke the traditional bonds of fealty and feudal obligation but, unlike the French, they only gradually replaced the traditional bonds with bonds of patriotism and nationhood. They were not quite a nation; their reluctant mobilisation of the colonial countryside had not fused them into one; and the multi-lingual, multi-cultural and socially divided underlying population resisted such a fusion.

The Persistence Of Nationalism (Detroit, 1985), p. 15. For a discussion of the American Civil War as the decisive moment in the formation of both national consciousness and nationalism in America, see S.-M. Grant, '"The Charter of its Birthright": the Civil War and American Nationalism', *Nations And Nationalism*, vol. 4, no. 2, July 1998.

41. L.L. Farrar Junior, K. McGuire and J.E. Thompson, 'Dog in the Night: the Limits of European Nationalism, 1789–1895', *Nations And Nationalism*, vol. 4, no. 4, pp. 550, 565.

42. Quoted in ibid., p. 555.

43. G. Mazzini, 'Instruzione Generale per gli Affrantellati nella *Giovine Italia*', quoted in B. Haddock, 'State and Nation in Mazzini's Political Thought', *History Of Political Thought*, vol. 20, no. 2, Summer 1999, pp. 321, 323.

44. E. Weber, *Peasants Into Frenchmen* (Stanford, 1977), p. 70.

45. R. Miliband, 'Barnave: a Case of Bourgeois Class Consciousness', I. Meszaros (ed.), *Aspects Of History And Class Consciousness* (London, 1971), pp. 22–3. Most discussions involve a similarly hierarchical conception of class consciousness, although with fewer levels. R.J. Morris lists, in ascending order, 'consensus', 'labour consciousness' and 'revolutionary class consciousness', *Class And Class Consciousness In The Industrial Revolution, 1750–1850* (London, 1979), p. 37. Michael Mann sees class consciousness involving four elements; an 'identity' of common interests, an 'opposition' to the interests of the capitalist class, a sense of 'totality'

which combines identity and opposition into a coherent world view of the worker's situation within society, and finally the vision of an 'alternative' type of society, *Consciousness And Action Among The Western Working Class* (London and Basingstoke, 1973), p. 13.

46. Miliband, 'Barnave: a Case of Bourgeois Class Consciousness', p. 23.

47. In this sense, Lenin was absolutely right to argue that: 'The history of all countries shows that the working class, exclusively by its own effort, is able to develop only trade union consciousness, i.e., the conviction that it is necessary to combine in unions, fight the employers, and strive to compel the government to pass necessary labour legislation, etc.' V.I. Lenin, 'What Is To Be Done', *Selected Works* (3 Volumes, Moscow, 1977), vol. 1, pp. 114, 121–2. The notion of 'trade union consciousness' is not, however, a particularly helpful one, since the type of reformist consciousness Lenin describes can and does exist outside of trade unions, whose members have always tended to be a minority of the world working class. Nevertheless, for an illuminating attempt to analyse class consciousness during the Industrial Revolution using strict Leninist categories, 'trade union consciousness' among them, see J. Foster, *Class Struggle And The Industrial Revolution* (London, 1974), esp. pp. 42–3.

48. K. Marx, *Capital* (3 Volumes, Harmondsworth, 1976), vol. 1, p. 680. For an attempt to draw out the gap between the potential explanation for reformism to be found in the theory of commodity fetishism and the actual ad hoc explanations advanced by Marx and Engels at various stages in their careers, see C. Johnston, 'The Problem of Reformism and Marx's Theory of Fetishism', *New Left Review* 119, January/February 1980. The significance of commodity fetishism and the related concept of alienation as the basis of the contradictory consciousness we call reformism has been demonstrated in detail by J. Rees, *The Algebra Of Revolution* (London and New York, 1998), pp. 87–97, 220–5, 240–4.

49. A. Gramsci, *Selections From The Prison Notebooks Of Antonio Gramsci*, edited and translated by Q. Hoare and G. Nowell-Smith (London, 1971), pp. 327, 333.

50. W. Reich, 'What Is Class Consciousness?', *Sex/Pol*, edited by L. Baxandall with an introduction by B. Ollman (New York, 1972), p. 313. By 'class consciousness' Reich means 'revolutionary class consciousness'.

51. G. Kerevan, 'Arguments Within Scottish Marxism', *Bulletin of Scottish Politics*, vol. 1, no. 2, spring 1981, pp. 118–19.

52. A. Callinicos, *Making History* (Cambridge, 1987), pp. 156–7.

53. B. Anderson, *Imagined Communities* (revised edition, London and New York, 1991), p. 36.

54. C. Harman, 'The Return of the National Question', *International Socialism* 56, second series, autumn 1992, pp. 42–3.

55. R.W. Davies, *The Industrialisation Of Soviet Russia* (4 Volumes, Houndmills, 1996), vol. 4, *Crisis And Progress In The Soviet Economy, 1931–1933*, pp. 485–8.

56. A.R. Luria, *Cognitive Development*, translated by M. Lopez-Morillas and L. Solotaroff, edited by M. Cole (London, 1976), pp. 12–4, 163–4.

57. G. Simmel, 'The Metropolis and Mental Life', *On Individuality And Social Forms*, edited with an introduction by D.N. Levine (Chicago and London, 1971), p. 325.

58. T. Nairn, 'The Modern Janus', *The Break-Up of Britain*, (second, revised edition, London, 1981), p. 354.
59. Kerevan, 'Arguments Within Scottish Marxism', pp. 118–19.
60. K. Marx, 'Critique of Hegel's Philosphy of Right. Introduction', *Early Writings*. Introduced by L. Colletti, translated by R. Livingstone and G. Benton (London, 1975), p. 244.
61. E. Gellner, 'Nationalism and Politics in Eastern Europe', *New Left Review* 189, September/October 1991, p. 121.
62. Breuilly, *Nationalism And The State*, p. 414.
63. N. Harris, *Of Bread And Guns* (Harmondsworth, 1981), p. 24.
64. P. Linebaugh and M. Rediker, 'The Many-Headed Hydra: Sailors, Slaves, and the Atlantic Working Class In the Eighteenth Century', *Journal Of Historical Sociology*, vol. 3, no. 3, September 1990, p. 245.
65. V.N. Voloshinov, 'The Word and Its Social Function', A. Shukman (ed.), *Bahktin School Papers* (Somerton, 1988), p. 147.
66. V.N. Voloshinov, *Marxism And The Philosophy Of Language*. Translated by L. Mateika and I.R. Titunik (London and Cambridge, Massachusetts, 1986), pp. 19, 23.
67. Colley, 'The Apotheosis of George III', p. 126.
68. A. Calder, 'Rewriting Scottish History', *Revolving Culture* (London and New York, 1994), p. 52.

Chapter 3: Was There a Scottish Nation Before 1707?

1. D. Murray, *The First Nation In Europe* (London, 1960), p. 10.
2. J. Foster, 'Nationality, Social Change and Class: Transformations of National Identity in Scotland', D. McCrone, S. Kendrick and P. Straw (eds), *The Making Of Scotland: Nation, Culture And Social Change* (Edinburgh, 1989), p. 35.
3. J. Foster, 'Capitalism and the Scottish Nation', G. Brown (ed.), *The Red Paper On Scotland* (Edinburgh, 1975), p. 142.
4. The medieval origin of nationalism is of course the theme of A. Hastings, *The Construction Of Nationhead* (Cambridge, 1997), although Foster also suggests that the nationalism he identifies in Scotland at the time of the Wars of Independence may have been more widespread, occurring in other parts of Europe where supposed 'populist anti-feudal struggle' took place. See 'Scottish Nationality and the Origins of Capitalism', T. Dickson (ed.), *Scottish Capitalism* (London, 1980) p. 45. Both this essay, and the book to which it forms the opening chapter, have been subjected to devastating criticism in Kerevan, 'Arguments Within Scottish Marxism'.
5. T.C. Smout, *A History Of The Scottish People* (Glasgow, 1969), p. 27.
6. G.W.S. Barrow, *Robert Bruce And The Community Of The Realm Of Scotland* (second edition, Edinburgh, 1976), p. 430.
7. Ibid., pp. 424–6.
8. Ibid., pp. xiv-v.
9. 'The Declaration of Arbroath', reproduced in A.A.M. Duncan, *The Nation Of The Scots And The Declaration Of Arbroath* (London, 1970), p. 34.
10. S. Reynolds, 'Medieval *Origines Gentium* and the Community of the Realm', *History*, vol. 68, no. 224, October, p. 377.
11. 'The Declaration of Arbroath', p. 36.

12. E.J. Cowan, 'Identity, Freedom and the Declaration of Arbroath', D. Broun, R.J. Finlay and M. Lynch (eds), *Image And Identity* (Edinburgh, 1998), p. 51.

13. S. Reynolds, *Kingdoms And Communities In Western Europe, 900–1300* (second edition, Oxford, 1997), p. 274.

14. Ibid., p. 275.

15. The use of 'nation' to identify the Scottish academic community abroad provides even less support for the existence of a premodern Scottish national consciousness. Local students at Aberdeen University in the early sixteenth century were also divided into the 'nations' of Mar, Buchan, Moray and Angus, all of which were northeastern feudal jurisdictions, but not even the most reverent northeastern patriot has yet argued that these regions have a past (or a future) as individual nation states (Hastings, *The Construction Of Nationalism*, p. 17.) In other words, we are dealing with a late medieval scholastic convention which sometimes corresponded to groups which later went on to form modern nations, and sometimes did not. When the University of Padua was founded in 1222, for example, the 'Natio Anglica' (i.e., the English 'nation') included all the inhabitants of the British Isles: English, Scots and Irish alike. As late as 1465 the 'nation' was still jointly that of the English and the Scots and it was only in 1534 that the English and Scottish students were split into separate 'nations', an arrangement which lasted until the 'nations' themselves were dissolved in 1738, 33 years after the Union of Parliaments. (A. Francis Stewart, 'The Scottish "Nation" At the University of Padua', *Scottish Historical Review* 3, 1906, p. 53.) The way in which the Scottish 'nation' was formed is itself of more than passing interest. The University was divided into two camps, the ultramontane (i.e., North of the Alps) and cismontane (i.e., south of the Alps). In March 1534 two nations were created, one of which was the Scottish nation in the ultramontane camp and the other a Piedmontese nation in the cismontane camp. The formation of the first was intended to maintain the electoral dominance of the ultramontane camp and appears not to have initially involved any Scottish people. The four members of the nation in 1534 – Bernardus Grivellus, Claudius Brocard, Ugetus Aruldus and Georgius Onis – were all described as 'Scouts', but the first two at least were French and, as Jonathan Woolfson writes: 'The irresistible conclusion is that the Scottish nation was created by a fraud perpetrated by French students.' In any event, the Scottish nation remained inquorate until 1592 and subject to struggle for control by the other nations. The final twist came in 1603 when, as a result of the accession of James VI to the throne of England, an Englishman – Simeon Foxe, son of John Foxe – was permitted to become its *consiliarius*. It is tempting to use these events as a metaphor, but I will resist the temptation. See J. Woolfson, *Padua And the Tudors* (Toronto, 1998), pp. 31–2.

16. T. Johnston, *The History Of The Working Classes In Scotland* (fourth edition, Glasgow, 1946), p. 25. Reference to 'the working class', in 1320 tends to support the view of John Maclean concerning 'the limitations of [Johnston's] theoretical equipment'. J. Maclean, 'Literary Note', *In The Rapids Of Revolution*, edited with an introduction and commentaries by N. Milton (London, 1977), p. 221.

17. Barrow, *Robert Bruce And The Community Of The Realm Of Scotland*, pp. 126, 326–7.
18. Kerevan, 'Arguments Within Scottish Marxism', p. 125.
19. Duncan, *The Nation Of The Scots And The Declaration Of Arbroath*, pp. 14–15.
20. R.J. Finlay, 'The Rise and Fall of Popular Imperialism In Scotland, 1850–1950', *Scottish Geographical Magazine*, vol. 113, no. 1, March 1997, p. 14.
21. G. Morton, 'What If?: the Significance of Scotland's Missing Nationalism in the Nineteenth Century', Broun, Finlay and Lynch (eds), *Image And Identity*, p. 161.
22. D. McCrone, 'Culture, Nationalism and Scottish Education: Homogeneity and Diversity', T.G.K. Bryce and W.M. Humes (eds), *Scottish Education* (Edinburgh, 1999), p. 235.
23. L. Patterson, *The Autonomy Of Modern Scotland* (Edinburgh, 1994), p. 66.
24. Quoted in R. Weir, 'The Scottish and Irish Unions: the Victorian View In Perspective', S.J. Connolly (ed.), *Kingdoms United?* (Dublin, 1999), p. 60.
25. R.D. Anderson, 'The History of Scottish Education, pre 1980', Bryce and Humes (eds), *Scottish Education*, p. 215.
26. R.G. Cant, 'Origins of the Enlightenment in Scotland: the Universties', R.H. Campbell and A.S. Skinner (eds), *The Origins And Nature Of The Scottish Enlightenment* (Edinburgh, 1982), esp. pp. 50–5.
27. T. Nairn, 'Empire and Union', *Faces of Nationalism* (London and New York, 1997), p. 206.
28. J. Steuart, *An Inquiry Into The Principles Of Political Economy*, edited with an introduction by A.S. Skinner, 2 Volumes, (Edinburgh and London, 1966), vol. 1, p. 108.
29. The founding text here is I.B. Whyte, *Agriculture And Society In Seventeenth Century Scotland* (Edinburgh, 1976), although Whyte is more cautious than some later writers. In the absence of any widely accepted conception of the Scottish bourgeois revolution, such writings occupy the same space in Scottish historiography as the work of 'revisionist' historians of the English Civil War and the French Revolution do in their respective nations.
30. C. Beveridge and R. Turnbull, *The Eclipse Of Scottish Culture* (Edinburgh, 1989), Chapter 3, 'The Darkness and the Dawn: Perceptions of Scottish Rural History'. Beveridge and Turnbull draw on Whyte in support of their thesis. See ibid., pp. 43–7.
31. D. Stevenson, 'The Effects of Revolution and Conquest on Scotland', R. Mitchison and P. Roebuck (eds), *Economy And Society In Scotland And Ireland, 1500–1939* (Edinburgh, 1988), pp. 53–5.
32. Davidson, 'Scotland's Bourgeois Revolution', C. Bambery (ed.), *Scotland, Class and Nation* (London, Chicago and Sydney, 1999), pp. 88–93.
33. Johnston, *The History Of The Working Classes In Scotland*, p. 146.
34. A. Gramsci, 'State and Civil Society', *Selections From The Prison Notebooks Of Antonio Gramsci*, edited and translated by P. Hoare and G. Nowell-Smith (London, 1971), p. 249.
35. B. Kay, *Scots: The Mither Tongue* (Edinburgh, 1986), p. 18.
36. K. White, 'Scotland, History and the Writer', *On Scottish Ground* (Edinburgh, 1998), p. 149.
37. J. Derrick McClure, 'The Concept Of Standard Scots', p. 92.

38. W. Dunbar, 'The Goldyn Targe', *The Poems Of William Dunbar*, edited by P. Bawcutt (2 Volumes, Glasgow, 1998), vol. 1, p. 192, lines 253–61.

39. White, 'Scotland, History and the Writer', p. 149. White adds: 'I can see in this no great cause for lamentation, and certainly no justification for trying to write systematically in Lallans, as some literati have done and are still doing.'

40. D. Murison, *The Guid Scots Tongue* (Edinburgh, 1977), p. 5.

41. Take, as a comparison, the following passage which appeared in the 'Country Diary' column of the *Guardian* (London), 23 December 1989, with reference to Oxfordshire: 'In my boyhood the old Oxfordshire dialect was still in general use, and was so different from what is now Standard English that visitors from other regions found it as incomprehensible as a foreign language.'

42. A.M. Scott, *Bonnie Dundee* (Edinburgh, 1989), p. 194.

43. C. Harvie, 'The Most Mighty of Goddesses: the Scots and the Law', *Travelling Scot* (Glasgow, 1999), p. 63.

44. G.M. Sutton, 'Stair's Aim In Writing the Institutions', D.M. Walker (ed.), *Stair Centenary Studies* (Edinburgh, 1981).

45. J.W. Cairns, 'Institutional Writings In Scotland Reconsidered', A. Kirafy and H.L. MacQueen (eds), *New Perspectives in Scottish Legal History* (London and Totowa, 1984), p. 78.

46. J. Dalrymple, *The Institutions Of The Law Of Scotland* (Edinburgh and Glasgow, 1981), p. 60. For similar claims as to the endogamous nature of the Scottish people see [J. Hodges], *The Rights And Interests Of The Two British Monarchies Inquir'd Into, And Clear'd With A Special Respect To An United Or Separate State* (London, 1703), pp. 2–3.

47. M. Lynch, *Scotland: A New History* (revised edition, London, 1992), p. 12. The origins of this process were famously mocked in the deathless prose of Sellar and Yeatman: 'The Scots (originally Irish, but by now Scotch) were this time inhabiting Ireland, having driven the Irish (Picts) out of Scotland; while the Picts (originally Scots) were now Irish (living in brackets) and vice versa. It is essential to keep these distinctions clearly in mind (and vice versa).' W.C. Sellar and R.J. Yeatman, *1066 And All That* (Harmondsworth, 1960), p. 13.

48. Dalrymple, *The Institutions Of The Law Of Scotland*, p. 1013.

49. N. Phillipson, *The Scottish Whigs And The Reform Of The Court Of Session, 1785–1830* (Edinburgh, 1990), p. 36.

50. Quoted in A.H. Williamson, *Scottish National Consciousness In The Age Of James VI* (Edinburgh, 1979), pp. 87–8.

51. C.G. Brown, *Religion And Society In Scotland Since 1707* (Edinburgh, 1997), p. 46.

52. Ibid., pp. 17, 45.

53. A point Nairn concedes when he writes that 'the Treaty of Union came just in time to bury a nascent Scottish nationalism, but could only put it in a shallow grave'. T. Nairn, 'Empire and Union', *Faces of Nationalism* (London and New York, 1997), p. 209.

54. Davidson, 'Scotland's Bourgeois Revolution', pp. 100–2.

55. [Hodges], *The Rights And Interests Of The Two British Monarchies Inquir'd Into, And Clear'd*, p. 9.

56. E.J. Hobsbawm, *The Age Of Empire* (London, 1987), p. 279 and J.G.A. Pocock, 'Deconstructing Europe', P. Gowan and P. Anderson. (eds), *The Question Of Europe* (London and New York, 1997), p. 306.

57. See, for example, M. Vajda, 'East-Central European Perspectives', J. Keane (ed.), *Civil Society And The State* (London and New York, 1988), pp. 343, 348–50.

58. N. Davis, *Europe* (New York, 1996), p. 25.

59. E.W. Said, *Orientalism* (Harmondsworth, 1985), p. 322.

60. D. Cannadine, *Class In Britain* (New Haven and London, 1988), p. 43. Needless to say, the Lowlands are described as being 'a modernising, Anglicised, urban world' in opposition to the Highlands, the truth of which depends on much more precise dating than Cannadine gives here.

61. *John of Fordun's Chronicle Of The Scottish Nation*, edited by W.F. Skene, *The Historians Of Scotland* (10 Volumes, Edinburgh, 1871–1880), vol. 4, p. 38.

62. J. Mair, *A History Of Greater Britain As Well England As Scotland, Compiled From The Ancient Authorities By John Mair, By Name Indeed A Scot But By Profession A Theologian*, translated and edited by A. Constable (Edinburgh, 1892), pp. 48–50.

63. W. Dunbar, 'The Flyting of Dunbar and Kennedie', *The Poems Of William Dunbar*, pp. 200–18. See, for example, lines 97–104.

64. P. Bawcutt, *Dunbar The Makar* (Oxford, 1992), p. 256.

65. R.A. Mason, 'Chivalry and Citizenship: Aspects of National Identity In Renaissance Scotland', *Kingship And Commonweal* (East Linton, 1998), pp. 96–7.

66. King James VI and I, 'Basilicon Doron', *Political Writings*, edited by J.P. Sommerville (Cambridge, 1994), p. 24.

67. S. Johnson, 'A Journey to the Western Isles of Scotland', *Johnson's Journey To The Western Isles Of Scotland And Boswell's Journal Of A Tour To The Hebrides With Samuel Johnson, LL.D*, edited by R.W. Chapman (Oxford, 1970), p. 40.

68. A. Fletcher, 'Two Discourses Concerning the Affairs of Scotland; Written in the Month of July, 1698', *Political Works*, edited by J. Robertson (Cambridge, 1998), p. 70.

69. A.I. MacInnes, 'Repression and Conciliation: the Highland Dimension, 1660–1688', *Scottish Historical Review* 180, October 1986, pp. 169, 171.

70. *The History Of The Affairs Of Scotland From The Restoration Of King Charles II In The Year 1660. And Of The Late Great Revolution In That Kingdom* (Edinburgh, 1690), pp. 128–9.

71. Ferguson, *The Identity Of The Scottish Nation* (Edinburgh, 1988), p. 45. See also pp. 301–6 for a summary of the argument. Establishing that the Scots were politically and culturally dominant during the formation of the kingdom is important, but for a Marxist, as opposed to a Scottish nationalist, it is not the central issue. *All* the tribes to which Ferguson refers lived in societies dominated by the same 'Asiatic' mode of production, and this ultimately determined the nature of social life in the early Scottish kingdom, not the language which the inhabitants spoke. An earlier and less developed version of the case made by Ferguson can be found in R.S. Rait, *An Outline Of The Relations Between England And Scotland (500–1707)*, London, 1901, pp. x–xxxviii, 1–5.

72. Kidd, *British Identities Before Nationalism*, p. 124.

73. *John Of Fordun's Chronicle Of The Scottish Nation*, p. 38.

74. Mair, *A History Of Greater Britain*, p. 48.
75. Kidd, *British Identities Before Nationalism*, p. 125.
76. One reason why the 'holy trinity' is so often invoked as the basis for national continuity is precisely because language could not play that role. 'Among the Scots, language long ago ceased to play a differentiating and unifying role, once Lallans had become the language of the Lowlands.' A.D. Smith, *The Ethnic Origins Of Nations* (London, 1986), p. 26.
77. C.W.J. Withers, 'The Scottish Highlands Outlined: Cartographic Evidence for the Position of the Highland Lowland Boundary', *Scottish Geographical Magazine*, vol. 98, no. 3, 1982, p. 154.
78. J. Walker, *An Economical History Of The Hebrides And Highlands Of Scotland* (2 Volumes, Edinburgh, 1808), vol. 1, p. 19.
79. *The Highlander's Complaint, Transmitted By A Gentleman Of That Country To His Friends At Edinburgh* (Edinburgh, 1737), p. 24.
80. D. Forbes, 'Some Thoughts Concerning the State of the Highlands [In the Lord President's Handwriting. Perhaps 1746]', *Culloden Papers ... From the Year 1625 to 1748*, (London, 1815), p. 297.
81. *John of Fordun's Chronicle Of The Scottish Nation*, p. 38.
82. *The History Of The Affairs Of Scotland*, p. 240.
83. H. MacKay, *Memoirs Of The War Carried Out In Scotland And Ireland 1689–1691* (Edinburgh, 1833), p. 16.
84. *Extracts From The Records Of The Synod Of Moray*, edited by W.M. Cramond (Elgin, 1906), p. 7.
85. J. Dawson, 'Calvinism and the Gaidhealtachd In Scotland', A. Pettigree, A. Duke and G. Lewis (eds), *Calvinism in Europe, 1540–1620* (Cambridge, 1994), p. 251.
86. C. Larner, *Enemies Of God* (London, 1981), p. 80.
87. M. Mann, *The Sources Of Social Power* (2 Volumes, Cambridge, 1986-), vol. 1, *A History Of Power From The Beginning To AD 1760*, p. 2.
88. J. Spalding, *The History Of The Troubles And Memorable Transactions In Scotland And England, From 1624 To 1645* (2 Volumes, Edinburgh, 1821), vol. 2, pp. 264–5. What little is known of Spalding's life is recounted in D. Stevenson, 'The Secretive Chronicler: Mr John Spalding', *King Or Covenant?* (East Linton, 1996).
89. D. Stevenson, *Alasdair MacColla And The Highland Problem In The Seventeenth Century*, (Edinburgh, 1980), p. 136.
90. G.W.S. Barrow, 'The Highlands in the Lifetime of Robert the Bruce', *The Kingdom of the Scots* (London, 1973), pp. 363–4.
91. A parallel can be drawn between the Highland society of 1688 (in relation to Scotland) and the Southern society of 1861 (in relation to the United States). As Greenfield writes:

> The South and the North, which were but the names of geographical sectors, the borders between which were established by convention and could be recharted, in the Southern consciousness became reified concepts, collective bodies possessed of antagonistic souls and pitted against each other as might be two warring persons.

But the South did not possess the cohesion to form a single nation separate from the states which comprised the North: 'Had the Confederacy survived, the secession might have brought into the world several

Southern nations, rather than one.' The universality of the nation state by 1861 means that Greenfield is probably right to assume it would have imposed itself on a victorious South in one form or another. See L. Greenfield, *Nationalism* (Cambridge Massachusetts, 1992), p. 479.

92. L. Colley, *Britons* (London, 1992), pp. 14–15.

93. A. MacDonald, 'Resurrection of the Old Scottish Tongue: the Author's Praise of the Old Gaelic Language', translated by and partially reproduced in M. Chapman, *The Gaelic Vision In Scottish Culture* (London and Montreal, 1978), pp. 60–1.

94. G. Wade, 'Report, etc., Relating to the Highlands, 1724', *Highland Papers Relating To The Jacobite Period 1699–1750*, edited by J. Allardyce (2 Volumes, Aberdeen, 1895), vol. 1, pp. 132–3. (Author's emphasis.)

95. I.L. MacDonald, 'The Battle of Inverlochy', D. Thomson, (ed.), *An Introduction To Gaelic Poetry* (London, 1974), p. 122.

96. A.I. MacInnes, 'Scottish Gaeldom, 1638–1651: the Vernacular Response to the Covenanting Dynamic', J. Dwyer, R.A. Mason and A. Murdoch (eds), *New Perspectives On The Politics And Culture Of Early Modern Scotland* (Edinburgh, n.d.), p. 77.

97. Stevenson, *Alasdair MacColla And The Highland Problem In The Seventeenth Century*, p. 23.

98. Quoted in G. MacDonald Fraser, *The Steel Bonnets* (London, 1974), pp. 49, 132. Given the similarities between Highland and Border society, prior to the latter being pacified in the early seventeenth century, it is worth noting that the inhabitants of that region displayed the same disregard for 'national' classifications.

99. *The Complaynt Of Scotland...With An Appendix Of Contemporary English Tracts*, re-edited from the original with an introduction and glossary by J.A.H. Murray (Edinburgh, 1822), p. 124. 'Nation' is used here in the 'racial' or 'ethnic' sense. The reference to language makes it clear that the Scotland referred to is Lowland Scotland.

Chapter 4: Highland versus Lowland, Scotland versus England

1. *Burt's Letters From The North Of Scotland*, with an introduction by R. Johnson (2 Volumes, Edinburgh, 1974), vol. 1, pp. 4–5.

2. Ibid., p. 5.

3. J. Swift, *Journal To Stella*, edited by H. Williams (2 Volumes, Oxford, 1974), vol. 2, Letter 43, 8 March 1711, p. 511.

4. *Burt's Letters From The North Of Scotland*, vol. 1, pp. 5–6. He also adds, however:

    On the other hand, some flattering Accounts that have been published, what with Commendation, and what with Concealment, might induce a Stranger to both Parts of the Island, to conclude that Scotland in general is the better Country of the two; and I wish it were so (as we are become one People) for the benefit of the whole.

5. Swift, *Journal To Stella*, vol. 1, Letter 14, 6 January 1710, p. 171.

6. N.C. Landsman, *Scotland And Its First American Colony, 1683–1765* (New Jersey, 1985), p. 169.

7. Mitchell to Forbes, 19 November 1745, *Culloden Papers...From The Year 1625 To 1748* (London, 1815), p. 253.

8. Quoted in J.T. Findlay, *Wolfe In Scotland In The '45 And From 1749 to 1753* (London, 1928), p. 295.

9. Carre to Marchmont, 10 September 1745, 'Marchmont Correspondence Relating to the '45', edited by C.F.C. Hepbourne Scott, *Miscellany Of The Scottish History Society* 5, 1933, p. 316. (Author's emphasis.)

10. A. MacDonald, 'A Fragment', *Highland Songs Of The Forty Five*, edited by J.R. Campbell, (Edinburgh, 1984), p. 117.

11. A. Gramsci, 'Notes on Italian History', *Selections From The Prison Notebooks Of Antonio Gramsci*, edited and translated by Q. Hoare and G. Nowell-Smith (London, 1971), pp. 58–9. The process described here, which Gramsci describes as one of 'passive revolution', is explicitly identified as a characteristic of the Italian Risorgimento in ibid., p. 109.

12. J. Henrisoun, 'Exhortation To the Scots To Conform Themselves to the Honourable, Expedient and Godly Union Between the Realms of England and Scotland', *The Complaynt Of Scotland...With An Appendix of Contemporary English Tracts*, re-edited from the original with an introduction and glossary by J.A.H. Murray (Edinburgh, 1822), p. 230.

13. R.A. Mason, 'The Origins of Anglo-Scottish Imperialism', *Kingship and Commonweal* (East Linton, 1998), pp. 243–61.

14. J. Wormald, 'The Creation of Britain: Multiple Kingdoms or Core and Colonies?' *Transactions Of The Royal Historical Society* 2, Sixth Series, 1992, p. 187.

15. There is an interesting indication in the correspondence between John Evelyn and Samuel Pepys of the way in which leading figures in the English state had grudgingly come to accept Scottish sovereignty by the late seventeenth century. In 1682 Evelyn wrote that he had changed his position on the supposed right of England to exercise dominion over the seas around the British Isles:

> One might query whether the Scots sea, and Scotland (to boot) be not a fee [i.e., a feudal estate held on condition of payment and homage to a superior] to England; for with as much reason we might challenge it, if the producing Rolls, Records and Acts of Parliament, and of Statutes to that purpose were of any importance; because we can show more to the purpose, than in the other case [i.e., of the Danegeld]: but how would then that Nation take it, and what become of their laws about Fishing?

Evelyn to Pepys, 19 September 1682, *Particular Friends: The Correspondence Of Samuel Pepys and John Evelyn*, edited by G.de L. Bedeyne (Rochester, 1997), p. 137. Pepys had recently ceased to be Secretary of the Admiralty.

16. Rycaut to Turnbull, 17 November 1697, *Papers Relating To The Ships And Voyages Of The Company Of Scotland Trading To Africa And The Indies, 1696–1707*, edited by G. Pratt Insh (Edinburgh, 1924), p. 13. Patterson was trying to gain English backing for the Darien expedition and this might well have led him to exaggerate the extent of his common feeling for the English people.

17. Patterson made a number of contributions to the 'pamphlet war' during the ratification process for the Treaty of Union on the pro-Union side. See, for example, 'L. Medway', *An Inquiry Into The Reasonableness Of A Union With Scotland...As Communicated To Lawrence Phillips, Esquire; Near York* (London, 1706).

18. Cromarty to Mar, 1 January 1706, W. Fraser, *The Earls Of Cromartie* (2 Volumes, Edinburgh, 1876), vol. 2, p. 2.

19. J. Anderson, *An Historical Essay Shewing That The Crown And Kingdom Of Scotland Is Imperial And Independent* (Edinburgh, 1705), 'Preface', no pagination, [p. i].

20. [Forbes] to Walpole, August 1716, *Culloden Papers*, p. 61.

21. [A. Wedderburn], 'Preface', *Edinburgh Review* 1, 1755, p. ii.

22. J. Dalrymple, *An Essay Towards A General History Of Feudal Property In Great Britain* (London, 1757), pp. 343–4.

23. W. Robertson, *The History Of Scotland During The Reigns Of Queen Mary And James VI Till His Accession To The Crown Of England* (fourteenth edition, 2 Volumes, London, 1794), vol. 2, p. 305.

24. C. Kidd, *Subverting Scotland's Past* (Cambridge, 1990), p. 247.

25. [R. Wallace], *Characteristics Of The Present Political State Of Great Britain* (New York, 1969, facsimile of the 1761 edition), p. 137.

26. B. Dobree, 'The Theme of Patriotism in the Poetry of the Early Eighteenth Century', *Proceedings Of The British Academy* 35, 1949, pp. 56, 60.

27. [Wallace], *Characteristics Of The Present Political State of Great Britain*, p. 115.

28. J.D. Young, *The Very Bastards Of Creation* (n.p., n.d. [Glasgow, 1997]), p. 26.

29. A Scotch journeyman cabinet maker to Bute, quoted in J. Brewer, 'The Misfortunes of Lord Bute: a Case Study in Eighteenth-Century Political Argument and Opinion', *Historical Journal*, vol. 16, no. 1, 1973, p. 7.

30. E.P. Thompson, *The Making Of The English Working Class* (Harmonsworth, 1980), p. 76.

31. 'Political Sketch 1760–1763', Countess of Ilchester and Lord Stavordale (eds), *The Lives And Letters Of Lady Sarah Lennox* (London, 1902), p. 68.

32. It is worth noting that not every attack on Jacobitism during this period invariably disguised an attack on the Scots as a nation: it is only in a historical perspective where Jacobitism is seen to represent Scottish nationhood that this is always assumed to be the case. In I. Gale 'A Brush With Bigotry', *Scotland On Sunday*, 16 March 1997, we learn that William Hogarth's painting of 1748 *O, The Roast Beef Of Old England* (*Calais Gate*) reveals a man 'consumed by hate. Hatred of the French, hatred of the papacy and, not least, hatred of the Scots.' It would be foolish to deny the elements of xenophobia in Hogarth's work. As a recent, outstanding, biography makes clear, when he visited France in 1744, his 'mental baggage was still crammed with the rhetoric of wooden shoes and slavery, despotism and foppery.' There was, however, a 'rational core' to his Francophobia (and its related Scotophobia) which ultimately derived from the fact that France *was* a feudal absolutist despotism, *was* dominated by a reactionary Catholic Church and *was* seeking to overturn the British state through support for Scottish Jacobitism. Hogarth's material interests were engaged in more than one respect. During the '45: 'Old fears of papist superstition, despotic laws and standing armies joined hands with the

moral fight against luxury and affectation – and with mercantile self-interest.' J. Uglow, *Hogarth* (London, 1997), pp. 462, 466. It should be noted however that Hogarth's admiring portrayal of the London based Huguenots – French speaking but Protestant – stands in stark contrast to the caricatures of *Calais Gate* or *The Invasion*: 'Hogarth contrasts the plain Huguenot worshippers with both the over-dressed French-imitating trendies and the loutish English commoners.' D. Widgery, *Some Lives!* (London, 1992), pp. 176–7.

33. L. Colley, *Britons* (London, 1992), p. 121.

34. A. Murdoch, 'Lord Bute, James Stuart Mackenzie, and the Government of Scotland', K.W. Schweizer (ed.), *Lord Bute: Essays In Re-Interpretation* (Leicester, 1988), p. 140.

35. Colley, *Britons*, p. 18.

36. These arguments are developed in the first five chapters of *Britons*, which, although they overlap in theme, are each mainly concerned with one of these elements. See ibid., Chapter 1 (Protestantism), Chapter 2 (war), Chapters 3 and 4 (empire), and Chapter 5 (monarchy).

37. Quoted in H.W. Meikle, *Scotland And The French Revolution* (New York, 1969, facsimile of the 1912 edition), p. 94.

38. H. Cockburn, *Memorials Of His Time*, new edition with introduction by his grandson, H.A. Cockburn (Edinburgh and London, 1909), pp. 74–5.

39. Colley, *Britons*, pp. 367–9.

40. I.B. Cowan, 'The Inevitability of Union – a Historical Fallacy?', *Scotia* 5, 1981, p. 2.

41. [J. Hodges], *The Rights And Interests Of The Two British Monarchies Inquir'd Into, And Clear'd With A Special Respect To An United Or Separate State* (London, 1703), p. 9.

42. Anderson, *An Historical Essay Shewing That The Crown And Kingdom Of Scotland Is Imperial And Independent*, p. 280.

43. Landsman, *Scotland And Its First American Colony*, pp. 189–90.

44. C. Cumming, 'Scottish National Identity in an Australian Colony', *Scottish Historical Review* 193, April 1993, p. 22.

45. Ibid., p. 35. One contributor to the *Melbourne Argus*, 5 July 1854, wrote of them that: 'They try to be English, and cannot succeed'. Quoted in ibid., p. 29.

46. R.K. Donovan, 'Voices of Distrust: the Expression of Anti-Catholic Feeling in Scotland, 1778–1781', *Innes Review* 30, 1979, pp. 62–4, 75–6. These years, after the defeat of Jacobitism, but before the infusion of fresh believers from the Irish emigration, were possibly the lowest point for Scottish Catholicism since the Reformation. At best, the Catholic population of the Lowlands might have increased slightly through the internal migration to the south and east by Highlanders displaced during phase one of the Clearances. See ibid., p. 63.

47. See G. Rude, 'The Gordon Riots: a Study of the Rioters and Their Victims', *Paris And London In The 18th Century* (London, 1970), pp. 289–292.

48. T. Paine, *The Rights Of Man*, edited with an introduction by H. Collins (Harmondsworth, 1969), p. 196.

49. Thompson, *The Making Of The English Working Class*, pp. 81–2.

50. J. Keane, *Tom Paine* (London, 1995), pp. 307–8.

51. D. Cannadine, 'The Context, Performance and Meaning of Ritual: the British Monarchy and the "Invention of Tradition", c. 1820–1977', E.J.

Hobsbawm and T. Ranger (eds), *The Invention Of Tradition*, (Cambridge, 1983), p. 120.

Chapter 5: Scotland After 1707: Oppressed Or Oppressor Nation?

1. A. Calder, *Revolutionary Empire* (New York, 1981), p. 387.
2. A. Callinicos, 'Marxism and Imperialism Today', *International Socialism* 50, second series, Spring 1991, pp. 5–8.
3. M. Hechter, *Internal Colonialism* (London and Henley, 1975), pp. 9–10, 80.
4. M. Hechter, 'Internal Colonialism Revisited', *Cencrastus* 10, Autumn 1982, p. 9.
5. J.D. Young, *The Rousing Of The Scottish Working Class* (London, 1979), p. 11.
6. K. Burgess et al, 'Scotland and the First British Empire 1707–1770's: the Confirmation of Client Status', T. Dickson (ed.), *Scottish Capitalism* (London, 1980), p. 90.
7. D. McCrone, 'Is Scotland Different?', *Understanding Scotland* (London and New York, 1992), p. 64.
8. C.A. Whatley, 'New Light On Nef's Numbers: Coal Mining and the First Phase of Scottish Industrialisation, c.1700–1830', A.J.G. Cummings and T.M. Devine (eds), *Industry, Business And Society In Scotland Since 1700* (Edinburgh, 1994), pp. 7, 15.
9. A.M. Durie, 'The Markets for Scottish Linen, 1730–1755', *Scottish Historical Review* 153–4, 1973, pp. 30, 38.
10. T.M. Devine, 'The Golden Age of Tobacco', T.M. Devine and G. Jackson (eds), *Glasgow* (Manchester and New York, 1995), vol. 1, 'Beginnings to 1830', pp. 140–4.
11. B.P. Lenman, *An Economic History Of Modern Scotland* (London, 1977), pp. 173, 280; J.G. Kellas, *Modern Scotland* (London, 1968), p. 244.
12. L. Brockliss, 'The Professions and National Identity', L. Brockliss and D. Eastwood (eds), *A Union of Multiple Identities* (Manchester and New York, 1997), p. 20.
13. L.B. Namier, *The History Of Parliament: The House Of Commons 1754–1790* (3 Volumes, London, 1964), vol. 1, p. 166; R.G. Thorne, *The History Of Parliament: The House Of Commons 1790–1820* (5 Volumes, London, 1985), vol. 1, p. 328.
14. S. Boyle et al, *Scotland's Future* (London 1989), p. 8.
15. E. MacAskill, 'Our Friends from the North', *The Guardian* (London), 8 May 1997.
16. K. Webb, *The Growth Of Nationalism In Scotland* (Glasgow, 1977), p. 93.
17. Young, *The Rousing Of The Scottish Working Class*, p. 41.
18. R. Heron, *Scotland Delineated, Or A Geographical Description Of Every Shire In Scotland, Including The Northern And Western Isles, With Some Account Of The Curiosities, Antiquaries And The Present State Of The Country* (Edinburgh, 1975, facsimile of the 1799 edition), p. 17.
19. W. Robertson, *The History Of Scotland During the Reigns of Queen Mary And James VI Till His: Accession To The Crown of England* (fourteenth edition, 2 Volumes, London, 1794), vol. 2, pp. 313–14.

20. C. Beveridge and R. Turnbull, 'Inferiorism', *The Eclipse Of Scottish Culture* (Edinburgh, 1989), p. 5.
21. F. Fanon, *The Wretched Of The Earth* (Harmondsworth, 1967), p. 160.
22. Hechter, *Internal Colonialism*, p. 64.
23. B. Kay, *Scots: The Mither Tongue* (Edinburgh, 1986), pp. 173–4.
24. C. Robinson, 'Notes Toward a Native Theory of History', *Review*, vol. 4, no. 1, Summer 1980, pp. 51, 53, 54.
25. P. Kane, 'Soul Brothers Under the Skin', *Tinsel Show* (Edinburgh, 1992), p. 168.
26. A.J.P. Taylor, 'Comment' [on Pocock, 'British History: a Plea for a New Subject'], *Journal Of Modern History*, vol. 47, no. 4, December 1975, p. 622.
27. J. Austen, *Mansfield Park*, edited with an introduction by T. Tanner (Harmondsworth, 1966), pp. 114, 120. Murray Pittock actually discusses the novel, but only to speculate on its relationship to English Jacobitism:

> When...the improving Rushworths cut down the oaks on their estate at Sotherton and close the chapel they are violating England and the organic heart of Englishness: but the symbolism their actions inherits is that of Stuart iconography, as Jane Austen, who came from a Jacobite family, may well have known.

M.G.H. Pittock, *Jacobitism* (London, 1998), pp. 136–7.
28. Brockliss, 'The Professions and National Identity', pp. 19–20.
29. D. Morse, *High Victorian Culture* (Houndmills, 1993), pp. 47–8.
30. C. Craig, *The Modern Scottish Novel* (Edinburgh, 1999), p. 30.
31. Hume to Elliot, *The Letters Of David Hume*, edited by J.Y.T. Greig (2 Volumes, Oxford, 1932), vol. 1, p. 470. In his reply Elliot insisted that 'we are both Englishmen; that is true British subjects, entitled to every emolument and advantage that our happy constitution can bestow'. G.F.S. Elliot, *The Border Elliots* (Edinburgh, 1897), p. 386–7.
32. P.H. Scott, 'David Hume, Le Bon David', *Defoe In Edinburgh And Other Papers* (East Linton, 1995), p. 68.
33. Quoted in L. Lunney, 'Ulster Attitudes to Scottishness: the Eighteenth Century and After', I.S. Wood (ed.), *Scotland And Ulster* (Edinburgh, 1994), pp. 65–6.
34. J.G. Basker, 'Scotticisms and the Problem of Cultural Identity in Eighteenth-Century Britain', J. Dwyer and R.B. Sher (eds), *Sociability And Society In Eighteenth Century Scotland* (Edinburgh, 1993), p. 89.
35. Craig, *The Modern Scottish Novel*, p. 28.
36. C. Harvie, *Scotland And Nationalism* (London, 1977), p. 29.
37. Quoted in J. Strawhorn, 'Ayrshire in the Enlightenment', G. Cruikshank (ed.), *A Sense Of Place* (Edinburgh, 1988), p. 189.
38. Lord Kames, *The Gentleman Farmer: Being An Attempt To Improve Agriculture By Subjecting It To The Test Of Rational Principles* (sixth edition, London, 1815), p. xix.
39. E.T. Svedenstierna, *Svedenstierna's Tour Of Great Britain 1802–3*, translated from the German by E.L. Dellow, with a new introduction by M.W. Flinn (Newton Abbot, 1973), p. 146.
40. G. Newman, *The Rise Of English Nationalism* (Houndmills, 1997), pp. 95, 152–3.

41. A. Murdoch, *British History 1660–1832* (Houndmills, 1998), p. 96.
42. L. Colley, *Britons* (London, 1992), p. 125.
43. J. Prebble, *The Highland Clearances* (Harmondsworth, 1969), p. 304. (Author's emphasis.)
44. K. Buchanan, 'The Struggle Against Satellisation In Scotland and Wales', *Monthly Review*, March 1968, p. 39.
45. C.W.J. Withers, *Gaelic In Scotland, 1698–1981* (Edinburgh, 1984), p. 111.
46. J. Campbell, *Invisible Country* (Oxford, 1984), p. 83. (Author's emphasis.)
47. P. Berresford Ellis and S. Mac a' Ghobhainn, *The Scottish Insurrection Of 1820* (London, 1970), p. 49.
48. J. Prebble, *Culloden* (Harmondsworth, 1967), p. 155.
49. MacNeil to MacDonald, 6 June 1816, 'The MacNeil Letters 1805–1825', J.L. Campbell (ed.), *The Book Of Barra* (London, 1936), p. 159.
50. MacNeil the Younger to MacDonald, 20 June 1825, ibid., p. 185.
51. Same to same, 8 August 1825, ibid., p. 186.
52. J. Hunter, *A Dance Called America* (Edinburgh, 1994), p. 237. Hunter recounts one of the more positive encounters between the Highland Scots and the Native Americans, in this case the MacDonalds of Glencoe and the Nez Perce, in his *Glencoe And The Indians* (Edinburgh, 1996).
53. There have been attempts to combine a recognition of Scotland's imperial role while still retaining the notion of Scotland as a colony. Formulations such as 'Scotland is a colonised nation as well as an imperial power' illustrate only too well the continuing need for formal, in addition to dialectical, logic. See A. Lincoln, 'Scott's *Guy Mannering*: the Limits and Limitations of Anglo-British Identity', *Scottish Literary Journal*, vol. 26, no. 1, June 1999, p. 61.
54. Colley, *Britons*, p. 130. The only major exception to this rule, to my knowledge, is to be found in *The Expansion Of England* (1888) by Sir John Seeley, yet the very obscurity into which this once famous text has fallen indicates how removed it was from the widespread perception that the Empire was British. But see also Matthew Arnold on the 'Celtic' races:

> But at any rate, let us consider that of the shrunken and diminished remains of this great primitive race, all with one insignificant exception, belongs to the English Empire; only Brittany is not ours; we have Ireland, the Scotch [sic] Highlands, Wales, the Isle of Man, Cornwall.

'On The Study Of Celtic Literature', *The Complete Prose Works Of Matthew Arnold* (11 Volumes, Michigan, 1962-), vol. 3, *Lectures And Essays In Criticism*, p. 384.
55. D. McCrone, 'We're A' Jock Tamson's Bairns: Social Class In Twentieth-Century Scotland', T.M. Devine and R.J. Finlay (eds) *Scotland In The Twentieth Century* (Edinburgh, 1996), p. 103.
56. D. Armitage, 'The Scottish Vision of Empire: Intellectual Origins of the Darien Venture', J. Robertson (ed.), *A Union For Empire* (Cambridge, 1995), p. 98. Armitage is concerned to revise the 'traditional' account of the Darien scheme that sees the project as doomed from the start. He emphasises instead that the establishment of a colony had been a cherished project for some Scots (including Patterson) for over a decade before 1695. His case is however weakened by a failure to give sufficient

weight to the profound crisis in Scottish society during the 1690s, without which it is unlikely the project would ever have been launched. Similarly, Armitage stresses the seriousness with which the political elite took the project, but their intellectual enthusiasm could scarcely compensate for the inability of the Scottish state to sustain such a venture.

57. S. Vetch, 'Canada Survey'd, or the French Dominions Upon the Continent of America Briefly Considered in Their Situation, Strength, Trade and Number, More Particularly How Vastly Prejudicial They Are to the British Interest, and a Method Proposed of Easily Removing Them', 27 July 1708, *Calendar Of State Papers, Colonial Series, America And West Indies, June, 1708–1709*, edited by C. Headlam (London, 1922), p. 51.

58. Devine, 'The Golden Age of Tobacco', p. 144.

59. D. Hancock, *Citizens Of The World* (Cambridge, 1995), p. 289.

60. The leading historian of the 'tobacco lords' notes, however, that they and the 'sugar princes' were by no means the most important section of the landowners with respect to improvement. See T.M. Devine, *The Tobacco Lords* (Edinburgh, 1990), pp. 26, 172–3 and 'Colonial Commerce and the Scottish Economy, c. 1730–1815', L.M. Cullen and T.C. Smout (eds), *Comparative Aspects Of Scottish And Irish Economic And Social History* (Edinburgh, 1977), pp. 182–3.

61. Hancock, *Citizens Of The World*, pp. 302–3.

62. A.L. Karras, *Sojourners In The Sun* (Ithaca and London, 1992), pp. 47, 48–9, 177.

63. R. Blackburn, *The Overthrow Of Colonial Slavery* (London and New York, 1988), pp. 46, 48–53. The most uncompromising proposals, inspired less by economic calculation and more by moral principle, were raised by a relatively obscure figure, George Wallace, in a book called *A System Of The Principles Of The Law Of Scotland* (1760).

64. A. Smith, *An Inquiry Into The Nature And Causes Of The Wealth Of Nations*, edited by A. Skinner (Harmondsworth, 1970), p. 184. See also p. 488, where this observation is repeated virtually word for word.

65. Ibid., p. 489. Moral considerations apart, Marx is simply more historically accurate in his account of the 'idyllic proceedings' which attended the 'genesis of the industrial capitalist':

> The discovery of gold and silver in America, the extirpation, enslavement and entombment in mines of the indigenous population of that continent, the beginning of the conquest and plunder of India, and the turning of Africa into a preserve for the commercial hunting of blackskins, are all things which characterise the dawn of the era of capitalist production.

K. Marx, *Capital*, (3 Volumes, Harmondsworth, 1976), vol. 1, p. 915.

66. Quoted in A. Hook, *Scotland And America* (Glasgow and London, 1975), pp. 56–7.

67. Contrary to what is claimed by John Murrin: 'To the extent that the settlers were self-conscious nationalists, they saw themselves as part of an expanding *British* nation and Empire.' J.M. Murrin, 'A Roof Without Walls: the Dilemma of American National Identity', R. Beeman, S. Botein and E.C. Carter II (eds), *Beyond Confederation* (Chapel Hill and London, 1987), p. 338.

68. Lee to Lee, 5 September 1774, quoted in P.J. Marshall, 'A Nation Defined by Empire, 1755–1776', A. Grant and K.J. Stringer, *Uniting The Kingdom?* (London and New York, 1995), p. 222.
69. See D. Walker Howe, 'Why the Scottish Enlightenment was Useful to the Framers of the American Constitution', *Comparative Studies In Society And History* 31, 1989, pp. 580–6, for a brief survey. (Some of the comparisons which Walker Howe draws between Scotland and colonial America should, however, be treated with caution, particularly in relation to Scottish and American 'slavery'. Slavery in Scotland was in fact a form of serfdom, which was confined to two groups of workers (coal miners and salt panners) and was already in decline even before the two Acts which banned first its extension (1775) and eventually its continuance (1799). Slavery in the American South was real, was the foundation of the economy and continued to expand territorially until the Civil War.) See also A. Hook, 'Introductory', *From Goosecreek To Gandercleugh* (East Linton, 1999), for a review of the controversy which the suggestion of Scottish influence on the Constitution aroused when made by Garry Wills in his book, *Inventing America* (1978).
70. Scott to Montagu, June 1822, *The Letters Of Sir Walter Scott*, edited by H.J.C. Grierson (12 Volumes, London, 1932–7), vol. 7, *1821–1823*, p. 185.
71. J.G. Parker, 'Scottish Enterprise in India, 1750–1914', R.A. Cage (ed.), *The Scots Abroad* (Beckenham, 1985), pp. 199–200.
72. E. Richards, 'Scotland and the Atlantic Empire', B. Bailyn and P.D. Morgan, (eds), *Strangers In The Realm* (Chapel Hill and London, 1991), p. 90.
73. G.J. Bryant, 'Scots in India in the Eighteenth Century', *Scottish Historical Review* 177, April 1985, p. 41.
74. J.T. Callender, *The Political Progress Of Great Britain; Or An Impartial Account Of The Principal Abuses In The Government Of This Country From The Revolution In 1688* (Edinburgh, 1792), Part 1, pp. 1–2. (Part 2 of this important work was never published.)
75. Young, *The Rousing Of The Scottish Working Class*, p. 41.
76. Lenman, *An Economic History Of Modern Scotland*, p. 192.
77. [W. Burns], *Scotland And Her Calumniators: Her Past, Her Present And Her Future* (Glasgow, 1858), pp. 19–20. For further information on Burns see H.J. Hanham, 'Mid-Century Scottish Nationalism: Romantic and Radical', R. Robson (ed.), *Ideas And Institutions Of Victorian Britain* (London, 1967), pp. 161–3.

Chapter 6: British Imperialism and National Consciousness In Scotland

1. M. Lynch, *Scotland: A New History* (revised edition, London, 1992), p. xiv.
2. J. Knox, *A View Of The British Empire, More Especially Scotland; With Some Proposals For The Improvement Of That Country, The Extension of Its Fisheries And The Relief Of The People* (London, 1784), p. lix.
3. G.J. Bryant, 'Scots in India in the Eighteenth Century', *Scottish Historical Review* 177, April 1985, p. 41.
4. G. Walker, *Intimate Strangers* (Edinburgh, 1995), p. 18.

5. D. Armitage, 'Making the Empire British: Scotland in the Atlantic Empire, 1542–1707', *Past And Present* 155, May 1997, pp. 39–40, 44–5, 63. Armitage argues that the initial Britishness of the Ulster colonists was diluted after the 1630s by the influx of Gaelic speaking Scots from the Borders and the southwest whose identity was more compatible with that of the native Irish population. This seems to give excessive credence to theories of ethnicity. In fact, the later Scottish settlers were incorporated into the existing colonial community without the slightest hesitation: their Presbyterianism proved stronger than any affinity to their fellow Gaelic speakers. See ibid., p. 46.

6. R.J. Finlay, 'The Rise and Fall of Popular Imperialism In Scotland, 1850–1950', *Scottish Geographical Magazine*, vol. 113, no. 1, p. 15. According to Finlay the other two prongs were the use of 'rural, Highland and historical symbols to represent the essence of the nation' and 'the widespread adoption of values and characteristics which were perceived to be intrinsically Scottish'. The first is certainly important, but, as we shall see below and in Chapter 7, was so even in the later eighteenth century. The second I find puzzling: if particular values and characteristics were already perceived to be 'intrinsically Scottish' (Finlay lists 'thrift, respectability, independence, temperance, the work ethic'), then why did they need to be 'widely adopted' in the first place? For a similar assessment of the role of Empire to Finlay see Walker, *Intimate Strangers*, pp. 17–23, who dates the significance of Empire from even later in the century.

7. Vetch, 'Canada Survey'd', pp. 42, 46, 50. (Author's emphasis.)

8. D.I. Fagerstrom, 'Scottish Opinion and the American Revolution', *William And Mary Quarterly*, third series, vol. 11, no. 2, April 1954, pp. 258–61.

9. J. Dwyer, *Virtuous Discourse* (Edinburgh, 1987), p. 40.

10. D.B. Swinfen, 'The American Revolution in the Scottish Press', O.D. Edwards and G. Shepperson (eds), *Scotland, Europe And The American Revolution* (New York, 1977), p. 71. The *Caledonian Mercury* was once more in the vanguard of making this case.

11. The same considerations arose at the French court during this period. Frank McLynn notes that 'there was an important section of opinion which held that the proper role for France was to assist England [sic] in the name of Monarchy to put down republican rebels in the colonies.' In the end, however, the realities of inter-state and inter-systemic competition prevailed and France threw its weight behind the rebels. F. McLynn, 'An Eighteenth Century Scots Republic? – An Unlikely Project from Absolutist France?', *Scottish Historical Review* 168, October 1980, p. 180.

12. Swinfen, 'The American Revolution in the Scottish Press', p. 71.

13. J.E. Cookson 'The Napoleonic Wars, Military Scotland and Tory Highlandism in the Early Nineteenth Century', *Scottish Historical Review* 205, April 1999, p. 63.

14. K. Brown, 'From Scottish Lords to British Officers: Elite Integration and the Army in the Seventeenth Century', N.M. McDougall (ed.), *Scotland And War AD79 To 1918* (Edinburgh, 1981), p. 149.

15. *John Peebles' American War 1776–1882*, edited by I.D. Gruber (Stroud, 1998), pp. 497 (30 November 1781), 186 (4 June 1778), 253 (21 March 1779). Peebles was an unusually widely educated man for an officer of his rank. In one entry he records that it was 'a fine warm day', during

which he 'took a long walk, dined alone, and read Montesquieu's *Persian Letters*', like a true son of the Scottish Enlightenment. See ibid., p. 508 (15 February 1782).

16. B.P. Lenman, *The Jacobite Clans Of The Great Glen* (second edition, Aberdeen, 1995), pp. 178–9.

17. M.G.H. Pittock, *The Invention Of Scotland* (London and New York, 1991), p. 62.

18. *Scots Magazine*, 22 December 1760, pp. 66–7.

19. A.I. MacInnes, 'Scottish Gaeldom: the First Phase of Clearance', *People And Society In Scotland*, edited by T.M. Devine and R. Mitchison (3 Volumes, Edinburgh, 1988–1990), vol. 1, *1760–1830*, p. 83.

20. T.M. Devine, *From Clanship To Crofter's War* (Manchester, 1994), p. 135.

21. Quoted in J.T. Findlay, *Wolfe In Scotland In The '45*, p. 226.

22. Quoted in ibid., p. 229.

23. *The Present Conduct Of The Chieftains And Proprietors Of Lands In The Highlands Of Scotland, Towards Their Clans And People, Considered Impartially* (Edinburgh, 1773), p. 6.

24. Knox, *A View Of The British Empire*, p. 15.

25. D. Stewart, *Sketches Of The Character, Manners, And Present State Of The Highlanders of Scotland; With Details Of The Military Services Of The Highland Regiments* (2 Volumes, Edinburgh, 1825), vol. 1, p. 318.

26. B.P. Lenman, *The Jacobite Risings In Britain 1689–1746* (London, 1980), p. 291.

27. J. Boswell, *Boswell's London Journal 1762–1763*, edited by F.A. Pottle (Harmondsworth, 1966), entry for 8 December 1762, p. 98. (Author's emphasis.)

28. J.T. Dunbar, *History Of Highland Dress* (Edinburgh and London, 1962), p. 12.

29. J. Boswell, 'The Journal Of A Tour To The Hebrides With Samuel Johnson, LL.D.', *Johnson's Journey To The Western Isles Of Scotland And Boswell's Journal Of A Tour To The Hebrides With Samuel Johnson, LL.D*, edited by R.W. Chapman (Oxford, 1970), p. 247.

30. Published in *Frazer's Bristol Journal*, 7 September 1776, and partially reproduced in M.W. Willard (ed.), *Letters On The American Revolution 1774–1776* (Port Washington, 1968), p. 334. (Author's emphasis. Parenthesis in the original.)

31. Quoted in L. Colley, *Britons*, (London, 1992), p. 120. Despite Barrington's boast that the Highland regiments were the least likely to rebel – there had indeed only been one mutiny, by the Black Watch, before 1751 – 15 were to follow between 1778 and 1804, indicating that the Highlanders were not the cannon fodder that His Majesty's Government had hoped. See J. Prebble, *Mutiny* (Harmondsworth, 1977), pp. 91–489.

32. Dundas to Eden, 5 September 1775, quoted in I. Adams and M. Somerville, *Cargoes Of Despair And Hope* (Edinburgh, 1998), pp. 137–8.

33. Quoted in B. Williams, *The Life Of William Pitt Earl Of Chatham* (2 Volumes, London, 1914), vol. 2, pp. 189–90.

34. Quoted in R. Clyde, *From Rebel To Hero* (East Linton, 1995), p. 161.

35. Scott to Abercorn, 25 November 1819, *The Letters Of Sir Walter Scott*, edited by H.J.C. Grierson (12 Volumes, London, 1932–7), vol. 6, *1819–1821*, pp. 29–30.

36. Scott to Morritt, 17 December 1819, ibid., p. 58.

37. Cookson, 'The Napoleonic Wars, Military Scotland and Tory Highlandism in the Early Nineteenth Century', pp. 61, 62.
38. M. Fry, 'A Commercial Empire: Scotland and British Expansion In the Eighteenth Century', Devine and Young (eds), *Eighteenth Century Scotland*, pp. 64–5.
39. J. Horn, 'British Diaspora: Emigration From Britain, 1680–1815', *The Oxford History Of The British Empire* (5 Volumes, Oxford and New York, 1998–), vol. 2, *The Eighteenth Century*, edited by P.J. Marshall, p. 31.
40. I.C.C. Graham, *Colonists From Scotland* (New York, 1956), pp. 185–9; J.M. Bumsted, *The People's Clearance* (Edinburgh, 1982), p. 9.
41. S. Johnson, 'A Journey To the Western Islands of Scotland', *Johnson's Journey To The Western Isles Of Scotland And Boswell's Journal Of A Tour To The Hebrides With Samuel Johnson, LL.D.*, p. 120.
42. Graham, *Colonists From Scotland*, p. 107.
43. D. Meyer, *The Highland Scots Of North Carolina, 1732–1776* (second edition, Chapel Hill, 1961), p. 142.
44. Graham, *Colonists From Scotland*, pp. 178–9.
45. Ibid., p. 108.
46. Meyer, *The Highland Scots Of North Carolina*, pp. 147–56.
47. Calder, *Revolutionary Empire*, p. 733.
48. B.S. Schlenther, 'Scottish Influences, Especially Religious, in Colonial America', *Records Of The Scottish Church Historical Society*, vol. 19, no. 2, 1976, p. 148.
49. Graham, *Colonists From Scotland*, p. 183.
50. Published in the *Gazeteer And New Daily Advertiser*, 13 July 1776, and partially reproduced in Willard (ed.), *Letters On The American Revolution 1774–1776*, pp. 314, 315, 318.
51. Hook, *Scotland And America*, pp. 50–1.
52. Quoted in D. Dobson, *Scottish Emigration To Colonial America, 1607–1785* (Athens and London, 1994), p. 166.
53. A. Young, *Political Essays Concerning The Present State Of The British Empire* (London, 1772), p. 1.

Chapter 7: Scottish History and Highland Mythology

1. M. Hroch, 'From National Movement To Fully-Fledged Nation', *New Left Review* 198, March/April 1993, pp. 6–7, 8–9.
2. Chapman, *The Gaelic Vision In Scottish Culture* (London and Montreal, 1978), pp. 27–8.
3. W. Ferguson, *The Identity Of The Scottish Nation* (Edinburgh, 1998), pp. 232–3, 238–40 and 'Samuel Johnson's Views on Scottish Gaelic Culture', *Scottish Historical Review*, vol. 127, no. 204, October 1998, pp. 184–5, 189–90.
4. G. Kristmannsson, 'The Subversive Loyalty of Ossian: Politics, Poetry and Translation in the Eighteenth Century', *Scotlands* 4.1, 1997, pp. 74, 76.
5. J. MacPherson, 'A Dissertation', *Temora, The Poems Of Ossian And Related Works*, edited by H. Gaskill with an introduction by F. Stafford (Edinburgh, 1996), pp. 205–6.
6. M. Forbes, *Beattie And His Friends* (Altrincham, 1990, facsimile of the 1904 edition), pp. 22–4. Although the episode gained Beattie the hostility

of Kames for many years, it did not affect his career: he held the post of Chair of Moral Philosophy at Marischal College in Aberdeen from 1760 to 1797.

7. J. Dwyer, *Virtuous Discourse* (Edinburgh, 1987), pp. 179–80.
8. J. Robertson, *The Scottish Enlightenment And The Militia Issue* (Edinburgh, 1985), p. 81.
9. J. MacPherson, *The Highlander: A Poem In Six Cantos* (Edinburgh, 1758), Canto 5, lines 177–80.
10. W. Scott, 'Report of the Highland Society Upon Ossian, Etc.', *Edinburgh Review And Critical Journal 12*, July 1805, p. 462.
11. W. Scott, 'Introduction to Canto First', *Marmion, The Poetical Works Of Sir Walter Scott* (12 Volumes, Edinburgh, 1880), vol. 7, p. 26.
12. Ibid., 'Introduction to Canto Third', p. 138.
13. C. Kidd, *Subverting Scotland's Past* (Cambridge, 1990), p. 270.
14. G. Lukacs, *The Historical Novel* (Harmondsworth, 1969), pp. 31–2. See also pp. 52–3. Lukacs often uses 'England' where he means 'Britain' or 'Scotland and England', and was notoriously inaccurate, both in his depiction of Scott's nationality (he refers to him as 'an English petty aristocrat') and the historical setting of at least one of the major novels (*Rob Roy* is said to take place at the end of the eighteenth century, rather than the beginning). The subtleties of the English-Scottish-British relationship have eluded writers closer to British culture than Lukacs, but dating *Rob Roy* after rather than before the '45 suggests that he had not entirely grasped the point Scott was making. There is nevertheless a great deal of value on Scott in *The Historical Novel*. For his inaccuracies, see ibid., pp. 58, 60, 62, 63.
15. There was, of course, one part of the world where the valedictory nature of his writing on the Scottish past was incorporated into the ideology of an existing ruling class: the Southern states of America. As William Cash writes: 'Walter Scott was totally taken over by the South and incorporated into the Southern people's vision of themselves.' (*The Mind Of The South* (New York, 1954), p 77.) The Southern white people, that is. Admiration for Scott was sustained until the Civil War destroyed slavery in the south. One South Carolina planter wrote, soon after enlisting: 'I am blessing old Sir Walter Scott daily for teaching me, when young how to rate knightly honour, and our noble ancestry for giving me such a state to fight for.' (J.M. McPherson, *For Cause And Comrades* (Oxford New York, 1997), p. 27.) Given the parallels I have drawn between the Jacobites and the Confederates elsewhere in this book, the identification by elements of the latter with Scott's portrayal of Scottish feudalism is extremely suggestive. Nevertheless, it should be noted that Scott was not only popular in the South. Contrary to what Mark Twain argues in *Life On The Mississippi*, Sir Walter cannot be blamed for inspiring the South to launch the Civil War in order to defend its identity. Andrew Hook does allow, however, that: 'Perhaps the South did respond to certain aspects of Scott's work with peculiar fervour; perhaps it is even true that the reading of Scott encouraged the South towards certain notions of its own social and cultural identity which had previously remained less well-defined.' A. Hook, 'Scott and America', *From Goosecreek To Gandercleugh*, (East Linton, 1999), p. 105.

16. T. Nairn, 'Scotland and Europe', *The Break-Up Of Britain* (second, revised edition, London, 1981), pp. 114–17; 'Old and New Scottish Nationalism', ibid., pp. 148–52. A similar point is made by Andrew Hook:

> The period 1814 to 1832 – the period that spanned the writing of the Waverly Novels – was a period of social and political counter-revolution in both Europe and America. On the face of it the writer to be idolised in such a period is hardly likely to be an exponent of revolutionary romanticism. On the whole it seems much more probable that Scott succeeded precisely because his romanticism, with its undoubted popular appeal, was in the end unthreatening because removed to the safety of the past.

'Scott and America', *Goosecreek To Ganduclergh*, p. 104.
17. J. Urry, *The Tourist Gaze* (London, 1990), p. 29.
18. Ibid., p. 4.
19. T.C. Smout, 'Tours of the Scottish Highlands From the Eighteenth to the Twentieth Century', *Northern Scotland*, vol. 5, no. 2, 1983, p. 100. Of the two subsequent stages, the third was under way 'by the middle of the nineteenth century [with] the age of vulgar tourism, facilitated on the one hand by the steam boat and the railway and on the other by the invention of the cheap shot gun, the guide book and the hotel.' And the fourth? 'Finally we arrive at the twentieth-century age of mass tourism.' Ibid..
20. P. Baines, 'Ossianic Geographies: Fingalian Figures on the Scottish Tour, 1760–1830', *Scotlands* 4.1, 1997, p. 45.
21. Ibid., p. 52.
22. Quoted in A. Hiley, '"Scotland's Name is Poetry in Our Ears": German Travellers in Scotland, c.1800–1860', *Scottish Archives* 2, 1996, p. 33.
23. T. Fontane, *Beyond The Tweed: A Tour Of Scotland In 1858* (London, 1998), pp. 110, 120.
24. E. Bowman, *The Highlands And Islands: A Nineteenth Century Tour* (Gloucester and New York, 1986), p. 32.
25. Hook, 'Scott and America', pp. 97–9.
26. Quoted in Hook, *Scotland And America*, p. 179.
27. Quoted in Hook, 'Scott and America', p. 102.
28. H.R. Trevor-Roper, 'The Invention of Tradition: the Highland Tradition of Scotland', Hobsbawn and Ranger (eds), *The Invention of Tradition*, p. 22.
29. M.G.H. Pittock, *Jacobitism* (London, 1998), p. 74.
30. D. Stevenson, *Alasdair MacColla And The Highland Problem In The Seventeenth Century* (Edinburgh, 1980), p. 294.
31. E. Cruikshanks, *Political Untouchables* (London, 1979), p. 106.
32. P. Monod, *Jacobitism And The English People* (London, 1989), p. 289.
33. Ibid., p. 87.
34. Trevor-Roper, 'The Invention of Tradition: the Highland Tradition of Scotland', p. 26.
35. J.M. McPherson, *The Battle Cry Of Freedom* (Oxford, 1988), p. 326.
36. B.I. Wiley and H.D. Millhollen, *They Who Fought Here* (New York, 1959), pp. 8–9. Apparently the mocking laughter with which their comrades greeted the Highlander's attempts to climb fences or dykes soon drove most of them back into trousers by 1862.

37. T.B. Macaulay, *The History Of England* (3 Volumes, Everyman's Library edition, London and New York, 1906), vol. 2, p. 452.
38. P.H. Scott, 'The Malachi Episode', W. Scott, *The Letters Of Malachi Malagrowther* (Edinburgh, 1981), pp. xxix-xxx.
39. Cookson, 'The Napoleonic Wars, Military Scotland and Tory Highlandism In the Early Nineteenth Century', *Scottish Historical Review* 205, April 1999, pp. 65–6.
40. J. Prebble, *The King's Jaunt* (Glasgow, 1989), p. 364.
41. C. Kidd, *British Identities Before Nationalism* (Cambridge, 1999), p. 145.

Chapter 8: The Reality of the Highlands: Social Assimilation and the Onslaught on Gaelic Culture

1. T.C. Smout, 'Problems of Nationalism, Identity and Improvement in Later Eighteenth Century Scotland', T.M. Devine (ed.), *Improvement and Enlightment* (Edinburgh, 1989), p. 14.
2. J. Ramsay, *Scotland And Scotsmen In The Eighteenth Century* (2 Volumes, Edinburgh and London, 1888), vol. 1, p. 396.
3. D.E. Meek, 'Scottish Highlanders, North American Indians and the SSPCK: Some Cultural Perspectives', *Records Of The Scottish Church History Society* 23, 1987–9, p. 384.
4. C.W.J. Withers, *Gaelic In Scotland 1698–1981* (Edinburgh, 1986), pp. 68–71, 83.
5. Quoted in ibid., p. 87.
6. W. Ferguson, 'The Problems of the Established Church in the West Highlands and Islands in the Eighteenth Century', *Records Of The Scottish Church History Society*, vol. 17. no. 1, 1969, pp. 30–1.
7. C.G. Brown, *Religion And Society In Scotland Since 1707* (Edinburgh, 1997), p. 90.
8. For the first position, see D.E. Meek, '"The Land Question Answered From the Bible"; the Land Issue and the Development of a Highland Theology of Liberation', *Scottish Geographical Magazine*, vol. 103. no. 2, 1987; for the second, see A.I. MacInnes, 'Evangelical Protestantism in the Nineteenth Century Highlands', G. Walker and T. Gallagher (eds), *Sermons And Battle Hymns* (Edinburgh, 1990), pp. 59–62.
9. Brown, *Religion And Society In Scotland Since 1707*, p. 90.
10. *The Statistical Account Of Scotland 1791–1700*, edited by Sir John Sinclair (20 Volumes, Wakefield, 1975–85), vol. 9, *Dunbartonshire, Stirlingshire And Clackmananshire*, with a new introduction by I.M.M. McPhail, pp. 7–8.
11. Ibid., vol. 8, *Argyle (Mainland)*, with a new introduction by M. Gray, p. 92.
12. M.W. Flinn et al, 'Emigration', M.W. Flinn, (ed.), *Scottish Population History From the Seventeenth Century to the 1930s*, (London, 1977), p. 474.
13. C.W.J. Withers, 'Kirk, Club and Culture Change: Gaelic Chapels, Highland Societies and the Gaelic Subculture in Eighteenth-Century Scotland', *Social History*, vol. 10, no. 2, May 1985, p. 179.
14. C.W.J. Withers, *Highland Communities In Dundee And Perth, 1787–1891* (Dundee, 1986), p. 42.

15. W. Scott, 'Review of the *Culloden Papers*', *Quarterly Review 18*, January 1816, p. 283.

16. 'Note Concerning Sutherland by Patrick Sellar: May 1816', *Papers On The Sutherland Estate Management, 1802–1816*, edited by R.J. Adams (2 Volumes, Edinburgh, 1971), vol. 1, pp. 175–6.

17. J.D. Lang, *Transportation And Colonization* (London, 1837), pp. i, v, quoted in D.S. MacMillan, *Scotland And Australia 1788–1850*, (Oxford, 1967), p. 310.

18. D. McLeod, *Gloomy Memories In The Highlands Of Scotland: Versus Mrs Harriet Beecher Stowe's Sunny Memories In (England) A Foreign Land: Or A Faithful Picture Of The Extirpation Of The Celtic Race From The Highlands Of Scotland* (New Delhi, n.d., facsimile of the 1892 edition), p. 207.

19. W. Allan, *The Invention Of The White Race* (2 Volumes, London and New York, 1994), vol. 1, *Racial Oppression And Social Control*, pp. 14–21, 32, 48, 65–6, 77–9, 92.

20. T.M. Devine, 'Why the Highlands Did Not Starve; Ireland and Highland Scotland During the Potato Famine', S.J. Connolly, R.A. Houston and R.J. Morris (eds), *Conflict, Identity And Economic Development*, (Preston, 1995), pp. 77–8.

21. J.S. Donnelly Junior, 'Excess Mortality and Emigration', T.M. Moody and W.E. Vaughn (eds), *A New History Of Ireland* (10 Volumes, Oxford, 1976), vol. 5, *Ireland Under The Union 1, 1801–70*, pp. 350–3.

22. T.M. Devine, *The Great Highland Famine* (Edinburgh, 1988), pp. 60–3, 79–80.

23. Devine, 'Why the Highlands Did Not Starve', pp. 79–88.

24. Trevelyan to Horne, 20 September 1846, quoted in T.M. Devine, 'Highland Landowners and the Potato Famine', L. Leneman (ed.), *Perspectives In Scottish Social History* (Aberdeen, 1988), p. 148. (Trevelyan's emphasis.)

25. [C.E. Trevelyan], 'The Measures for the Relief of the Distress Caused by the Great Irish Famine of 1846–7', *Edinburgh Review And Critical Quarterly* 87, January 1848, pp. 229–30, 314, 320.

26. T. Eagleton, 'Heathcliff and the Great Hunger', *Heathcliff And The Great Hunger* (London and New York, 1995), p. 26.

27. R. Southey, *Journal Of A Tour In Scotland In 1819* (Edinburgh, 1972, facsimile of the 1929 edition), pp. 136–7, 208–9.

28. T.B. Macaulay, *The History Of England* (3 Volumes, Everyman's library edition, London and New York, 1906), vol. 2, pp. 493–4.

29. H. Miller, *My Schools And Schoolmasters* (Collins Illustrated Pocket Edition, London and Glasgow, n.d.), p. 375.

30. J. Pinkerton, *An Inquiry Into The History Of Scotland Preceding The Reign Of Malcolm III Or To The Year 1056, Together With A Dissertation On The Sythians And The Goths* (new edition, 2 Volumes, Edinburgh, 1814), vol. 1, p. 73.

31. Scott to Stafford, 19 November 1811, *The Letters Of Sir Walter Scott*, edited by H.J.C. Grierson (12 Volumes, London, 1932–7), vol. 3, *1811–1814*, p. 21.

32. R. Mitchison, 'Patriotism and National Identity In Eighteenth Century Scotland', T.M. Moody (ed.), *Nationality And The Pursuit Of National Independence* (Belfast, 1978), p. 92.

Chapter 9: Burns and Scott: Radical and Conservative Nations

1. R. Burns, 'A Man's a Man For a That', *The Complete Illustrated Poems, Songs and Ballads Of Robert Burns* (London, 1990), p. 490.
2. T. Crawford, *Boswell, Burns And The French Revolution* (Edinburgh, 1990), pp. 63, 77.
3. W. Scott, 'For a' That an' a' That', *The Poetical Works Of Sir Walter Scott* (12 Volumes, Edinburgh, 1880), vol. 10, pp. 360–2.
4. R. Burns, 'Such a Parcel of Rogues In a Nation', *The Complete Illustrated Poems, Songs and Ballads Of Robert Burns*, p. 410.
5. R. Burns, 'Robert Bruce's March To Bannockburn', ibid. p. 457.
6. Burns to Thompson, August 1793, *The Complete Letters Of Robert Burns*, edited and introduced by J.A. Mackay (Ayrshire, 1987), Letter XXVI (582), p. 639.
7. Ibid., (Editorial note.)
8. M. Butler, 'Burns and Politics', R. Crawford (ed.), *Robert Burns And Cultural Authority* (Edinburgh, 1997), p. 100.
9. W. Donaldson, *The Jacobite Song* (Aberdeen, 1988), p. 87.
10. Ibid., p. 86.
11. 'Letter to the Edinburgh Evening Courant', 8 November 1788, *The Complete Letters Of Robert Burns*, p. 488.
12. C. Bewley, *Muir Of Huntershill* (Oxford, 1981), pp. 171–5.
13. T. Crawford, 'Political and Protest Songs in Eighteenth-Century Scotland II: Songs of the Left', *Scottish Studies*, vol. 14, no. 2, 1970, pp. 218–9.
14. Quoted in ibid., pp. 119–20.
15. Burns to Graham, 5 January 1793, *The Complete Letters Of Robert Burns*, p. 437.
16. R. Burns, 'Does Haughty Gaul Invasion Threat?', *The Complete Illustrated Poems, Songs And Ballads Of Robert Burns*, pp. 503–4.
17. Crawford, *Boswell, Burns And The French Revolution*, p. 73.
18. Berresford Ellis and Mac a' Ghobhainn, *The Scottish Insurrection Of 1820* (London, 1970), p. 55. The authors follow Hugh MacDiarmid in making this unsupported assertion.
19. Crawford, *Boswell, Burns and the French Revolution*, pp. 63, 69; J. Morris, 'Robert Burns, the Patriot Bard', C. Bambery (ed.), *Scotland, Class And Nation* (London, Chicago and Sydney, 1999), p. 170.
20. A. Calder, 'Burns, Scott and the French Revolution', *Revolving Culture* (London and New York, 1994), p. 74.
21. Ferguson, *The Identity Of The Scottish Nation* (Edinburgh, 1998), p. 314.
22. Morris, 'Robert Burns, the Patriot Bard', pp. 170, 172.
23. J.G. Lockhart, *The Life Of Sir Walter Scott, Bart.* (London, 1893), p. 143.
24. W. Scott, 'A Letter to the Editor of the *Edinburgh Weekly Journal*, from Malachi Malagrowther Esq., on the Proposed Change of Currency, and Other Late Alterations, as They Affect, or are Intended to Affect, the Kingdom of Scotland', *The Letters Of Malachi Malagrowther*, pp. 13, 17.
25. P.H. Scott, 'The Malachi Episode', ibid., p. xvii–xviii.
26. Scott, 'A Letter...from Malachi Malagrowther', pp. 47–8.
27. Lincoln, 'Scott's Guy Mannering', p. 53.
28. J. Hogg, *A Tour Of The Highlands In 1803: A Series Of Letters By James Hogg, The Ettrick Shepherd, Addressed To Sir Walter Scott, Bart.* (Edinburgh, 1986, facsimile of the 1888 edition), pp. 6, 42, 43.

29. N.T. Phillipson, 'Nationalism and Ideology', J.N. Wolfe (ed.), *Government And Nationalism In Scotland* (Edinburgh, 1969), pp. 184, 186.
30. P.H. Scott, 'The Distortions of Unionism', *Scotlands* 5.1, 1998, pp. 114–15. Although most of the material in this article (a response to J. Stevenson, 'Scott, Scotland and the Roman Past', *Scotlands* 4.2, 1997.) simply goes over the familiar quotations from Sir Walter that Scott has been reproducing for years, the tone reaches new heights of vituperation. Whatever errors were made by Stevenson in her original article – and there are a few – nothing could justify the reckless accusations of political bias which he descends to here.
31. Mitchison, 'Patriotism and National Identity In Eighteenth Century Scotland', p. 94.
32. Scott, 'A Letter...From Malachi Malagrowther', pp. 49–50.
33. Scott to Scott, 3 December 1819, *The Letters Of Sir Walter Scott*, edited by H.J.C. Grierson (12 Volumes, London, 1932–7), ibid., vol. 6, *1819–1821*, p. 39; same to same, 17 December 1819, ibid., p. 55.
34. C. Harvie, 'Scott and the Image of Scotland', R. Samuel (ed.), *Patriotism: The Making And Unmaking of British National Identity* (3 Volumes, London, 1989), vol. 3, *Minorities And Outsiders*, p. 180.
35. [J. G. Lockhart], *Peter's Letters To His Kinsfolk* (2 Volumes, Edinburgh, 1819), vol. 1, p. 208.

Chapter 10: Class Consciousness and National Consciousness In the Age of Revolution

1. L. Brockliss and D. Eastwood, 'Introduction: a Union of Multiple Identities', Brockliss and Eastwood (eds), *A Union of Multiple Identities* (Manchester and New York, 1977), p. 3.
2. R.J. Finlay, 'Caledonia or North Britain? Scottish Identity in the Eighteenth Century', D. Broun, R.J. Finlay and M. Lynch (eds), *Image And Identity* (Edinburgh, 1998), p. 151.
3. P. Berresford Ellis and S. Mac a' Ghobhainn, *The Scottish Insurrection Of 1820* (London, 1970), p. 296.
4. J.D. Young, *The Rousing Of The Scottish Working Class* (London, 1979), p. 45.
5. R.J. Finlay, 'National Identity: From British Empire to European Union', A. Cooke, I. Donnachie, A. MacSween and C.A. Whatley (eds), *Modern Scottish History 1707 To The Present*, (5 Volumes, East Linton, 1998), vol. 2, *The Modernisation Of Scotland, 1850 To The Present* p. 26.
6. T.M. Devine, *The Scottish Nation, 1700–2000*, (Harmondsworth, 1999), p. 106.
7. R. Mitchison, *A History Of Scotland* (London, 1970), p. 345.
8. I. Wallerstein, 'One Man's Meat: the Scottish Great Leap Forward', *Review*, vol. 3, no. 4, Spring 1980.
9. In 1701 Daniel Defoe cautioned his English readers against the contempt they felt towards foreigners for 'what they are to-day, we were yesterday, and tomorrow thay will be like us'. 'Explanatory Preface to the Ninth Edition of *The True-Born Englishman*', *The Novels And Selected Writings Of Daniel Defoe* (Oxford, 1927), vol. 13, p. 24.

10. K. Marx, 'Preface to the First Edition', *Capital* (3 Volumes, Harmondsworth, 1976), vol. 1, p. 91. This very condensed formula was not, of course, his last word on the subject. In 1877 Marx wrote a letter to the Russian journal *Otechesivenniye Zapiski* criticising the interpretation of *Capital* made in its pages by the Populist N.K. Mikhailovsky. Marx proposes two hypotheses. First, that the Russian peasant commune *might* provide the launching pad for the advance to communism in Russia, but the possibility of that happening was *already* being undermined by the development of capitalism. Second, that even if the commune failed to play this role, capitalist development would in any event not proceed in the same manner as in England or France, contrary to what was asserted by Mikhailovsky in his desire to turn a 'historical sketch of the genesis of capitalism in Western Europe into a historic-philosophical theory of general development, imposed by fate on all peoples, whatever the historical circumstances in which they are placed'. 'Letter to *Otechesivenniye Zapiski*', *Collected Works* (50 Volumes, London, 1975–), vol. 24, pp. 199, 200.

11. See, for example, Nairn, 'The Modern Janus', *The Break-Up Of Britain*, (second, revised edition, London, 1981), pp. 334–5.

12. L.D. Trotsky, *The History Of The Russian Revolution* (London, 1977), p. 27. Certain aspects of the theory of Combined and Uneven Development appeared, over 20 years after Trotsky died, in one of the most important non-Marxist works of development economics, A. Gerschenkron, *Economic Backwardness In Historical Perspective* (Cambridge, Mass., 1962), pp. 7–11, which notes the speed with which backward states can rise to the level of the more advanced, given certain conditions, but places too great an emphasis on the technological, rather than the social, aspects of this process. Gerschenkron did not consider the Scottish experience, but for a brief attempt to do so using his explanatory framework, see C.A. Whatley, *The Industrial Revolution In Scotland* (Cambridge, 1997), pp. 17, 39.

13. W. Scott, *Waverley; Or, 'Tis Sixty Years Since*, edited by A. Hook (Harmondsworth, 1972), p. 492. (Author's emphasis.)

14. [Wedderburn], 'Preface', *Edinburgh Review* 1, 1755, p. ii.

15. [Wallace], *Characteristics Of The Present Political State of Great Britain* (New York, 1969, facsimile of the 1761 edition), p. 107.

16. A. Callinicos, 'Exception Or Symptom? The British Crisis and the World System', *New Left Review* 169, May/June 1988, p. 103.

17. [Wallace], *Characteristics Of The Present Political State of Great Britain*, pp. 137–8.

18. Lord Kames, 'Preface', *The Gentleman Farmer: Being An Attempt To Improve Agriculture By Subjecting It To Rational Principles* (sixth edition, Edinburgh, 1815), p. xii.

19. 'A Supplement, Containing An Account Of The Present State Of Agriculture, And The Improvements Recently Introduced', ibid., p. 537.

20. L. Timperly, 'The Pattern of Landholding in Eighteenth Century Scotland', M.L. Parry and T.R. Slater (eds), *The Making Of The Scottish Countryside* (London, 1980), p. 141.

21. Whatley, *The Industrial Revolution In Scotland*, p. 56.

22. See T.C. Smout, 'Where Had the Scottish Economy Got To By the Third Quarter of the Eighteenth Century?', I. Hont and M. Ignatieff (eds), *Wealth And Virtue* (Cambridge, 1983). Smout concludes that:

> This is not a quarter-century of 'industrial revolution', but it can be not inaptly described as an era of pre-industrial growth, during which Scotland resembled a number of late-eighteenth-century European countries (Denmark, for example, and some of the German states) rather than her more precocious yoke-fellow in the Union, England.

Ibid., p. 71.

23. E.T. Svedenstierna, *Svedenstierna's Tour Of Great Britain 1802–3*, translated from the German by E.L. Dellow, with a new introduction by M.W. Flinn (Newton Abbot, 1973), p. 137.

24. W.W. Knox, *Industrial Nation* (Edinburgh, 1999), pp. 35–6.

25. K. Marx, *Capital* (3 Volumes, Harmondsworth, 1976), vol. 1, pp. 457, 489, 493, 497, 508.

26. H. Braverman, *Labour And Monopoly Capital* (New York, 1974), p. 169.

27. A. Slaven, *The Economic Development Of The West Of Scotland* (London, 1975), pp. 84, 86, 87.

28. N. Murray, *The Scottish Handloom Weavers, 1790–1850: A Social History* (Edinburgh, 1978), p. 4.

29. Slaven, *The Economic Development Of The West Of Scotland*, pp. 87–8.

30. Murray, *The Scottish Handloom Weavers*, pp. 18–22, 23.

31. C.W.J. Withers, *Urban Highlanders* (East Linton, 1998), pp. 86, 140; Murray, *The Scottish Handloom Weavers*, pp. 31–5.

32. A. Webster, 'An Account of the Number of People in Scotland in the Year One Thousand Seven Hundred and Fifty Five', *Scottish Population Statistics Including Webster's Analysis Of Population 1755*, edited by J.G. Kyd (Edinburgh, 1975), pp. 77, 79.

33. R. Tyson, 'Contrasting Regimes: Population Growth in Ireland and Scotland During the Eighteenth Century', Connolly, Houston and Morris (eds), *Conflict, Identity And Economic Development*, p. 64–7.

34. Tyson, 'Contrasting Regimes', pp. 66–7; R. Mitchison et al, 'The Eighteenth Century', Flinn (ed.), *Scottish Population History*, p. 302.

35. R.E. Tyson, 'Demographic Change', T.M. Devine and J.R. Young (eds), *Eighteenth Century Scotland: New Perspectives* (East Linton, 1999), p. 196.

36. Devine, *The Scottish Nation*, pp. 106–7.

37. J. De Vries, *European Urbanisation 1500–1800* (London, 1984), pp. 39, 45; Mitchison et al. 'The Eighteenth Century', p. 313.

38. C. Tilly, 'Did the Cake of Custom Break?', J.M. Merriman (ed.), *Consciousness And Class Experience In Nineteenth-Century Europe* (New York and London, 1979), p. 27.

39. I.D. Whyte, 'Urbanisation in Eighteenth-Century Scotland', Devine and Young (eds), *Eighteenth Century Scotland*, pp. 179 (quotation), 184.

40. W.H. Fraser, *Conflict And Class* (Edinburgh, 1988), p. 14.

41. T.M. Devine, 'The Urban Crisis', T.M. Devine and G. Jackson (eds), *Glasgow*, (2 Volumes, Manchester and New York, 1995), vol. 1, *Beginnings to 1830*, p. 407.

42. *Report On The Select Committee Enquiring Into The Condition Of The Poorer Classes In Ireland*, Appendix G, *Report On The State Of The Irish Poor In Great Britain*, 1836 (40), XXXIV, p. xxxv.
43. A. Dickson and W. Speirs, 'Changes in the Class Structure in Paisley, 1750–1845', *Scottish Historical Review* 167, April 1980, pp. 160–1.
44. Devine, 'The Urban Crisis', pp. 402–17.
45. Trotsky, *The History Of The Russian Revolution*, p. 33.
46. Ibid., p. 55.
47. Thompson, *The Making Of The English Working Class*, p. 13.
48. L.D. Trotsky, 'Where Is Britain Going?', *Collected Writings And Speeches On Britain*, edited by R. Chappell and A. Clinton (3 Volumes, London, 1974), p. 37.
49. Fraser, *Conflict And Class*, Chapter 2.
50. Scott to Montagu, 2 January 1820, *The Letters Of Sir Walter Scott*, edited by H.J.C. Grierson (12 Volumes, London, 1932–7), vol. 6, *1819–1821*, p. 103.
51. 'The Warder, No. VII', *Blackwood's Edinburgh Magazine* 7, 1820, pp. 100–1.
52. Scott to Morritt, 19 May 1820, *The Letters Of Sir Walter Scott*, vol. 6, *1819–1821*, p. 190.
53. H. Miller, *My Schools And Schoolmasters* (London and Glasgow, n.d.), pp. 374–5.
54. Knox, *Industrial Nation*, pp. 59–60.
55. J. Paterson, *Autobiographical Reminiscences* (Glasgow, 1871), p. 67.
56. Scott to Sidmouth, 23 August 1819, quoted in Mitchell, *The Irish In The West Of Scotland*, p. 105.
57. Devine, *The Scottish Nation*, p. 489.
58. Ibid., p. 487.
59. Mitchell, *The Irish In The West Of Scotland*, pp. 90–6.
60. Gallagher, *Glasgow: The Uneasy Peace* (Manchester, 1987), p. 2.
61. E.W. McFarland, *Ireland And Scotland In The Age Of Revolution* (Edinburgh, 1994), p. 244.
62. Mitchell, *The Irish In The West Of Scotland*, p. 99.
63. Ibid., p. 104.
64. See McFarland, *Ireland And Scotland In The Age Of Revolution*, Chapter 6 and Mitchell, *The Irish In The West Of Scotland*, Chapter 2.
65. Mitchell, *The Irish In The West Of Scotland*, pp. 105–6. See also pp. 103, 258.
66. Devine, *The Scottish Nation*, pp. 196–7.
67. M. Fry, *Patronage And Principle* (Aberdeen, 1987), p. 7.
68. W. Straka, 'Reform in Scotland and the Working Class', *Scottish Tradition* 2, 1972, p. 32.
69. Fry, *Patronage And Principle*, p. 7
70. Devine, *The Scottish Nation*, p. 197.
71. *An Address To The People Of Scotland, On Ecclesiastical And Civil Liberty* (Edinburgh, 1782), pp. 19–20.
72. Cockburn, *Memorials Of His Time*, new edition with introduction by his grandson, H.A. Cockburn (Edinburgh and London, 1909), pp. 74, 78–82.
73. Daer to Grey, 17 January 1793, 'The Scottish Reform Movement and Charles Grey, 1792–94: Some Fresh Correspondence', *Scottish Historical Review* 119, April 1956, p. 34.

74. Palmer to Grey, 29 October 1793. ibid., pp. 37–8.

75. J.D. Brims, 'The Scottish "Jacobins", Scottish Nationalism and the British Union', R.A. Mason (ed.), *Scotland And England, 1286–1815* (Edinburgh, 1987), p. 256.

76. Thompson, *The Making Of The English Working Class*, pp. 88, 135.

77. Fraser, *Conflict and Class*, Chapters 3–6. Quotations on pp. 83, 96, 98–9.

78. H. Perkin, *The Origins Of Modern English Society, 1780–1880* (London and Henley, 1969), p. 213.

79. Fraser, *Conflict And Class*, p. 109.

80. Murray, *The Scottish Handloom Weavers*, p. 99.

81. Quoted in F.K. Donnelly, 'The Scottish Rising of 1820: a Re-Interpretation', *Scottish Tradition* 6, 1976, p. 29.

82. Knox, *Industrial Nation*, p. 52.

83. Although several smaller local risings did in fact take place in England, involving 300–500 people in Barnsley and 200 in an abandoned attack on Attercliffe barracks. See, for example, J. Stevenson, *Popular Disturbances In England, 1700–1870* (New York, 1979), pp. 216–7.

84. T. Clarke and T. Dickson 'Class and Class Consciousness In Early Industrial Capitalism: Paisley, 1770–1850', T. Dickson (ed.), *Capital And Class In Scotland* (Edinburgh, 1982), p. 41.

85. Daer to Grey, 17 January 1793, 'The Scottish Reform Movement and Charles Grey, 1792–94: Some Fresh Correspondence', pp. 35–6.

86. Brims, 'The Scottish "Jacobins", Scottish Nationalism and the British Union', p. 261.

87. Quoted in W.M. Roach, 'Alexander Richmond and the Radical Reform Movement In Glasgow In 1816–17', *Scottish Historical Review* 151–2, 1972, p. 4.

88. W. Aiton, *A History Of The Rencounter At Drumclog And The Battle Of Bothwell Bridge In The Month Of June, 1679, With An Account Of What Is Correct, And What Is Fictitious In* The Tales Of My Landlord *Respecting These Engagements, And Reflections On Political Subjects* (Hamilton, 1821), pp. 7–8, 99.

89. R. Brown, *The History Of Paisley* (2 Volumes, Paisley, 1885), vol. 2, pp. 184–5.

90. P. Holt, 'Review of *The Scottish Insurrection Of 1820*', *Journal Of The Scottish Labour History Society* 3, November 1970, p. 36.

91. [J.T. Callender], *A Critical Review Of The Works Of Dr Samuel Johnston Containing A Particular Vindication Of Several Eminent Characters* (Edinburgh, 1783), pp. 53–4.

92. C. Stevenson Black, *The Story Of Paisley* (Paisley, n.d.), p. 187.

93. 'Address to the Inhabitants of Great Britain and Ireland', 1 April 1820, reproduced in Berresford Ellis and Mac a' Ghobhainn, *The Scottish Insurrection of 1820*, plate facing p. 96.

94. Ibid., pp. 140–5.

95. Holt, 'Review of *The Scottish Insurrection Of 1820*', p. 35.

96. H. Cockburn, *Journal Of Henry Cockburn, Being A Continuation Of The Memorials Of His Time, 1831–1854* (2 Volumes, Edinburgh, 1924), vol. 1, pp. 33–4.

97. *The Scotsman*, 11 August 1832.

98. Thompson, *The Making Of The English Working Class*, pp. 757–8, 760.

99. T.C. Smout, 'Problems of Nationalism, Identity and Improvement in Later Eighteenth-Century Scotland', T.M. Devine (ed.), *Improvement and Enlightenment* (Edinburgh, 1989), p. 12.

100. R.C. Gammage, *History Of The Chartist Movement 1837–1854* (London, 1969, facsimile of the 1894 edition), p. 33. Gammage also reports a mass meeting from the same year in Newcastle where the banners bore, among other quotations, several from Burns. See ibid., p. 23.

101. E. Evans, 'Englishness and Britishness, c.1790-c.1870', Grant and Stringer (eds), *Uniting The Kingdom?*, p. 232.

102. 'Song: the Deluge of Carnage at Length Has Subsided', *Radical Renfrew: Poetry From The French Revolution To The First World War*, selected, edited and introduced by T. Leonard (Edinburgh, 1990), p. 91.

103. P.J. Taylor, 'The English and Their Englishness: "a Curiously Mysterious, Elusive and Little Understood People"', *Scottish Geographical Magazine*, vol. 107, no. 3, 1991, pp. 148–9.

104. Marx to Meyer and Vogt, 9 April 1870, *Political Writings*, edited and introduced by D. Fernbach (3 Volumes, Harmondsworth, 1973), vol. 3, *The First International And After*, pp. 168–9.

105. E.J. Hobsbawm, 'What Is the Worker's Country?', *Worlds Of Labour* (London, 1984), pp. 42, 51.

106. Mitchell, *The Irish In The West Of Scotland*, p. 258 and passim. Devine follows Mitchell in arguing against the notion of the Catholic Irish as strikebreakers (except in restricted areas of Lanarkshire and Ayrshire) or of the working class being divided on communalist lines during this period. Devine, *The Scottish Nation*, pp. 490–1.

107. J. Connolly, 'North East Ulster', *Collected Works* (2 Volumes, Dublin, 1987), vol. 1, p. 386.

108. Pocock, *British History*, p. 615.

109. Miller, *My Schools And Schoolmasters*, p. 374.

110. Gallagher, *Glasgow: The Uneasy Peace*, pp. 33–4.

111. Hanham, 'Mid-Century Scottish Nationalism', pp. 148–9.

112. G. Morton, 'What If?: the Significance of Scotland's Missing Nationalism in the Nineteenth Century', Brown, Finlay and Lynch (eds), *Image and Identity*, p. 167.

113. T. Nairn, 'From Civil Society to Civil Nationalism: Evolutions of a Myth', *Faces Of Nationalism* (London and New York, 1997), p. 79. Nairn goes so far as to claim that the peculiarities of Scottish development mean it was alone in producing a 'civil society'.

114. G. Morton, *Unionist Nationalism* (East Linton, 1998), pp. 9, 190, 193.

115. C. Tilly, *Popular Contention In Great Britain, 1758–1834* (London and Cambridge Mass., 1995), pp. 364–7, 383–4.

116. Smout, 'Problems of Nationalism, Identity and Improvement in Later Eighteenth-Century Scotland', p. 11.

117. Kidd, *Subverting Scotland's Past*, p. 209.

118. Mitchison, 'Patriotism and National Identity In Eighteenth Century Scotland', T.M. Moody (ed.), *Nationality And The Pursuit of National Independence* (Belfast, 1978), pp. 93–4.

119. Prebble, *The King's Jaunt* (Glasgow, 1989), p. 17.

120. Scott to Croker, 19 March 1826, *The Letters of Sir Walter Scott*, vol. 9, *1823–1826*, pp. 471–2.

Conclusion

1. J.G. Kellas, *The Scottish Political System* (second edition, Cambridge, 1975), p. 119.
2. J. Brand, 'National Consciousness and Voting in Scotland', *Ethnic And Racial Studies*, vol. 10, no. 3, July 1987, pp. 336–7.
3. *The Scotsman*, 5 June 1998; L. Bennie, J. Brand and J. Mitchell, *How Scotland Votes* (Manchester, 1997), p. 133.
4. Bennie, Brand and Mitchell, *How Scotland Votes*, pp. 139, 140.
5. D. McCrone, 'Opinion Polls In Scotland, July 1998-June 1999', *Scottish Affairs* 28, Summer 1999, p. 40; D. Denver and I. Macallister, 'The Scottish Parliament Elections 1999: an Analysis of the Results', ibid., p. 12.
6. T.C. Smout, *A Century Of The Scottish People 1830–1950* (Glasgow, 1987), pp. 237, 238.
7. B. Crick, 'Essays on Britishness', *Scottish Affairs* 2, Winter 1993, p. 76.
8. J. McMillan, 'Foreign Lessons In Pressing for Home Rule', *Scotland On Sunday*, 22 August 1993.
9. See, for example, R.J. Finlay, 'The Rise and Fall of Popular Imperialism In Scotland, 1850–1950' *Scottish Geographical Magazine*, vol. 113, no. 1, p. 20 and G. Kerevan, 'Switch-Off Time for Ukania', *The Scotsman*, 4 January 1999.
10. J. MacGregor, 'The Tories Treat Us With Disdain', *Radical Renfrew: Poetry From The French Revolution To The First World War*, selected, edited and introduced by T. Leonard (Edinburgh, 1990), p. 89.

Afterword

1. T. Eagleton, *Ideology* (London and New York, 1991), p. 189.
2. C. Craig, *The Modern Scottish Novel*, p. 10.
3. D. McCrone, S. Kendrick and P. Straw, 'Introduction: Understanding Scotland', McCrone, Kendrick and Straw (eds), *The Making Of Scotland*, p. 3.
4. M.G.H. Pittock, *The Myth Of The Jacobite Clans* (Edinburgh, 1995), pp. 117–18.
5. C. Beveridge and R. Turnbull, *Scotland After Enlightenment* (Edinburgh, 1997), pp. 65–6.
6. A. Livingston, *Scotland On Sunday*, 12 April 1998, letter responding to C. McArthur, 'Scotland May Rue the Day', *Scotland On Sunday*, 5 April 1998. McArthur had suggested that the adoption of 6 April as 'Tartan Day' by the US Congress might not necessarily be the best way to represent Scotland abroad. The majority of responses opposed his position, although only Mr Livingston was prepared to suggest that the two leading proponents of High Structuralism were directly responsible for postmodernism.
7. Nairn, 'Empire and Union', *Faces of Nationalism* (London and New York, 1997), p. 207.
8. Those who claim, as Beveridge and Turnbull do, that the contemporary nationalist movement has no truck with this, might reflect on the support given by the SNP to the British state during the Gulf War of 1990–91, and the continued opposition of the Party to the slightest diminution of 'our

Scottish regiments', who played such a glorious role in defending Western oil interests during that conflict. In 1991 the Scottish National Party was asked for its position on the merger of the Gordon Highlanders and the Queen's Own Highlanders during the Kincardine and Deeside by-election. The SNP candidate, the late Allan Macartney, informed readers of the *Deeside Piper*: 'The Scottish National Party is the only party with an OFFICIAL policy to save all the Scottish regiments, including the Gordons.' What particularly aroused the ire of Dr Macartney was the fact that 'Scottish troops bore the brunt of the danger of the front-line in the Gulf, but are now expected to bear the brunt of the cuts.' The idea that opposing the imperialist onslaught on Iraq (against a dictator whom the West had helped into power in the first place) might have been an issue of greater importance than saving one of the regiments involved in it, does not seem to have occurred to the SNP, or if it did the thought was ignored for electoral considerations. For the correspondence see D. Fairgrieve, *A Regiment Saved* (Edinburgh, 1993), p. 46. This book is mainly concerned with the campaign to save the King's Own Scottish Borderers, who were originally raised to fight Claverhouse in 1689, saw action at Culloden and participated in most subsequent imperialist policing operations; or, as the author puts it: 'In recent years the Regiment has served with distinction in Malaya, Berlin, Belize and Northern Ireland.' Ibid., p. 17.

9. See E.J. Hobsbawm, 'Identity History is Not Enough' and 'Post-Modernism in the Forest', *On History* (London, 1997) and R.J. Evans, *In Defence Of History* (London, 1997), pp. 80–102, 108–116, 124–8, 138–52, 181–90, 195–223, 233–49. Evans makes a number of unnecessary concessions to postmodernism which mar this otherwise useful book. ('They have opened up possibilities of self-renewal for the historical discipline, suggesting a way out of the impasse into which social determinism, above all its Marxist variants, had run by the beginning of the 1990s.' Ibid., p. 243.) A belief that certain determinations act to shape society does not make one a determin*ist*. Some of the theoretical issues involved in postmodernist approaches to history are more satisfactorily discussed in A. Callinicos, *Theories And Narratives* (Cambridge, 1995), pp. 65–75, 179–211, a reading of which should make the more ignorant claims about supposed Marxist determinism impossible – although on past experience this scenario is probably too optimistic. See also J. Molyneux, 'Is Marxism Deterministic', *International Socialism 68*, second series, autumn 1995.

10. Hobsbawm, 'Identity History Is Not Enough', p. 271. The view that Scotland is an oppressed nation will not stand up to examination, but there is no doubt that many members of its lumpen-*intellegentsia* regard themselves in precisely that light, albeit as subjects of 'cultural' oppression rather than the political or economic varieties. See Chapter 5 above.

11. Ibid., p. 277.

12. Craig, *The Modern Scottish Novel*, p. 32.

13. R.J. Finlay, 'Heroes, Myths and Anniversaries in Modern Scotland', *Scottish Affairs* 18, Winter 1997, p. 123.

14. C. Small, '"The Strong Command, the Weak Obey..."', L. Scott-Moncrieff (ed.), *The '45: To Gather An Image Whole* (Edinburgh, 1988), p. 186.

15. L. Grassic Gibbon, 'Glasgow', L. Grassic Gibbon and H. MacDiarmid, *Scottish Scene Or The Intelligent Man's Guide To Albyn* (London and Melbourne, 1934), pp. 118–19.

Index

Compiled by Sue Carlton